BUSINESS RESEARCH METHODS FOR CHINESE STUDENTS

T0323099

Sara Miller McCune founded SAGE Publishing in 1965 to support the dissemination of usable knowledge and educate a global community. SAGE publishes more than 1000 journals and over 800 new books each year, spanning a wide range of subject areas. Our growing selection of library products includes archives, data, case studies and video. SAGE remains majority owned by our founder and after her lifetime will become owned by a charitable trust that secures the company's continued independence.

Los Angeles | London | New Delhi | Singapore | Washington DC | Melbourne

BUSINESS RESEARCH METHODS
FOR CHINESE STUDENTS

A PRACTICAL GUIDE TO YOUR RESEARCH PROJECT

Huiping Xian
Yue Meng-Lewis

Los Angeles | London | New Delhi
Singapore | Washington DC | Melbourne

Los Angeles | London | New Delhi
Singapore | Washington DC | Melbourne

SAGE Publications Ltd
1 Oliver's Yard
55 City Road
London EC1Y 1SP

SAGE Publications Inc.
2455 Teller Road
Thousand Oaks, California 91320

SAGE Publications India Pvt Ltd
B 1/I 1 Mohan Cooperative Industrial Area
Mathura Road
New Delhi 110 044

SAGE Publications Asia-Pacific Pte Ltd
3 Church Street
#10-04 Samsung Hub
Singapore 049483

Editor: Kirsty Smy
Assistant editor: Lyndsay Aitken
Production editor: Nicola Carrier
Copyeditor: Sharon Cawood
Indexer: Silvia Benvenuto
Marketing manager: Alison Borg
Cover design: Shaun Mercier
Typeset by: C&M Digitals (P) Ltd, Chennai, India
Printed in the UK

© Huiping Xian and Yue Meng-Lewis 2018

First published 2018

Apart from any fair dealing for the purposes of research or private study, or criticism or review, as permitted under the Copyright, Designs and Patents Act, 1988, this publication may be reproduced, stored or transmitted in any form, or by any means, only with the prior permission in writing of the publishers, or in the case of reprographic reproduction, in accordance with the terms of licences issued by the Copyright Licensing Agency. Enquiries concerning reproduction outside those terms should be sent to the publishers.

Library of Congress Control Number: 2017949655

British Library Cataloguing in Publication data

A catalogue record for this book is available from the British Library

ISBN 978-1-47392-665-3
ISBN 978-1-47392-666-0 (pbk)

At SAGE we take sustainability seriously. Most of our products are printed in the UK using responsibly sourced papers and boards. When we print overseas we ensure sustainable papers are used as measured by the PREPS grading system. We undertake an annual audit to monitor our sustainability.

CONTENTS

LIST OF FIGURES AND TABLES

FIGURES

TABLES

ABOUT THE AUTHORS

 HUIPING XIAN, PhD, is a lecturer in the Work, Employment, People and Organisation Division at Sheffield University Management School. She received her doctorate from Manchester Metropolitan University, United Kingdom. At Sheffield, Huiping is programme director for both BA Business Management (with Sino British College) and MSc Human Resource Management. Previously, Huiping also lectured at Manchester Metropolitan University and Bournemouth University. Huiping has contributed to teaching research methods and supervising dissertations at these universities. Huiping is also an active researcher and has published a number of academic papers in international journals. Her research interests include women's careers, HRM issues in Chinese organisations, qualitative research methods, cross-cultural research and translation issues in international research. Her recent projects include 'Developing Women's Careers in Japan', which is funded by the British Academy.

 YUE MENG-LEWIS, PhD, is a senior lecturer in Marketing and Sport Marketing at Coventry University Business School. She completed her doctoral studies at Leeds University Business School, and has previously worked as a lecturer in Marketing at Henley Business School, University of Reading, and as a senior lecturer in Marketing Communications at the Media School, Bournemouth University. Her research interests focus on consumer psychology, sponsorship, ambush marketing, organisational behaviour and quantitative methods. Her work has been published in leading marketing and management journals, and has contributed to book chapters and case studies in key marketing textbooks. Yue teaches research methods at both undergraduate and postgraduate levels.

PREFACE

The idea for this book originated from our experiences in teaching and supervising Chinese postgraduate students. Since 2000, the number of Chinese students studying abroad has increased by 20% each year (Ministry of Education, China). In 2013, around a quarter of students at UK universities were from China, among whom 36% registered in business-related programmes (UK Council for International Student Affairs). The same picture can be found in institutions in other English-speaking countries, such as the USA, Canada, Australia and New Zealand. Australia, for example, had approximately 35,000 Chinese students enrolled in the broad field of 'Management and Commerce' in 2010 (Australian Bureau of Statistics). In the last decade, Chinese students have also populated English-taught programmes delivered in non-English speaking countries, such as Germany, Spain, France and Sweden. Chinese students are particularly interested in business-related masters degrees, including the MA, MSc and MBA, which often require the completion of evidence-based research.

Despite the large number of research method textbooks on the market, there is no such book that serves the needs of this student population. This book is designed to support Chinese students who study business and management programmes at both postgraduate and undergraduate levels. It aims to provide straightforward and user-friendly guidance to Chinese students with research methods in their dissertations. This book is suitable for students across business and management disciplines, including accounting, general management, human resources management, industrial relations, information systems, international business, leadership, marketing, operations management, organisational studies, sports management, strategic management and work psychology.

We understand that, for many of you, this is the first time you will carry out an evidence-based research project. Completing a dissertation within a short period of time can be very challenging for Chinese students who study abroad. Many of you are confronted with cultural and language difficulties, while trying to acquire sufficient knowledge to use various research methods and meet the academic requirements of overseas universities. We have written this text to ease your anxiety and make the journey more enjoyable! This user-friendly book is written to suit the unique learning style of Chinese students. We both successfully completed a masters degree and a PhD at a UK university. Now, as lecturers, we have daily conversations with Chinese students. Equipped with 'first-hand' knowledge of the difficulties and struggles that many students encounter, we include such tailor-made features as Chinese explanations of key concepts and terms, short illustrative examples and tips for doing research in China, to guide you through the research process. We hope this book will help you to develop the confidence and necessary knowledge to succeed in your studies.

ACKNOWLEDGEMENTS

We would like to thank the commissioning editors and the editorial team at SAGE who provided us with support throughout the writing of this book. We are grateful to the many anonymous reviewers, whose insightful comments and suggestions contributed to improvements in the final text.

Huiping Xian would like to thank Professors Phil Johnson and Catherine Cassell for their encouragement and feedback, especially at the beginning of this book project. She would also like to thank her colleagues at Sheffield University Management School for sharing their book-writing experiences and providing helpful advice and support.

Yue Meng-Lewis would like to thank her husband, Gavin Lewis, not only for his continuous encouragement and support in writing the book, but also for his great help with proofreading. Gavin also kindly contributed to the design of the front cover for this book.

1

INTRODUCTION

1.1 PURPOSE OF THE BOOK

A large number of books on research design and methods have been published on the market. However, to the best of our knowledge, there has been no text particularly addressing the needs of Chinese scholars and students. From our experience (first as students, now as supervisors), Chinese students face three challenges when managing their research projects. The first issue relates to the dissimilarity between the English and Chinese languages. Many technical terms (for example, positivism or grounded theory) found in traditional method books have no direct translation in the Chinese language. Most Chinese students find it difficult to comprehend these terms. The second issue is associated with the unique social context of China. Traditional textbooks of research methods are often written by Western authors and based on Western samples. Yet, Chinese students frequently find it problematic to apply these methods in Chinese society without modifications. Third, the majority of Chinese students have no prior experience of conducting evidence-based research. As a result, they struggle to understand the nature of research and meet the requirements of UK universities.

By adopting two important pedagogical strategies for supporting Chinese learners, namely unity of knowledge and doing, and practical reasoning (Chen, 2016), this text has been designed to tackle these problems. To address the first issue, we provide short lists of Chinese explanations of key terminologies throughout the book to enhance understanding. To address the second issue, we use examples of Chinese research from our own work and examples drawn from top journals in the disciplines concerned to illustrate how these methods can be applied in the Chinese context. We believe this may help Chinese students quickly make sense of the various methods. To address the third issue, we include sections on the key components of research projects in both Chapter 2 and Chapter 10, and on the generic requirements of dissertations throughout this book.

1.2 WHAT IS RESEARCH?

Although the focus of this book is helping Chinese students conducting research in the Chinese context, we believe it is useful to provide a brief review of what the term 'research' means in English. In the 16th century, the English term 'research' was mostly associated with the act of searching for either a specific person or thing. In this case, the target was well defined, with little room for accidental discoveries. Since then, a wider range of investigation has been incorporated into the idea of research, emphasising both the outcome and the process. Increasingly, research has been conducted by individuals for the purpose of advancing knowledge. The 18th and 19th centuries saw the establishment of many new educational institutions and learned societies, which aimed to discuss and diffuse knowledge (Bishop, 2006). The essence of research was associated with reason, objectivity, truth and empiricism, as opposed to irrationalism, subjectivity, ignorance and faith.

Depending on their discipline and perspective, modern scholars have defined 'research' in various forms, with little consensus in the literature. For example, Sharp and Howard (1996: 6) see it as 'seeking through methodical processes to add to one's own body of knowledge and, hopefully, to that of others, by the discovery of non-trivial facts and insights', while Wilson (2014) suggests that most definitions share three common understandings. First, research is a process of enquiry and investigation. In *The Metaphysics*, Aristotle wrote that 'all men, by nature, have the desire to know'. This means that research is about raising a set of questions with regard to a chosen subject and aiming to answer these questions by gathering information and analysing data. In doing so, researchers discover new facts, test new ideas or revise theories and applications. Thus, research is a way of knowing, and the whole process is 'a disciplined way of coming to know something about our world and ourselves' (Bouma, 2001: 5). Second, research is systematic and methodical. This means that a good piece of research has a clear focus and follows a vigorous process and logical steps to achieve its goals. The difference between research and our direct experience is that research is controlled and carried out systematically (Lowe, 2007). Frequently, the research process includes the collecting, recording, analysing and interpreting of information. It requires systematic thinking and logical reasoning skills. Third, research increases knowledge. Rose (1927: 118) suggests that 'academic research has been the fountain from which the most important knowledge regarding our surroundings has come'. Research can be seen as an organised effort to acquire knowledge regarding natural and social phenomena.

KEY CONCEPTS IN CHINESE: RESEARCH

研究通常指针对一个具体的课题或问题，收集资料，使用科学有效的方法收集，分析数据，并解释结果，最后找出问题解决方案的过程。研究的目的是为了发现新事物，新现象，提出新理论，揭示自然事物或社会现象的内在规律。研究经常会促成发明和创新。

To manage a research project successfully, researchers must have knowledge, intellectual abilities, techniques and professional standards to do research, as well as personal qualities and skills. Throughout this book, we will introduce you to different methods (方法) and methodologies (方法论) and take you through the research process step by step. However, here we would also emphasise the importance of a researcher's personal attitudes and qualities. In our experience, some Chinese students failed to achieve a desired mark for their dissertation because they had not developed the right attitudes during this process. A good researcher (including postgraduate student):

- is independent, self-reliant and takes responsibility for self and the project
- approaches the research project with enthusiasm and passion
- is proactive and keen to find solutions in the face of obstacles
- shows integrity and ethics
- is willing to receive constructive criticism
- is self-reflective and commits to continuing development.

KEY CONCEPTS IN CHINESE: METHOD AND METHODOLOGY

方法和方法论在很多书里有提到。有些书会把这两个词混着用，但其实这两个词意思上有很大差异。方法（Method）指的是收集或分析数据时用的具体的方法。如本书第6章里讨论的几种收集数据的常用方法（如问卷，访谈，等）。方法论（Methodology）指研究人员在从事一项科研项目时采取的总体的研究方法。研究报告和学术论文里一般包含一章研究方法论，里面包括一些固定的元素，如该研究员具体采纳的研究哲学（Research Philosophy），数据收集方式（如问卷，访谈，实地 观察等），取样方式（sampling），和分析方法等。这些元素要互相支持，才能构成有效和科学的研究方法论，从而使得最后的研究结果有意义。

1.3 BUSINESS AND MANAGEMENT RESEARCH IN THE CHINESE CONTEXT

Business and management research can be linked to any aspect related to business and managerial issues, including (but not limited to) human resource management (HRM), marketing, business strategy, finance, entrepreneurship, logistics and operation management, international business, e-business, and so on. It aims to enhance management efficiency and inform business-related decision-making so as to improve the overall performance of a business. Research can have both academic and industrial significance. Some projects try to fill a research gap in the literature, while others start with a real-life problem in an organisation. Moreover, many projects cover more than one particular area in business and management. For example, a study looking at a company's brand might investigate both employer branding (HRM) and its reputation in the minds of consumers (marketing).

In general, business and management research tend to emphasise the logic and objectivity of research. For example, Zikmund et al. (2009: 5) define business research as 'the application of the scientific method in searching for the truth about business phenomena. These activities include defining business opportunities and problems, generating and evaluating ideas, monitoring performance and understanding the business process'. They indicate that all business research involves *scientific methods*, and requires the researcher to be objective, detaching themselves from the research process, and use knowledge and evidence to reach objective conclusions about the real world.

KEY CONCEPTS IN CHINESE: BUSINESS RESEARCH

本书主要关注的是商业研究，是指运用科学方法去寻求对于特定商业行为的解释和真相。主要的研究活动包括：寻找、定义商业机会和问题；提出、衡量计划建议；追踪、监控业绩，以及研究、学习商业过程。研究需要运用科学的方法，也就是需要研究者通过观察，去运用相关理论、知识和证据得到对现实世界现象的客观解释和结论。

Traditionally, business and management research has been dominated by studies conducted in developed economies, which are primarily North America and Western Europe. As a result, much management knowledge is the product of scholarly work in such settings (Lau, 2002; Tsui, 2004). However, three decades of rapid economic development in Asia have given rise to academic interests in the region, especially in the 'Greater China' area, which, many believe, includes mainland China, Hong Kong, Taiwan, Macao and Singapore. There is now a general recognition that Western-originated knowledge may not be applicable in Asia. Tsui (2004) calls for high-quality contextualised research, not simple replications or studies that test Western models or findings, to contribute to global management knowledge. Consequently, the last three decades have also witnessed the emergence of new scholarship in Greater China in mainstream business and management journals and books.

Peng and colleagues' early review of nine top-tier American and European journals identified a total of 59 Greater China-related articles for the period of 1978–1997 (Peng et al., 2001): two articles were published in the 1970s, 13 in the 1980s and 44 in the 1990s. These articles cover a range of business and management disciplines, including organisational behaviour, strategic management and international management. More recent reviews in specific disciplines reveal a similar trend. For example, Cooke's (2009) examination found 256 papers related to HRM issues in mainland China in 34 major English journals during the period between 1998 and 2007. In the advertising and communication field, So's (2010) review of 23 communication journals showed that China was mentioned 60 times in article titles between 1990 and 1999, and 108 times between 2000 and 2009. This sounds like good news!

Now, the bad news. Although the amount of articles is large in quantity, a number of authors note the lack of quality in many empirical studies, which tend to be simple and descriptive (Cooke, 2009; Tsui, 2004). Thus, only a few made their way into top-ranking international journals. Lau (2002) highlights several barriers that Asian scholars face when publishing in international journals. One such barrier is that Asian scholars and students (including those from China) traditionally receive little training in Western research methodology and academic writing. Our aim in producing this textbook is thus to offer an insight into conducting business and management research in the Chinese context and the essential skills required to navigate it successfully at postgraduate level. Although this book has a clear focus on mainland China, we believe many of the issues discussed here are applicable to other Chinese regions such as Hong Kong, Macau, Taiwan and Singapore, given the fact that these societies share a similar language and culture.

1.4 HOW TO USE THIS BOOK

This book aims to provide an intermediate level guide to the research methods and processes in business and management subjects. While it is not designed to replace traditional core texts, we suggest it be used as a practical guide for Chinese students who are managing a research project for their dissertation at both undergraduate and postgraduate levels. Incorporating the Chinese cultural beliefs of learning by doing in real contexts and learning with appropriate adaptation and flexibility (Chen, 2016), this book contains extensive discussion of tacit knowledge of conducting research in the Chinese context based on our experience. It may also be of interest to international scholars who plan to conduct research in such a context. This book adopts a student-centred approach to overcome the language and cultural barriers faced by Chinese students. The following pedagogical features are included to assist self-guided study:

- clear definitions of key terms in the text
- boxed definitions and/or explanations of key concepts/terms in Chinese following their English counterparts to enhance understanding
- further reading references with a short review of their contents at the end of each chapter
- short illustrative examples (such as a questionnaire in Chinese or a coding system) from the authors' previous work or academic journal articles
- tips on how to use different methods in the Chinese context and advice on how to produce high-quality research from the authors' own experience within each chapter
- a list of useful resources about Chinese research (including academic journals, websites, national and international databases) in Appendix 1.

The remainder of this chapter outlines the structure and key features of the book, as follows.

Chapter 1 (this chapter) provides the rationale for writing this book and introduces students to the basic ideas around research. We believe it is important for students to have an overview of business and management research in the Chinese context and the difficulties of doing research in such a context.

Chapter 2 deals with considerations for developing a research topic and planning a research project. Practical issues include how to formulate research aims and objectives, how to connect theories and methods and how to apply Western theories in the Chinese context. Advice is also given on how to write a research proposal.

Chapter 3 discusses the fundamental concepts of research philosophy (epistemology and ontology) and examines the various philosophical perspectives that can inform business and management research, namely positivism, realism, pragmatism and interpretivism. Deductive, inductive and abductive research approaches are also reviewed and discussed in relation to how they contribute to international and context-related research.

Chapter 4 explores the nature of qualitative and quantitative research design. In particular, it will focus on the most common approaches taken by Chinese students, including survey, experiment, case study method and grounded theory. Issues around assessing your own research will also be discussed.

Chapter 5 is concerned with sampling issues, such as different kinds of sampling techniques and what can be inferred from different kinds of sample.

Chapter 6 discusses some of the best-known methods for collecting data, including the use of questionnaires, interviews, focus groups and documents. As Chinese students may collect data in China while overseas, practical advice will be given on how to use online-based tools to collect data.

Chapter 7 comprehensively discusses the process of analysing qualitative data. Critical steps such as reading, data-reducing, coding and interpreting will be explored. The chapter then examines different approaches to the analysis of qualitative data, such as content analysis, discourse analysis and narrative analysis.

Chapter 8 presents a range of the most useful tools for analysing quantitative data, including descriptive quantitative analysis, correlation and regression, and tests of measurement and quality. The approach taken is non-technical. Step-by-step guidance for using IBM® SPSS® Statistics software (SPSS)[1] to process data is also illustrated with examples.

Chapter 9 focuses on the cultural and language issues around conducting research in the Chinese context. It also deals with some translation issues in both quantitative and qualitative research, such as interview language, translating questionnaires and interview data.

Chapter 10 deals with issues in the writing-up stage of the research, including key components and general requirements of a dissertation, writing style, referencing (both English and Chinese sources) and bibliography management. Issues of managing relationships with supervisors will also be discussed.

---

[1]SPSS Inc. was acquired by IBM in October, 2009.

1.5 OVERVIEW OF THE RESEARCH PROCESS

The research journey is often described as a linear and sequential process, which involves a series of steps and stages. Each step relies on the completion of the preceding steps for support and stability. In reality, however, research is never a straightforward process (Ang, 2014). Your research ideas and questions change during the process. Often, you will have to go back to previous steps to make changes according to new ideas. This moving backwards and forwards between stages means you may engage with more than one stage at the same time. Nevertheless, to ensure the findings are scientifically rigorous and the conclusion robust, your research needs to be planned and conducted systematically (Gelling, 2015). There are certain essential steps and stages that you will need to go through, regardless of which method is taken (see Figure 1.1). Here, we briefly discuss a six-stage model to give an overview of a typical research process. Subsequent chapters will provide more in-depth discussions of each stage.

Figure 1.1 The research process

Stage 1: Developing research questions

This stage involves early readings of literature to identify your research area and formulate your aims and objectives. Students usually start with an idea that they are personally interested in or already have some knowledge of. Some reading of the literature will help you to identify a research gap and narrow down the research topic. If your research is about a phenomenon in China, the local research context should be discussed to some extent.

Stage 2: Reviewing literature

This stage involves searching and critically reviewing relevant literature. A critical review requires you to analyse the strengths and problems of existing research, further justify your research gap and questions, and refine your aims and objectives. You may use both Chinese and Western literature as long as they are from credible sources.

Stage 3: Research design

At this stage, you are to choose an appropriate and feasible research methodology that can help you to answer your research questions. Your research design should also take into account your personal skills and experiences (e.g. doing interviews or handling numerical data) as well as access to potential participants. For example, you may need to negotiate organisational access in order to distribute your questionnaires. You should also obtain ethics approval before collecting data.

Stage 4: Data collection

Data can be collected quantitatively or qualitatively through a range of techniques (e.g. questionnaire, interview, observation, focus group, documents). You may want to do a pilot study, on a smaller scale than the main study, to ensure your research instruments are effective and robust.

Stage 5: Analysis

Different techniques and skills are required to process and analyse quantitative and qualitative data. Quantitative data are numerical and used on an aggregate level to test hypotheses, whereas qualitative data are often textual and focusing on people's subjective experiences.

Stage 6: Writing up

Although we present it as the last stage here, in reality writing is ongoing. You should start writing different chapters as early as possible. Students are advised to draft Introduction and Literature Review chapters before collecting data. The final writing-up stage is to complete the whole dissertation and make sure everything is consistent.

REFERENCES

Ang, S.H. (2014) *Research Design for Business and Management.* London: Sage.

Bishop, R. (2006) Research. *Theory, Culture and Society* 23: 570–1.

Bouma, G.D. (2001) *The Research Process.* Melbourne: Oxford University Press.

Chen, X. (2016) Challenges and strategies of teaching qualitative research in China. *Qualitative Inquiry* 22: 72–86.

Cooke, F. (2009) A decade of transformation of HRM in China: A review of literature and suggestions for future studies. *Asia Pacific Business Review* 47: 6–42.

Gelling, L. (2015) Stages in the research process. *Nursing Standard* 29(27): 44–9.

Lau, C.-M. (2002) Asian management research: Frontiers and challenges. *Asia Pacific Journal of Management* 19: 171–8.

Lowe, M. (2007) *Beginning Research: A Guide for Foundation Degree Students.* London: Routledge.

Peng, M.W., Lu, Y., Shenkar, O., et al. (2001) Treasures in the China house: A review of management and organizational research on Greater China. *Journal of Business Research* 52: 95–110.

Rose, R.E. (1927) Research. *Science* 66: 117–22.

Sharp, J.A. and Howard, K. (1996) *The Management of a Student Research Project.* Gower: Aldershot.

So, C.Y.K. (2010) The rise of Asian communication research: A citation study of SSCI journals. *Asian Journal of Communication* 20: 230–47.

Tsui, A. (2004) Contributing to global management knowledge: A case for high quality indigenous research. *Asia Pacific Journal of Management* 21: 491–513.

Wilson, J. (2014) *Essentials of Business Research: A Guide to Doing Your Research Project.* London: Sage.

Zikmund, W.G., Babin, B.J., Carr, J.C., et al. (2009) *Business Research Methods.* Fort Worth, TX: South-Western Cengage Learning.

2
DEVELOPING A RESEARCH TOPIC

2.1 OVERVIEW

As suggested in Chapter 1, research helps us develop our understanding on a particular topic. Through our research, we are able to develop insights and come up with effective plans and strategies to inform our decisions. The research process is guided by rules and principles, with the ultimate goal of making confident statements or conclusions through our observations, interrogation of previous studies and critical discussions. In this chapter, we will consider some key issues at the initial stage of a research project. We will also provide advice on writing a research proposal.

Example 2.1

HOW DOES DISSERTATION RESEARCH DIFFER FROM RESEARCH FOR OTHER ASSIGNMENTS?

It is very likely that you have taken a few modules involving a research element by the point of beginning a dissertation. Nevertheless, there are many differences in expectation when comparing dissertation research and your research at other levels of study:

- time frame: dissertation research takes a much longer time than a regular essay assignment; normally between three and six months
- length: a typical degree or masters dissertation is 10,000–12,000 words in length, while a degree or masters coursework assignment with a research element normally requires only 3,000 words
- primary data: the majority of dissertation research in business and management involves primary data collection and analysis. Nevertheless, primary data collection is normally not required for degree-level assignments; at postgraduate level, only a small amount of primary data may be expected for an individual module

(Continued)

- academic underpinning: it is expected that dissertation research demonstrates a good level of integration of the relevant theories and literature; up-to-date research findings from peer-reviewed journal articles should be included
- structure: dissertation research is required to be structured in a specific way; however, the structural requirements for other coursework assignments may be much more flexible.

2.2 CHOOSING A RESEARCH TOPIC AND DEVELOPING IT INTO RESEARCH QUESTIONS

Gaining an understanding of why you should conduct a piece of research will enhance your motivation to finish the research project. For many students, successfully completing a dissertation may not be the only motivation. A research project can be seen as a 'personal voyage of exploration' (Davies and Hughes, 2014: 17). It may be a topic that you discuss with your prospective employers in your job interviews. Blaxter et al. (2001: 12) suggest the following ways of turning a research project into something more exciting:

- changing your research project to something you are more interested in; 选取一个你感兴趣的课题
- focusing on the skills you will develop through undertaking the research, rather than the output; 关注在你通过做此课题所将学到的技能，而不仅仅是研究结果
- incorporating within the research some knowledge acquisition of relevance to you; 在做此研究的过程中，获取和这个领域相关的知识
- seeing the research project as part of a larger activity, which will have knock-on benefits for your work, your career, your social life or your life in general; 这项研究也许会对你的职业规划，工作，或者生活也起到积极的作用
- finding someone who will support you and push you through until you finish; 要知道，你至少还能得到导师的支持和帮助，更不用说来自同学和家人的。
- promising yourself a reward when it is successfully completed; 许给自己一个愿望，试想，'如果我成功的完成了这个课题'。

2.2.1 Choosing a research topic

Some students are inspired by a particular unit or lecturer, or by incidents they have observed previously in the workplace. A good research topic should be of interest to you, innovative, challenging, engage your readers and inform your existing knowledge or understanding.

Originality (原创性)

Many of the definitions of research outlined in Chapter 1 imply that there is an expectation that research will discover something new or make an original contribution to knowledge. Research projects carried out for a university degree in the UK, either at undergraduate or postgraduate level, often require some degree of originality. For example, you may find the following general terms in the marking criteria: 'an original piece of research'; 'an original contribution to existing knowledge'; 'evidence of original thinking'.

Example 2.2

WHAT IS ORIGINALITY?

什么样的课题具有原创性？它可以是：

1. 提供了前所未有的新信息，别人没有做过的。
2. 承接继续了其他有原创性的研究。
3. 接手你导师的原创性课题。
4. 运用了独创的研究手段和方法。
5. 在测试别人提出的观点时展示了原创性。
6. 做了前人未做过的实证研究。
7. 对已知的信息和结果做出新的解释。
8. 在本国运用在其他国家的观察研究模式。
9. 在一个领域运用其他领域惯用的研究方法和技术。
10. 在一个老课题的基础上，尝试带来新的发现。
11. 跨学科课题，运用不同的研究方法。

Source: adapted from Blaxter et al. (2001)

At postgraduate level, the demand for originality in a dissertation is much higher than at undergraduate level. In other words, postgraduate dissertations are expected to make an original contribution to the development of knowledge. Undergraduate dissertations allow students to test out existing ideas or perhaps even refine ideas (Finn et al., 2000).

Types of research

Many UK higher education dissertation projects require a certain level of academic/theoretical grounding. You can choose to conduct either a piece of academic research or a piece of practical/consultant research, as long as it demonstrates your understanding and integration of the relevant literature and theories. In general, academic research allows us to expand the limits of knowledge by adding to theory through the research project. This kind of academic research is conducted to improve our understanding of an issue without an immediate application to business. On the other hand, a piece of applied research seeks to analyse and find a solution to a business or management problem. For example, you may conduct a case study of a particular brand and look at how it uses social media to create consumer equity. (See Table 2.1.)

Table 2.1   Academic research 学术研究 versus professional research 实践研究

学术研究	实践研究
主要发表在学术期刊，会议，或者书籍上的	主要形式为行业或公司报告；发表在公司网站或者杂志上的
由高校或者学术研究机构发起和主导的	由咨询公司或者公司内部发起和主导的
有文化，社会重大意义的	对本产业或公司起商业策略上的指导意义
带给我们新的知识	带给我们对本产业或企业更深入的了解
以理论建立为基础的	市场调查，顾客，员工调查为基础的
对实践有一定意义的	不一定要对理论有贡献，主要贡献在于对本产业或者企业
寻求普遍化，研究结果有概括推广意义	研究独立的案例，不寻求研究结果上的推广性
解决 *Why* is this happening? 和/或 *How* has it happened? 的问题	解决 *What* is the problem? 的问题
e.g. the role of humour in influencing how consumers respond to print advertisements	e.g. students' brand perceptions of UK universities

Another way to distinguish between different types of research is to focus on the research aim (see Table 2.2). For your dissertation, you may only want to concentrate on one of these types, but two or more research types can be included in the same project.

Table 2.2   Descriptive, explanatory and evaluative research

Research type	Aim	Example
1. Descriptive research 描述性研究	Finding out, describing what is 勘查并说明情况。常常是受特定公司或者组织的委托所开展的	The legacy of the London 2012 Olympic Games; changes in beauty icons in Hollywood films over the last 60 years
2. Explanatory research 解释性研究	Explaining *how* and *why* things are the way they are (and using this to predict) 试图解释特定的现象或趋势	The motives of fans in attending football games; the main purposes as to why people purchase counterfeit goods as gifts
3. Evaluative research 评估性研究	Evaluation of policies and programmes 目的是为了衡量一项措施或者活动是否成功、有效	Whether a particular marketing communications campaign has been cost-effective; the effectiveness of traditional legal measures in the context of ambush marketing in the Olympic Games

Source: adapted from Veal and Darcy (2014)

Relevance (相关性)

You may have a wide range of research topics to choose from within your own subject area. Given the interdisciplinary nature of business studies, you may also get inspiration from psychology, sociology, economics, cultural studies, and even linguistics and semiology. However, you still need to show the relevance of your study to the general knowledge within your discipline. The examiners may question the genuineness of the research if you fail to show this link. For example, if a marketing student conducted a piece of research that only cited studies from the natural sciences, the student may fail the dissertation because the study would be of little relevance to the body of knowledge in marketing and consumer research. Business studies as a subject in the *social sciences* deals with 'people as individuals and social beings with relationships to groups and communities' (Veal and Darcy, 2014: 5). In other words, social science research deals with *people* and their social behaviour.

Value (研究价值)

It is important to demonstrate that your research is worth doing. When you are developing a research topic, try to think how it contributes to existing knowledge or practice. Consider, for example, how your research findings can be beneficial to a particular organisation, an industry, a market segment, policy-makers, other stakeholders, or society as a whole, and what value your study adds. Of course, you need to find a balance between the insightfulness of the study and your ambition.

Using your own advantages (运用你自己的优势)

As a Chinese student studying in the UK, the advantages may lie in your understanding of the Chinese culture and people, the Chinese market (consumers) and your knowledge of the country's political, economical, technological and business environment. You may also be familiar with business practices in Chinese enterprises and organisations. In addition, you probably have access to data collection in China through your personal or family contacts. You should try to utilise these advantages when you are designing a research project. China is the world's second biggest economy and many developmental issues have attracted worldwide attention. Here, based on the review of China-related research topics that have been published in recent years, we propose a few research topics within the business and management discipline that may be of academic interest:

- Chinese investment in Europe
- China's state-owned enterprises
- China's collectivist culture
- China's one-child population
- mega events hosted in China
- the 'made-in-China' label
- the controlled economy and financial markets
- Chinese social hierarchy and the distribution of wealth and power.

2.2.2 Developing your research question(s)

We are confronted by questions all the time. Is doing a university degree worthwhile? Should I buy organic food? Is there life on Mars? As mentioned earlier, research requires discipline, in that it is rigorously determined and dependent on rigorous methods of data collection and analysis (Bouma, 2001). Therefore, to conduct a piece of research, we first need to ask the right questions.

TOP TIPS 小建议

很多中国学生对于所谓的'研究问题'的概念感到无所适从，但这又是所有毕业论文都要求的。理解这个词其实不难，你一定在开始做一项研究开始就曾问过自己很多问题，比如：我究竟要研究学习什么？我为什么要选择这个方向？这个课题有意义吗？这样的问题会进一步启发你去寻找答案，指导你进一步开发你的研究课题。

Moving from a general research topic to a research question is a crucial step. Campbell et al. (1982) suggest that the selection of research questions often involves a considerable amount of uncertainty and intuition. Therefore, through our observations and literature search we should be able to identify something that is currently poorly understood, either practically or theoretically, could be of some value to our existing knowledge and could be converted into a defined research question.

--------- **Example 2.3** ---------

KEY CHARACTERISTICS OF GOOD RESEARCH QUESTIONS

According to Robson (2011: 62), good research questions have the following characteristics:

好的研究问题具备以下几个特征：

- 清晰明确的定义问题 （clear and unambiguous）；
- 展示你的研究目的 （去探索explore，描述describe，解释explain，或者加强理解 increase understanding某个问题）；
- 是能够通过你的研究和数据给予解答的问题；
- 不是琐碎细小而杂乱的； 而是
- 有逻辑的，从相互关联的一组问题中提炼的（并非是随机选取的问题）。

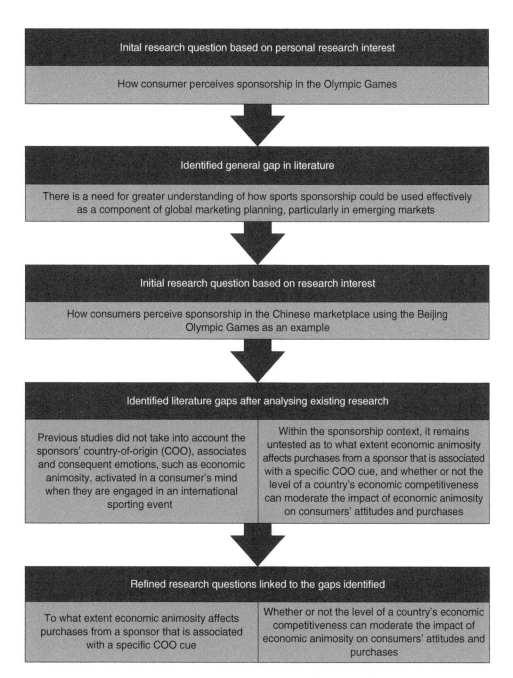

Figure 2.1   An example of linking the research questions to the gap in literature

Source: Meng-Lewis et al. (2013: 1911)

Once you have a research idea and are starting to formulate it into research questions, you will need to go further into researching and analysing the topic, and investigate its possibilities. You are now entering the initial stage of searching and reviewing the literature in order to refine your research question and identify research possibilities. Through reading and analysing what has been done in this particular subject area, you are developing an understanding of the gaps in the literature – that is, what has not been done and would be worthwhile looking into. Your research questions should be closely connected to the gaps in the literature that you have identified.

As illustrated in Figure 2.1, in order to develop good research questions, first of all you need to relate the question to the purposes of your research and be very familiar with your research area. It is important to develop researchable questions (Bouma, 2001). Don't be over-ambitious, and try to limit your research scope to certain times, places, groups of people, conditions, and so on. For example, the question 'What factors influence consumers' online shopping experiences?' is a very large topic and would be extremely difficult to manage within your dissertation time frame. A more manageable research question would be something like, 'How does e-word of mouth affect consumers' purchase intentions through *Taobao* amongst Chinese university students?' In essence, your research question needs to be very focused, narrow and refined.

In addition, you will need to consider whether the research question can be answered through your empirical research. Make sure that the research question is observable and measurable from the data that you obtain. For example, if you set out to answer the question of 'whether loyal customers are *happier* about a service than normal customers', you may find that *happiness* is not truly measurable using a single scale, because of its multi-dimensional nature (The Globe and Mail, n.d.). However, consumers' *perceived service quality* is a measurable construct and there are existing measurement scales that you can adopt. Therefore, it may be more achievable to change the question to one of 'how customers' perceived service quality is affected by their loyalty to a company'.

TOP TIPS 小建议

在提出研究问题时，不要过早去想适用的研究方法 (research methods)。在你的研究问题还没有清晰明确的定义下来，还没有熟悉此研究领域的文献之前，不要去想研究方法。因为这会影响到你对于研究问题范围和主题的设定。

2.3 FORMULATING RESEARCH AIMS AND OBJECTIVES

In addition to your research questions, you are often required to formulate a research aim (研究目的) and a set of objectives (研究目标). Your research question(s) and research aim(s) complement each other and tell your readers what your research is about. Table 2.3 provides some examples of research questions and the related research aims. Research objectives (Table 2.4) inform the research aim and are a more precise breakdown of the general purpose of the research.

Table 2.3 Examples of research questions, related research aims and objectives

Research question	Research aim	Research objectives
How effective is Guanghua Management School's marketing activities in China?	To investigate the effectiveness of Guanghua Management School's marketing activities in China	To understand the selection criteria when students make the decision of where to study; to identify the marketing activities in GMS; to assess the awareness level of GMS's marketing activities amongst their current students; to explore students' views about how marketing activities could be improved
What are the key components needed to create a successful viral video?	To recognise and understand the key components needed to create a successful viral video	To analyse the content characteristics across 100 successful viral videos and the similarities between them; to understand the key factors a consumer faces when deciding to share a viral video; to recognise the main distribution channels for sharing, and identify the channel most likely to achieve success; to create a framework entailing the essential components to a successful viral video
How does the attractiveness of the sales assistant affect consumers' purchase behaviour?	To examine whether the attractiveness of the sales assistant has a positive effect on the purchase behaviour of the customer	To investigate if the attractiveness of the sales assistant has an impact on consumers' perceived trustworthiness; to investigate if the attractiveness of the sales assistant has an impact on consumers' perceived expertise; to find out if the attractiveness of the sales assistant has an impact on consumers' purchase intention

Table 2.4 Tips on developing good research objectives

Good research objectives should be ...	Good research objectives shouldn't be ...
transparent （清楚，清晰的定义）	lacking in focus （没有重点）
specific （具体化）	too broad a scope （太宽泛，不具体）
relevant （与你的研究问题和目的相关）	too narrow a scope （具体在一个很狭隘的点上，没有太多研究的意义）
measurable （在允许的时间范围内能够测量的）	immeasurable, unachievable （很难通过此研究解答提出的研究问题）
answerable（能够实现的，可以解答的）	lacking interconnectivity （研究目的的制定有漏洞，不能完整的解答研究问题）

Source: Cameron and Price (2009); Saunders et al. (2016)

KEY CONCEPTS IN CHINESE: RESEARCH AIMS AND RESEARCH OBJECTIVES

研究目的（aims）是对你要做这个课题的简要评述。常常是用一句话阐述你要做什么，以及希望达到的什么结果。

研究目标 (objectives) 是指通过此研究具体要达到的目的。一篇论文通常要制定3-5个研究目标。做完论文后，你要在Conclusion里讨论你如何达到了这些目标。

The example in Figure 2.2 shows some typical problems that Chinese students have when developing research aims and objectives, and how they can be solved.

There is a further issue with the example in Figure 2.2. After removing the objectives that are inappropriate and combining the ones that have the same meaning, the research scope seems too narrow. In this case, your supervisor may suggest you go back to the literature and look for any additional variables within consumer behaviour studies that should be considered. Alternatively, you may be advised to find a Chinese company as a case study.

A more appropriate research aim and its objectives are shown in Example 2.4.

Example 2.4

RESEARCH AIM AND OBJECTIVES

Research aim

To examine the effectiveness of Lining's current CSR activities in terms of consumers' brand perceptions, attitudes and purchase intentions.

Research objectives

1. To identify the factors influencing Chinese consumers' perceptions of the Lining brand and its current CSR activities.
2. To assess the impact of Lining's CSR activities on Chinese consumers' perceived brand image, attitudes and purchase intentions.
3. To make recommendations on effective CSR management for Lining.

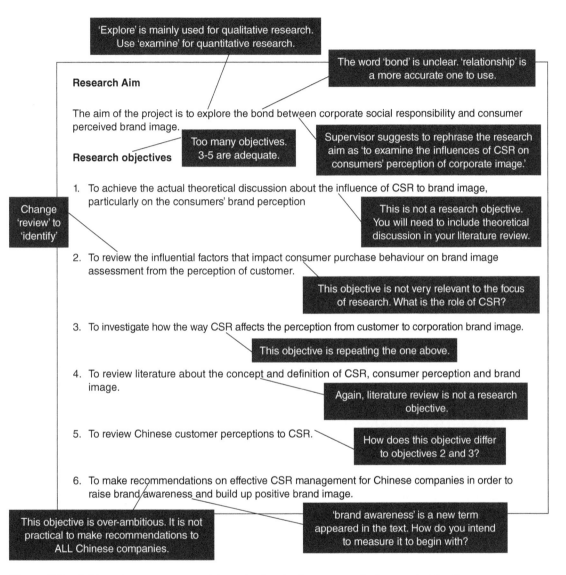

Figure 2.2 Addressing common problems in developing research aims and objectives

2.4 CONNECTING THEORIES TO METHODS

2.4.1 What is a theory?

In Chapter 1, we mentioned that business research involves the use of scientific methods to develop knowledge. Theory building helps researchers to achieve this purpose. Theory（理论）can be defined as 'an explanation of observed regularities' (Bryman and Bell, 2011: 7). It provides formal, logical explanations of some phenomenon through describing how things correspond to the phenomenon and how they relate to each other. Theories are those generalisations that help us better understand reality and allow us to identify the logic behind the things we observe (Zikmund et al., 2009).

Whetten (1989) describes four essential elements of a theory as follows:

1. *What*, 此理论检验了哪些变量 (variables) 或者概念 (concepts)? 比如在 Table 2.3 中的第三个例子里，从设定的研究问题和研究目标中我们可以看出来，要检验的变量是 attractiveness of the sales assistants 和 purchase behaviour (perceived trustworthiness, perceived expertise and purchase intention).

2. *How*, 这些变量或者概念之间的关系是什么？在以上例子里，研究者要检验的是 attractiveness of the sales assistants 和 consumers' purchase behaviour 之间的因果关系 (causality)。所以，理论是研究变量之间的因果关系，或者不同概念之间是如何相互作用的。

3. *Why*, 为什么这些变量或者概念之间有此关系？我们如何解释这种关系？继续沿用以上例子，研究者发现 attractiveness of the sales assistants 并没有对顾客的 purchase intention 产生统计学上的重大影响 (not statistically significant)，这与之前他基于现有的文献理论所做出的假设 (hypothesis) 并不相符。于是，研究者就必须对于他所得到的这个结果做出合理的解释。由此可见，我们需要解答的问题可能是：why does/(does not) this relationship exist in my data?

4. *Who, Where, When* 这些条件局限制约了研究者提出的理论假设。比如以上实例是针对一个英国的服装连锁品牌 Hollister 所做的实证研究。我们要考虑这些研究结果是否适用于其他的品牌？或者有不同的文化背景的人群？是否适用于二十年以后的情况？这些都是我们提出或者验证一个理论的制约因素 (limitations)。

2.4.2 How a theory informs research questions, objectives and methods

It is crucial for researchers to recognise the importance of theories in any research, even from the very early stages, i.e. when writing your research question and research objectives. Saunders et al. (2016) suggest that theories are helpful when formulating a research question in that they give it a sound theoretical explanation. This allows you to identify other research around similar research topics in the literature. You may discover how other scholars have formulated their research questions, aims and objectives; and how their research contributes to our knowledge. For masters students, it may become a good shortcut for developing your own research question and objectives by applying an existing theory to a different scenario or context, such as China.

The nature of your research is dependent on whether you are *testing* a theory or *developing* a theory. This is the distinction between *deductive* （演绎）and *inductive* （归纳）*research*. Chapter 3 provides an in-depth discussion of these two approaches as well as a third approach – abduction （溯因法）.

> ## TOP TIPS 小建议
>
> - 演绎是从一般到个别的推理方法。是以现有理论为基础，去考察验证某个特殊的对象。它着重于理论的检验，是由'理论➜观察 / 结果'的过程。
> - 归纳是从个别到一般的推理方法。是从若干个个别事实中概括总结出一个理论。它着重于理论的创建和发展，是由'观察 / 结果➜理论'的过程。

2.5 APPLYING WESTERN THEORIES IN THE CHINESE CONTEXT

2.5.1 Why do business research in China?

According to the World Bank Group (2014), China represents 16.7 per cent of the world economy and about 19 per cent of the world's population. Therefore, few international companies can afford to ignore the Chinese market. While investment opportunities in China are abundant, there is a longstanding recognition that China's social, economic and cultural environment is fundamentally different from that of the West. As we have argued in Chapter 1, it would be problematic to assume that Western management concepts, mostly American in origin, can be transferable and applicable to China without modifications. In response to China's continuing economic growth in the world, and the lack of understanding of its market, increasing academic and managerial attention has been paid to this country.

2.5.2 Which are the most researched areas relevant to China?

The significant economic reforms undertaken over the last few decades have brought dramatic changes within Chinese society. As a result, there has been a substantial increase in the number of academic studies on business- and management-related topics. Quer et al. (2007) identify two broad areas in business and management research conducted in the Chinese context.

The first is at an individual level and involves the behaviour of consumers, employees or households. In the marketing discipline, for example, owing to China's increasingly opened-up society and market, dramatic changes in Chinese consumer behaviour have become evident. Since the 1990s, academic attention has been paid to Chinese consumer research. To date, research in this area has covered a wide range of topics, looking at the behaviours of acquisition, the use and disposition of products/goods, as well as factors around these behaviours such as consumer lifestyle. At a macro level, research has been done to describe or categorise consumers according to their attitudes, activities, opinions and demographics. For example, Dickson and colleagues (2004) identify six market segments of Chinese consumers based on their potential to buy foreign apparel.

At a micro level, consumer research is often associated with the recognition and cognition of marketing stimuli, communications between brands/organisations and consumers, and behaviour at different stages of the decision-making process. For example, Zhou and Belk (2004) analyse upscale Chinese consumers' understanding of global and local television and print advertising.

More recent Chinese consumer research also takes into consideration the impact of personal values (e.g. individualism vs collectivism) and consumer values on consumption behaviours (i.e. functional, emotional, social and epistemic) and life satisfaction (Xiao and Kim, 2009). With the growing amount of research into business ethics being conducted worldwide, more research has also been carried out in this area in relation to Chinese consumers. For example, Tian et al. (2011) explore how Chinese consumers respond to corporate social responsibility (CSR). Chan et al. (2008) identify the factors affecting Chinese consumers' intentions to bring their own shopping bags when visiting a supermarket. Another area, which has attracted much attention from researchers, is the country-of-origin effect on Chinese consumers. These studies often examine the impact of Chinese consumers' ethnocentrism and/or animosity on their attitudes towards foreign and domestic brands, product judgements and purchase intentions (e.g. Klein et al., 1998; Kwok et al., 2006).

The second area identified by Quer et al. (2007) is at the organisational level and refers to management and organisational research. Three broad categories have been identified based on the systematic review of management and organisational research in Greater China: organisational behaviour, strategic management and international management (Peng et al., 2001). The researched subjects include, for example, how state-owned enterprises (SOEs) operate in the marketised sectors that follow different 'rules of the game'; the study of small and medium-sized enterprises (SMEs); and foreign investment enterprises and how they adapt to Chinese culture.

The focus of organisational research has been around studying the operations and performance of Chinese enterprises. Researchers have approached organisational research from either a cultural or an institutional perspective. The cultural approach takes into consideration the influences of Chinese culture and Confucian values (e.g. the respect for authority, family/group orientation, and preference for personal relations – *guanxi*) on organisational behaviour. The institutional approach introduces a broader range of variables within the institutional framework（制度框架，通常指社会层面的）to explain relations between organisations and environments – for example, the institutional pressure and power from central and local governments over economic activities and Chinese firms (e.g. Lu, 1996).

Strategic management research looks at the business strategies of various types of Chinese enterprises – for example, the important role of 'trust' in family-based networks (e.g. Tsang, 2002) and the importance of diversification strategies for family firms' performance (e.g. Tsang, 2001). With regards to SOEs, attention has been paid to how firms adapted to the 'game of market competition' following the Chinese economic transition in the 1970s (Peng, 2000). In addition, the business strategies of Chinese private firms, collective firms, and township and village enterprises are of interest to researchers.

Regarding research into international management, attention has been focusing on comparative organisational behaviour at both the micro and macro levels. At a micro level, research compares the managerial values, organisational commitment and negotiation behaviours of Chinese and Western firms. The issues and challenges in using Western models and instruments in micro-competitive research have led to an increased amount of indigenous research in order to capture the essence of Chinese values (e.g. Farh et al., 1998). At a macro level, comparative international management research has looked at strategic alliances and joint ventures based on case studies and surveys involving Chinese companies and foreign partners. More specifically, entry modes, partner selection, government control, ownership structure, investment timing, standardisation versus localisation, technological leadership and organisational learning have been investigated.

FURTHER READING

Frontiers of Business Research in China 《中国工商管理研究前沿》, Journal, ISSN: 1673-7326 (Print, Springer); 1673-7431 (Online)，高等教育出版社编辑出版，德国Springer出版公司负责海外发行的全英文管理学季刊。FBR发表中国企业管理领域的最优秀研究成果以及最新进展和动态。

2.5.3 Current and future issues

The vast majority, if not all, of these researchers have employed the experience, theories and research methodologies devised elsewhere – predominantly from developed and industrialised countries in the West – as paradigms for studying and understanding developments in China (Roy et al., 2001). There have been some discussions about the appropriateness of applying Western theories to the Chinese context (Shenkar and Von Glinow, 1994). The findings indicate that theories developed in the West require significant adjustment before they can be used effectively to assess the structure and processes of Chinese enterprises, and employee attitudes and behaviours within Chinese organisations.

Another piece of research, which reviews issues around conducting research in China (Roy et al., 2001), suggests a few areas of potential concern, including probability sampling, government controls, the lack of reliable secondary data, survey instrument design and survey implementation. Despite the tremendous differences and disparities in managerial practices, cultures, structures and multinational institutions, the academic attention paid to these differences is minimal. There have been concerns regarding the recent trend of imitating American theories and methods in China, as this trend may have the unintended consequence of stifling diversity and innovation in management knowledge (Van de Ven and Jing, 2012).

Although for undergraduate or postgraduate dissertation projects, adapting and applying foreign theories and methods to the Chinese context may have advantages, in some cases these 'borrowed' theories and methods may not be sensitive to the local context. *Indigenous research*, as a context-sensitive approach to unique local phenomena, is hence recommended. The central idea is that business and management researchers should pay attention to 'the differences and disparities in managerial practices, cultures, structures, and institutions across regions and countries' (Van de Ven and Jing, 2012: 124).

KEY CONCEPTS IN CHINESE: INDIGENOUS RESEARCH

本土研究，是对于当地的特定现象进行的科学研究。这种研究运用当地语言，当地人，和具有地域含义的抽象概念（constructs）来验证或者建立理论。这些理论又都具有一定的共性：都是能解释和预测在当地特有的社会文化影响下的一些特定现象。

Source: Tsui (2004)

Pan et al. (2012) formulate a specific problem of the lack of measures that capture Chinese cultural dimensions. They use a grounded theory-building approach with the extensive engagement of interdisciplinary Chinese scholars to identify five major schools and 35 measures of Chinese cultural traditions, and then trace these back to original writings in the literature. Following good psychometric methods of test construction, the researchers conducted a pilot study of the initial instrument, followed by two large samples consisting of 2,658 respondents in Beijing and 716 participants in 27 Chinese provinces. The research nicely addresses the problem. It contributes a newly developed instrument of the Structure of Chinese Cultural Traditions (SCCT) that measures a unique indigenous model of Chinese businesses. It also expands our general knowledge on cross-cultural research by showing that the SCCT is complementary, but cannot be reduced to generic values as generated by the Schwartz Value Survey.

When conducting research in China, it is important to appreciate and respect the unique values of indigenous people and their context – that is, they may not act in the same ways as research conducted in other contexts. Identifying and recognising the uniqueness of Chinese culture, its people and organisations can greatly help in understanding the research topic being studied.

Methodologically, indigenous research requires research methods that engage and bridge the perspectives of various stakeholders in China. Some examples of indigenous research conducted in China are as follows:

- Silin's (1976) study investigated how large private firms in Taiwan were controlled by individual leaders, based on a year-long field study.
- Yan and Gray (1994) looked at the issue of bargaining power in joint ventures between partners from the United States and China, using case studies where data were collected through interviews and archives.
- Joy (2001) explored gift-giving practices in Hong Kong and how social ties were developed through this ritual, using in-depth interviews.
- Ma (2012) investigated how authority relations influenced the organisational restructuring of Chinese SOEs. Interviews were conducted with the SOEs' managers.

2.6 NEGOTIATING ACCESS WITH CHINESE ORGANISATIONS

As soon as you have identified a research topic, it is important to think about how you would gain access to the data. Research data can be obtained from primary or secondary sources (see Chapter 6 for detailed discussion about the types of data and main methods of data collection). Gaining permission to access documents and people may not always be a straightforward process. Often, you need to undertake a considerable amount of work before you can actually start collecting your data. This requires patience and negotiation skills. The two most cited reasons for refusing research access are staff time and confidentiality (Buchanan et al., 1988). There are a number of issues that you should keep in mind while negotiating with Chinese organisations.

Point of entry. In our experience, many Chinese students secure access through the networks and connections of their extended family. Other students acquire access to the organisation that they have been working for part-time alongside conducting their research projects. As the Chinese culture respects hierarchy and seniority, ideally your point of entry should be senior organisational members, who have the authority to grant permission. In this case, *guanxi* is essential in building trust and establishing credibility with Chinese organisations and people.

Preparation. At the very least, you should let the organisation know what your research is about and how it may be able to help you. You should also customise the access request letter and prepare for any potential questions raised by the organisation. As Jones (2014: 74) suggests, 'approaching an organisation without any indication of what is to be studied is unlikely to elicit a positive response, as the organisation will be unable to judge what aspects of its activities will be subject to scrutiny, and whether it would be happy to allow this, or the resources, such as staff time, that this may involve'. Ideally, the more material you can provide, the easier it is for the organisation to make a decision. In practice, it is very rare to know in advance exactly how your research will proceed. Although your research design can be flexible at this initial stage, it is unethical to promise to do one thing but end up doing something completely different. Thus, it may be better to have not too specific a description at this stage.

Selling your project. In most cases, you have to convince the organisation to participate in your study. There are two general approaches. The first one is to show why they are 'qualified'. This is particularly useful when you seek to understand best practices within organisations. As you are focusing on the positive aspects of the organisation, you may be able to get the PR department involved to help you distribute questionnaires or arrange interviews. The second approach is to identify the benefits of research for that organisation. It is not uncommon for some organisations to expect some return from their participation. As an independent researcher, you can, for example, provide feedback on the management activity you observe. You can also persuade organisations by sharing your results, for example offering a report on the research findings. Having said this, as a student, you should avoid 'over-selling'. It is unlikely that a student's dissertation can solve a significant problem in a prospective organisation.

Persistence. It may take longer than you think to get a decision. The granting of access may be slow paced for many reasons, for example the manager could be away, or your request may coincide with a busy period in the organisation's business activities. Without being seen as 'pushy', you could try to have some follow-up communication with your contact in the organisation. In some cases, you need to be flexible in your research design. For example, if an organisation refuses your request to send a large-scale survey to their employees, you may change your method of data collection to one of conducting a small number of in-depth interviews with managers/employees. Moreover, demonstrating your competence and integrity as an external researcher may help to establish your credibility.

Confidentiality agreement. As will be discussed in the next section, ensuring confidentiality and anonymity can ease the minds of managers, as commercial organisations may be concerned that their sensitive information (such as marketing plans, employee salary, accounting reports) may be leaked to competitors. On this point, Western and Chinese organisations use different methods. Western organisations sometimes require researchers to sign a formal, written confidentiality agreement (Jones, 2014). In Chinese organisations, trust is often established on a personal and informal basis. Although you may not need to sign a legal document, it is still considered good practice to promise confidentiality, even verbally.

After securing access to potential participants and data, and prior to your data collection, you should obtain *informed consent* from your participants.

TOP TIPS 小建议

Gaining access to Chinese organisations (based on Saunders et al., 2016 and personal experience):

- 在和相关公司或机构联络前，充分了解他们的相关信息；
- 预留充分的时间；
- 运用现有的关系，并且通过他们发展建立更多的关系；
- 给对方提供关于你研究课题和希望达到的研究目标清晰明确的解释；
- 尽可能通过对话交流和实际行动消除、减少对方的疑虑；
- 找出哪些是对于对方有利的结果；
- 运用适当的语言和举止去交流协商；
- 一步一步的逐渐争取数据；
- 强调并确保数据的保密性和匿名性；
- 建立你自己作为一个客观研究员的信誉。

2.7 ETHICAL CONSIDERATIONS

Ethics refers to the moral values or principles that guide a code of conduct for human beings. It relates to the ways in which people behave and, to put it simply, it is about 'doing the right thing'. Ethical rules are formed when people make value judgements about what is right and wrong and about where the boundary lies between acceptable and unacceptable behaviour. Research ethics deal with the manner and principles in which research is conducted and how the results or findings are reported. They are guided by legal, professional, cultural and personal obligations (Cameron and Price, 2009).

Students studying within UK universities must comply with their university's ethical standards. Each university has an ethics committee which is responsible for the research activities carried out by students and academic staff. As part of your dissertation project, you are expected to submit your ethics application form, which is reviewed, first of all, by your supervisor.

KEY CONCEPTS IN CHINESE: RESEARCH ETHICS

道德是关于人类价值和行为的一个哲学分支，是依靠人们对于信念传统和社会习惯形成的价值规范和行为准则。学术道德是指在从事科研工作和进行学术活动时所应遵守的道德规范。学术道德是做研究、治学的最基本要求，是学者的学术良心，并且受到法律、职业、文化和个人准则的约束以及社会道德舆论的监督。

2.7.1 Ethical principles and suggestions

As a researcher, you take responsibility for your participants/respondents, those sponsoring or commissioning your research and the wider research community. Students studying at UK universities should adhere to the following principles which set out the responsibilities and values relevant to your research. You, as a researcher, are encouraged to follow these principles and consider the wider consequences of your work, and to engage critically in good practice in your research.

Integrity and honesty

You should comply with all legal and ethical requirements relevant to your field of study. You should declare any potential or actual conflicts of interest relating to research and, where necessary, take steps to resolve them. Researchers should make every effort to stick to the research plan and produce the desired results. Your results and findings must be trustworthy. You should be honest in relation to your own research and that of others. You must be honest about your research purpose and processes, what data will be recorded and how they will be used. 'Informed consent' must be obtained prior to your data collection. You should do your utmost to ensure the accuracy of data and results by dealing with the data collected or provided to you, in an accurate and unbiased way. It is also important to acknowledge the contributions of others involved in your research.

Respect and fairness

Treating the people involved in your research with respect requires you to think about the ways in which your research may be seen as undermining others' values and credibility. Researchers should not discriminate against other people on the basis of their personal identities, including their ethnicity, gender, age, religion, disability, sexual orientation, social background or political beliefs. Furthermore, you should always give credit to the original authors of your cited sources.

Voluntary participation

While doing your research, one of the most important ethical principles is that coercion should not be used to force people into participating in the research (Collis and Hussey, 2014). You should also not attempt to extend the scope of participation without seeking further permission. Your participants have the right not to answer any question(s); not to provide any data requested; to modify the nature of their consent; and to withdraw from participation and withdraw the data they have provided (Saunders et al., 2016).

Privacy and confidentiality

You need to protect the privacy of your research respondents and ensure the confidentiality of research data, whether relating to individuals, groups or organisations. It is very important to protect the anonymity of the individuals or organisations that are involved. For example, you should use quotes from your interview data only with explicit permission of the respondent; and you should remove or change all names or other identifiers. In principle, you should offer anonymity and confidentiality to all the participants in your research to protect their privacy and encourage greater freedom of expression and more open responses. When researching sensitive organisational issues, you are expected not to share your data with anyone, including your contact person and senior managers within that organisation.

TOP TIPS 小建议

在问卷开头，你应加入以下语句：

你回答的内容不会联系到你或你公司的名字。未经许可，所以资料会严格保密。

At the top of the questionnaire you plan to distribute, you should include the following sentence:

> Neither your name nor the name of your company will be associated with your responses. Unless you have given permission otherwise, your contact details and all data you provide will be treated in the strictest confidence. (Collis and Hussey, 2014: 33)

Harm to participants and researchers

You should ensure the safety of everyone involved in your research, including yourself, the research subjects, patients, participants and others. You need to avoid any potential physical and psychological harm to your research participants throughout the research process. Meanwhile, it is important to consider your personal safety when exposing yourself to new situations and meeting people you do not know. Consider the following scenario:

Yu Wang is doing her undergraduate dissertation with a research objective to find out brand choices and alcohol consumption behaviour amongst pub goers. On her ethics application form, she states that she plans to visit three pubs on a Friday night, to observe and interview people there. In order to increase the response rate, she plans to offer drink vouchers to her participants.

There are a number of ethical concerns around her research design. First is the protection of the researcher. It may not be safe for her to collect data among people who may have consumed a large amount of alcohol. The second issue is related to the quality of her data. People who are under the influence of alcohol may not be in a suitable state to answer her questions. The third issue is her incentive for participation. It is not considered ethical to encourage people who are already drinking alcohol to consume more alcohol.

2.7.2 Ethics application procedure and important forms

Students and staff at UK universities are required to apply for ethics approval via the University Research Ethics Procedure, particularly when they wish to conduct research that involves human participants and personal data. You will normally be asked to complete an ethics application form, an information sheet and a consent form. Only after your ethics application is approved should you be allowed to conduct your research. At most universities, retrospective approval, i.e. obtaining approval after you conduct your research, is not allowed. The purposes of obtaining ethical approval are:

- to protect the rights and welfare of participants and minimise the risk of physical and mental discomfort, harm and danger from research procedures
- to protect your rights as a researcher to carry out legitimate investigations, as well as the reputation of the university for research conducted by its students
- to minimise the potential for claims of negligence made against you, your university and any collaborating individuals or organisations
- to safeguard quality, because increasingly external funding bodies and refereed journals require a statement of ethical practice in applications for research funds and as a precondition of publication
- to avoid the likelihood of problems occurring during the course of the research.

A consideration of research ethics is likely to influence your research design. Properly considered research ethics can strengthen your research design. As such, ethical approval and research design should be considered at the same time.

An example of an ethics application form is provided in Appendix 2 of this book.

2.7.3 Participant information sheet

Throughout this chapter, we have mentioned 'informed consent' a few times. In Western research practice, it is recommended that consent is obtained from research participants if the research involves face-to-face interviews, focus groups, direct observation or similar methods of data collection. In social science research ethics, informed consent is commonly seen as the key to respecting the participant's autonomy. Increasingly, universities and researchers also see obtaining informed consent as a precaution against potential accusation, litigation, and compensation claims. In order to gain participants' consent, researchers are expected to provide their participants with an *information sheet* containing brief and clear details of the research (what the research is about, the requirements and implications), participants' or respondents' rights, how the data will be analysed, reported and stored and whom to contact in the case of concerns (Saunders et al., 2016). The information sheet should use language that is readily understood by the general public.

While there is broad agreement that informed consent is useful in protecting participants, concerns have also been raised that it makes the research process too formalised, bureaucratic and complex (O'Neill, 2003). In a collectivist society like China, social relations are often personal and based on mutual trust and cooperation. It may seem pompous to go through informed consent procedures with participants for a postgraduate dissertation. Moreover, informed consent, typically involving signatures in documents (i.e. a consent form), can lead to displacing the traditional Confucian ethics of *xin* (信) – verbal or tacit understandings between gentlemen based on their reputation. In this case, research participation may be seen as legal and contractual rather than informal and voluntary. In our experience, Chinese participants often become reluctant to disclose information if the researcher insists on signing the consent form, for the fear that they may face legal consequences. As such, we suggest that researchers should still fully explain the purpose of the research to their participants and obtain verbal consent without demanding their signatures.

In the participant information sheet in Example 2.5, the researcher outlines the nature and aim of her research, explains exactly what participation means in her research practice (when, where, who, what) and states clearly the inclusion and exclusion criteria for the study. She also describes the benefits for participants and explains how privacy and confidentiality would be maintained.

Example 2.5

INFORMATION SHEET

Consumer perceptions of corporate social responsibility and how it affects perceived brand image: A case study of Li Ning

I would like to invite you to participate in my research, which is concerned with your awareness and understanding of Li Ning's activities in relation to its corporate social responsibility, and how these may contribute to your perception of the company's brand image.

The research is carried out for my postgraduate dissertation at XXX University. It is hoped that the research could provide insights into how corporate social responsibility practices have been conducted within Chinese companies and how consumers respond to them.

You are invited to complete a structured online survey between 1 and 15 October 2017. The survey will take approximately 5-10 minutes to complete. You should be over 16 years of age and have some prior knowledge of Li Ning to be eligible for this survey. All participants will be entered into a prize draw and the winner will receive a £50 gift voucher.

The data collected via the survey will be used in my written dissertation. All data will be treated confidentially and no participant in this research will be individually identifiable in the dissertation or any other publications.

(Continued)

Your participation in this research is entirely voluntary. You are completely free to discontinue your participation in this research at any time. By completing this survey, it will be assumed that consent has been provided. You may also skip any question(s) you do not want to answer.

If you have any concerns about your involvement in the project, please contact my supervisor (Professor A, email address). If you would like further information about this research study, please contact me directly at (your email address).

Researcher: Fei Li   Date:

Postgraduate student, XXX University

Supervisor: Date:

Business School, XXX University

2.7.4 Consent form

In general, a consent form should contain the full title of the project and the name, position and contact details of the researcher. If the researcher is a student, the name, position and contact details of the supervisor should also be provided. An example of an informed consent form can be found in Appendix 3.

The form should be signed and dated by both parties. The participant should receive a copy of the consent form, the participant information sheet and any other written information provided to the participants. A copy of the signed and dated consent form should be kept with the project's main documents, which must be kept in a secure location.

If you are conducting research through the internet, informed consent may be obtained by contacting an online community's moderator or administrator; or by specifically asking the individual participant, if you use an online questionnaire or interview.

KEY CONCEPTS IN CHINESE: INFORMED CONSENT

研究知情同意书是参与研究的对象表示自愿提供信息资料并授权研究者使用其信息资料的文件证明。在签署知情同意书的过程中，要确保研究对象充分了解此项研究的基本信息，允许他们提出自己的疑问，并被给予充分的时间自主决定是否参与此项研究。从事研究的人员在开始数据收集前，有责任去主动获得研究对象的知情同意书。但在中国，有时参与者会误认为这是某种法律文件，签了以后反而会处处小心翼翼，不敢畅所欲言。

TOP TIPS 小建议：怎样成功通过学术道德审查

- 想清楚你计划要做的全部步骤和整个过程，并尽可能清楚地用文字表述出来。列清楚每一步要做的事情。
- 避免使用术语或缩写，要记得你的评审和研究对象可能不了解你的专业，你的叙述应该是通俗易懂的。
- 不要夸大研究目的。想清楚你的研究目的，你本身是否具有相应的知识和技能？你是否有充分的时间去实现所有的研究目标？
- 考虑收集数据的方法，并考虑到可能出现的危险。对数据的安全性，保密性也要有所考量。
- 考虑如何使用收集到的数据。是要运用在毕业论文，还是有可能发表？这些数据会被重复、继续使用在其他的一些研究课题上吗？
- 最后，要记得给你自己预留充分的时间在准备学术道德审查的资料上面。并且做好再次、甚至多次修改提交的思想准备。

Research ethics checklist:

- 你的研究参与者何时签署同意书，或者你如何以其他方式征得了他们的同意？
- 研究过程或者结果是否会伤害参与者或者更广泛的人群（包括你自己）？
- 你如何安全妥善地保存了关于参与者（个人和公司）的个人／保密信息？
- 你如何确保你的参与者（个人和公司）都是匿名？
- 在你的研究过程中，你是否遵守了你所在研究领域的行为准则？
- 在你大规模的发送集体邮件时，你是否取得了此机构组织的许可？

2.8 WRITING A RESEARCH PROPOSAL

A written research proposal is often required when you are doing a dissertation project for either your undergraduate or postgraduate degree in the UK. It is normally used for supervisor allocation so that the staff's expertise fits the student's research topic. At some universities, your proposal counts for a certain percentage of the dissertation mark (e.g. typically 10%). There are also many other reasons for writing a research proposal. First of all, the proposal helps to clarify and organise your ideas. It presents the research question and highlights the importance of the research. Second, it shows how your research fits in with existing knowledge through the literature review. It provides a discussion and critique of other related research in the chosen area. Third, it suggests the data needed for solving the research question and how the data will be collected, analysed and interpreted. In essence, it demonstrates that your research is achievable.

KEY CONCEPTS IN CHINESE: RESEARCH PROPOSAL

研究计划（proposal），有时也翻译成'开题报告'，是在研究项目开展初期撰写的一份可行性报告。主要涵盖对所要研究的主题和问题的描述和解释，对研究方法及研究对象的探讨，以及研究进度的制定。

The key components of a research proposal include the following:

1. *Context of the research*. Why are you doing this research? What is the background? What is your research question? What is the value of the research?

2. *Theoretical basis*. What is the academic grounding of the research? What is the gap in the literature?

   You need to demonstrate your knowledge of the literature in your selected research area by identifying key authors or important literature.

3. *Research aim and objectives*. What are you trying to find out?

   You need to relate your research aim and objectives to your research question. You may need to discuss with your supervisor the development of *achievable and measureable* research objectives.

4. *Methodology and methods*. How are you going to achieve your objectives? What are the research approaches and methods to be used? Who is your target audience or sample? How should you collect and analyse the data?

   Make sure that you provide justification for the selected sample. For example, why are you going to draw surveys from the 18–25-year-old population?

5. *Ethical considerations and consents*. Have you had your research ethics form approved? Have you obtained the consent of your respondents?

   If you are going to collect data from China, have you thought through the possible risks?

6. *Timescale*. When are you going to carry out each stage of the research?

7. *Limitations*. Are there any methodological or theoretical limitations?

TOP TIPS 小建议

你的研究计划书是一份草拟稿（working document），在你开展研究的过程中是可以不断修改和完善的。不过，在你和导师已经确定的最初版本上，也不要做出太多重大的修改，因为这可能会耗费你很多时间和精力，而你的主要任务是在规定的时间内完成论文。

FURTHER READING

Hair, Jr., J.F., Celsi, M., Money, A., Samlouel, P. and Page, M. (2016) *Essentials of Business Research Methods*, 3rd edition. Oxon: Routledge. Chapter 4 identifies the characteristics of a quality research topic and provides guidance on how to convert research ideas into research questions.

Jankowicz, A.D. (2005) *Business Research Projects*, 4th edition. London: Thomson Learning. Chapter 2 takes readers through the process of turning the initial idea into a useable research question.

REFERENCES

Blaxter, L., Hughes, C. and Tight, M. (2001) *How to Research*, 2nd edition. Buckingham: Open University Press.

Bouma, G.D. (2001) *The Research Process*, 4th edition. Melbourne: Oxford University Press.

Bryman, A. and Bell, E. (2011) *Business Research Methods*. Oxford: Oxford University Press.

Buchanan, D., Boddy, D. and McCalman, J. (1988) Getting in, getting on, getting out and getting back. In A. Bryman (ed.) *Doing Research in Organisations*. London: Routledge, 53–67.

Cameron, S. and Price, D. (2009) *Business Research Methods: A Practical Approach*. London: Chartered Institute of Personnel and Development (CIPD).

Campbell, J.P., Daft, R.L. and Hulin, C.L. (1982) *What to Study: Generating and Developing Research Questions*. Beverly Hills, CA: Sage.

Chan, R., Wong, Y. and Leung, T. (2008) Applying ethical concepts to the study of 'green' consumer behavior: An analysis of Chinese consumers' intentions to bring their own shopping bags. *Journal of Business Ethics* 79(4): 469–81.

Collis, J. and Hussey, R. (2014) *Business Research: A Practical Guide for Undergraduate and Postgraduate Students*, 4th edition. London: Palgrave Macmillan.

Davies, M. and Hughes, N. (2014) *Doing a Successful Research Project: Using Qualitative or Quantitative Methods*. London: Palgrave Macmillan.

Dickson, M.A., Lennon, S.J., Montalto, C.P., et al. (2004) Chinese consumer market segments for foreign apparel products. *Journal of Consumer Marketing* 21(5): 301–17.

Farh, J.-L., Tsui, A.S., Xin, K., et al. (1998) The influence of relational demography and guanxi: The Chinese case. *Organisation Science* 9(4): 471–88.

Finn, M., Walton, M. and Elliott-White, M. (2000) *Tourism and Leisure Research Methods: Data Collection, Analysis, and Interpretation*. London: Longman.

Jones, M. (2014) *Researching Organisation: The Practice of Organisational Fieldwork*. London: Sage.

Joy, A. (2001) Gift giving in Hong Kong and the continuum of social ties. *Journal of Consumer Research* 28(2): 239–56.

Klein, J., Ettenson, R. and Morris, M. (1998) The animosity model of foreign product purchase: An empirical test in the People's Republic of China. *Journal of Marketing* 62(Jan.): 89–100.

Kwok, S., Uncles, M. and Huang, Y. (2006) Brand preferences and brand choices among urban Chinese consumers: An investigation of country-of-origin effects. *Asia Pacific Journal of Marketing* 18(3): 163–72.

Lu, Y. (1996) *Management Decision-making in Chinese Enterprises*. London: Macmillan.

Ma, D. (2012) A relational view of organisational restructuring: The case of transitional China. *Management and Organisation Review* 8(1): 51–75.

Meng-Lewis, Y., Thwaites, D. and Pillai, K.G. (2013) Consumers' responses to sponsorship by foreign companies. *European Journal of Marketing* 47(11/12): 1910–30.

O'Neill, O. (2003) Some limits of informed consent. *Journal of Medical Ethics* 29(1): 4–7.

Pan, Y., Rowney, J. A., and Peterson, M. F. (2012) The structure of Chinese cultural traditions: An empirical study of business employees in China. *Management and Organization Review*, 8(1): 77–95.

Peng, M., Lu, Y., Shenkar, O., et al. (2001) Treasures in the China house: A review of management and organisational research on Greater China. *Journal of Business Research* 52(2): 95–110.

Peng, M.W. (2000) *Business Strategies in Transition Economies*. Thousand Oaks, CA: Sage.

Quer, D., Claver, E. and Rienda, L. (2007) Business and management in China: A review of empirical research in leading international journals. *Asia Pacific Journal of Management* 24(3): 359–84.

Robson, C. (2011) *Real World Research: A Resource for Users of Social Research Methods in Applied Settings*, 3rd edition. Chichester: Wiley.

Roy, A., Walters, P. and Luk, S. (2001) Chinese puzzles and paradoxes: Conducting business research in China. *Journal of Business Research* 52(2): 203–10.

Saunders, M., Lewis, P. and Thornhill, A. (2016) *Research Methods for Business Students*, 7th edition. Harlow: Pearson.

Shenkar, O. and Von Glinow, M. (1994) Paradoxes of organisational theory and research: Using the case of China to illustrate national contingency. *Management Science* Jan.(1): 56–72.

Silin, R. (1976) *Leadership and Values: The Organisation of Large-scale Taiwanese Enterprises*. Cambridge, MA: Harvard University Press.

The Globe and Mail. (n.d.) *Happiness is not Truly Measurable*. Available at: www.theglobe andmail.com/globe-debate/editorials/happiness-is-not-truly-measurable/article4098416 (accessed 21 October 2015).

Tian, Z., Wang, R. and Yang, W. (2011) Consumer responses to corporate social responsibility (CSR) in China. *Journal of Business Ethics* 101(2): 197–212.

Tsang, E.W.K. (2001) Internationalizing the family firm: A case study of a Chinese family business. *Journal of Small Business Management* 39(1): 88–93.

Tsang, E.W.K. (2002) Learning from overseas venturing experience. *Journal of Business Venturing* 17(1): 21–40.

Tsui, A. (2004) Contributing to global management knowledge: A case for high quality indigenous research. *Asia Pacific Journal of Management* 21(4): 491–513.

Van de Ven, A.H. and Jing, R. (2012) Indigenous management research in China from an engaged scholarship perspective. *Management and Organisation Review* 8(1): 123–37.

Veal, A. and Darcy, S. (2014) *Research Methods in Sport Studies and Sport Management: A Practical Guide*. Oxon: Routledge.

Whetten, D. (1989) What constitutes a theoretical contribution? *Academy of Management Review* 14(4): 490–5.

World Bank Group (2014) China – World Bank Data. Available at: https://data.worldbank.org/country/china (accessed 6 October 2016).

Xiao, G. and Kim, J. (2009) The investigation of Chinese consumer values, consumption values, life satisfaction, and consumption behaviors. *Psychology & Marketing* 26(7): 610–24.

Yan, A. and Gray, B. (1994) Bargaining power, management control, and performance in United States–China joint ventures: A comparative case study. *Academy of Management Journal* 37(6): 1478–1517.

Zhou, N. and Belk, R. (2004) Chinese consumer readings of global and local advertising appeals. *Journal of Advertising* 33(3): 63–76.

Zikmund, W., Babin, B., Carr, J., et al. (2009) *Business Research Methods*. Mason, OH: South-Western, Cengage Learning.

3
RESEARCH PHILOSOPHY AND APPROACHES

3.1 EPISTEMOLOGY AND ONTOLOGY

Research philosophy is important in designing and evaluating research. First, it is useful for researchers to clarify research design. Danermark et al. (2002) suggest that our understanding of the social world depends on our ontological and epistemological assumptions. Over the years, various authors have attempted to use metaphors to explain the relationship among research philosophy, methodology and methods. Popular ones include Saunders et al.'s (2015) research onion and Easterby-Smith et al.'s (2015) tree ring. Briefly, it is argued that the research methods and techniques adopted in a project depend on the assumptions of the methodology, and the decisions made around it, which often rely on a researcher's understanding of epistemology and ontology. There is no specific knowledge or sophisticated technique that can guarantee, by itself, that results will be reliable, valid and relevant in social research. These authors suggest that the method, object and purpose of investigation must be considered simultaneously and in relation to each other. Second, research philosophy helps researchers to understand their own roles in the research process and thus develop more robust theories and knowledge.

The primary aim of this chapter is to present an overview of the various philosophical stances that guide social research. Before we move on to discuss some of the most common perspectives, it is useful to first define two key terms that we use throughout this chapter, namely ontology（存在论）and epistemology（认识论）. Ontology for social scientists is about the nature of reality and existence. Epistemology for social scientists is about the nature of knowledge.

KEY CONCEPTS IN CHINESE: RESEARCH PHILOSOPHY

研究哲学，是指导研究的思想方法或哲学。 在研究哲学（主要是认知论和存在论）的引导下，我们才得以提出适合的研究方法 (research methodology)。

3.1.1 Ontology

This branch of philosophy deals with the nature of the social phenomenon under investigation. Central to the discussion of ontology is whether something (or the phenomenon that we are interested in) actually exists, regardless of whether or not we know it or have experience of it, or it is only our perception. In other words, it is about whether something is real or illusory (Johnson and Duberley, 2000). There are broadly two different views. Various authors refer to them in different terms. For example, Johnson et al. (2006) call this objective versus subjective ontology, while Easterby-Smith et al. (2015) use realist versus relativist ontology. From an objective or realist point of view, social concepts such as leadership, culture and discrimination can be seen as 'real' and they exist independently of our personal knowing. They guide our behaviour and have a real impact on people's lives and work experience. Some of these concepts can be difficult to measure, and people in different societies, age groups, gender categories, and so on, may experience such social phenomena differently, but we cannot deny their existence. Neither can we change the reality of their consequences. By doing research, we are attempting to discover the truth. This stream of thinking takes 'reality as it is'.

On the contrary, a subjective or relativist ontology assumes that what we believe to be reality is a product of what we know. Having an understanding of certain social concepts depends largely on our personal background, the society we grow up in or the social class we belong to. Leadership, for example, has been defined more than a thousand times. These definitions vary according to the context they originated in. Therefore, there is no single 'reality' of leadership waiting to be discovered. Rather, there can be many different perspectives depending on the observer's position. This stream of thinking sees reality as socially constructed, and what counts for the truth can vary from place to place and from time to time (Collins, 1983). Thus, the task of doing social research should not be just about gathering facts and searching for patterns, but also about understanding how people give meaning to their experience. Some authors go even further by suggesting that what we see as social reality is no more than something we create through language and discourse (讨论). According to this perspective, so-called 'truth' only exists in people's perceptions.

KEY CONCEPTS IN CHINESE: ONTOLOGY

西方研究哲学里讨论的两大焦点是存在论和认识论。存在论 (Ontology) 讨论的主要问题是究竟我们研究的社会现象是否有唯一的，客观存在的真相或现实。或者简单的说法是究竟客观真理是否存在。对该问题总体来说有两种相反的观点。一种观点认为有客观真理的存在，即唯物论 (objectivism)。很多社会概念没有物理的形状，但它们客观并独立地存在着。这些概念影响我们对事物的看法，规范着我们的行为。虽然不

同的人（或观察者）由于来自社会不同的阶层，有不同个人背景，但是对同一个社会现象的体会，理解却会不一样。如性别歧视，同一社会里一般女性比男性体会更深。但我们不能因为自己没经历过歧视就否认这些社会现象的存在。

　　相反，另一种观点认为所谓真理是主观存在的，　即唯心论（subjectivism）。它认为真理会随着人的主观意识的改变而改变。正因为社会里每个人对这些现象的理解都不一样，所以现实的存在是多重的。有些学者甚至认为真理根本不存在。持不同观点的哲学家对同一个社会现象的存在论会有完全不同的观点。比如，企业文化是一个看不见也摸不着的东西。有的人认为企业文化是实在和客观存在的，因为它约束了我们在企业里的言行举止。但有的人认为企业文化是虚幻的，可能每名员工都有不同的认识，所以它只存在于我们的意识形态里。

3.1.2 Epistemology

While ontology is about whether truth exists, epistemology is about how to access truth. Epistemology refers to a set of assumptions about ways of understanding the world. Duberley et al. (2012) call it the 'knowledge of knowledge'. These authors suggest that 'epistemology is the study of the criteria by which we can know what does and does not constitute warranted or scientific knowledge' (p. 16). Similar to the debate in ontology, there are also two opposing views about how social science research should be conducted. Again, different scholars label these views differently. Johnson et al. (2006) refer to objectivist versus subjectivist epistemology, whereas Easterby-Smith et al. (2015) use positivist versus social constructivist epistemology. An objectivist epistemology requires an objective ontology that assumes an external reality out there. It entails that the properties of social concepts can be measured through objective approaches, and that researchers can maintain a neutral position in the research process. If knowledge developed in the research process is to be significant, it should be based on externally observable evidence. Thus, this view discounts subjectively inferred evidence, such as feelings, reflections or perceptions.

By contrast, a subjectivist view of epistemology presupposes people's experience as legitimate evidence. Authors of this tradition focus on the ways people make sense of the world and how they communicate and interact with each other. The purpose of social science is to appreciate the different experiences that people have, rather than merely discovering external causes or patterns of behaviour. Moreover, a subjectivist epistemology recognises that researchers are actively engaging in the research process, thus bring in their personal understandings and feelings. This is in stark contrast to an objectivist view that researchers can play neutral and detached roles. A strong version of subjectivist or constructivist epistemology believes that knowledge is created through intersubjectivity, that is, meanings are co-constructed in the research process between the researcher and the researched.

KEY CONCEPTS IN CHINESE: EPISTEMOLOGY

存在论探讨的是现实是否客观存在，而认识论探讨的是如何能认知现实，不管是单一的还是多重的现实。在社会科学里，认识论主要研究的三个问题是：第一，提出新的理论需要有科学的证据，那什么才算科学的证据；第二，为什么这些证据是有效的；第三，研究者在这过程中能否保持中立的状态。正如存在论有客观和主观两种观点，认识论也有客，主两种观点。客观论者认为社会的概念是可以从外部观察和测量的。研究者在科研的过程中应该是客观中立的。只有通过系统的，大规模的收集数据才能发现社会中人的行为的规律。这样发展的知识才是质量有保证的。而主观论者则认为社会现象是由人而产生，这些现象大多不能从外部观察，因为这涉及到人的内在的情感、认知和对事物的喜好，以及人与人之间的交流和交往。但这正是社会科学需要研究的重点。而且，研究者做为社会里的一员，自己本身对某项事物肯定带有一定认识和偏向，所以研究者很难保持中立或绝对的客观。

Ontological and epistemological positions may be culturally bound. Reflecting on their experience of a UK–China collaborative research project, Easterby-Smith and Malina (1999) note that Chinese researchers are interested in obtaining accurate data and factual information in interviews, whereas their UK counterparts place a greater emphasis on people's perception and interpretation of events. These scholars also observe that Chinese researchers expect an agreed-upon answer to each question and look for similarities and patterns between cases, while British researchers' interests lie in exploring the different accounts of various informants in the same company. Thus, they suggest that Chinese researchers are more likely to take a realist stance, while British researchers hold a constructionist view.

3.2 PHILOSOPHICAL PERSPECTIVES

The ontological and epistemological assumptions we discussed above provide foundations for the philosophical perspectives we shall explore below. Here we focus on the four positions that students are most familiar with: positivism, realism, interpretivism and pragmatism.

3.2.1 Positivism (实证主义)

Positivism in social science adopts the philosophical stance of the natural scientists. It relies heavily on Popper's (1959) falsificationism (证伪论), which emphasises objective data collection to test hypotheses. It also proposes that researchers should, by all means, act against their personal feelings and attachments in order to develop unbiased theories. Positivists commit to an objectivist epistemology, which assumes that there is a neutral point at which an observer can stand back and observe the external world objectively (Johnson and Duberley, 2000). In the research process, knowledge of the external social and natural world can be transferred from a passive knower (the subject) to an independent researcher. Positivists also accept a realist ontological position which entails that there is an objective world out there beyond our senses, and that the job of the researcher is to 'pursue truth', or to fit our theories closer and closer to the one objective reality that we presume (Mitroff and Pondy, 1978). Positivist research entails the evaluation of an underlying commitment to a correspondence of truth. The aim is to ensure a distance between the researcher and the researched, so that the research process and findings can be value-free (Johnson et al., 2006). Positivism has been influential in business and management research and becomes the guiding principle of most quantitative research. Johnson et al. (2006) comment on key steps in quantitative research, which include (1) selecting a sample (often large) to participate in a survey or an experiment; (2) using valid and reliable measurements for each variable; (3) testing hypotheses; and (4) generalising findings to a wider population. In so doing, positivist researchers would be able to produce rational, reliable, theoretically derived and generalisable knowledge.

Yet, some researchers use positivism to guide qualitative research too. Neo-empiricism（新经验主义）is sometimes called 'qualitative positivism', as researchers who subscribe to this school use non-quantitative methods within largely positivistic assumptions (Prasad and Prasad, 2002). Neo-empiricists also adopt an objectivist epistemology and assume the possibility of the unbiased and objective collection of qualitative empirical data. But they reject falsificationism in favour of induction. Often, neo-empiricists are interested in the subjective meanings that people use to make sense of their everyday worlds and rely on qualitative methods to investigate the implications of those interpretations for social interaction (Johnson et al., 2006). While adopting an interpretive stance, neo-empiricists emphasise the neutrality of the researcher and maintain the idea that there is a world out there to be discovered and explored by an objective means. Because the quality of research can only depend on the researchers' own objective judgement in the process, a key task for the researcher(s) is to establish the credibility of their own behaviours, so as to justify the findings. This can be done through methodological reflexivity (Alvesson and Sköldberg, 2000). That means minimising bias by deploying strategies such as multiple researchers, multiple sources of data collection, cross-referencing and mixed methods.

KEY CONCEPTS IN CHINESE: POSITIVISM

实证主义来源于珀朴的证伪论，即任何理论可以当作是真的直到被证实是假科学为止。如一千多年来人们一直以为地球是平的，直到有人用实例证明地球是圆的。地圆论证明了地平论是假科学。珀朴认为科学研究就是不断地用新的证据而推翻伪科学，从而不断地接近真理。实证主义承认客观的存在论和认识论。即

(Continued)

认可客观存在，独立于人的认知以外的现实。所以实证论者认为探讨真相的过程也应该采取客观的手段，研究人员不应该带进自己的偏见和感情。接受实证主义的研究者大多采用定量研究法，主要步骤包括：提出假设；找出对社会概念的测量；通过发问卷，做实验等向一定的人群收集数据；用复杂的统计方法分析数据；最后用结果支持或否定假设。他们认为这样的得出的结果较大程度代表客观现实。

有少数的实证主义者也采用定性研究法。他们认为有些概念带有主观性，所以不能用测量的方法去研究。这类研究会采用访谈，观察等方法收集数据。但最终目的也是为了寻找客观现实，所以他们更强调研究人员的中立和客观的地位。往往他们的研究方法论包括很多用于减少主观偏见的手段，如研究员之间互相监督，采用多个来源收集数据，尽量运用电脑之类的客观的分析手段以减少误差。

3.2.2 Realism （现实主义）

Realism adopts an objective ontology, which assumes a reality independent of our cognition. Similar to positivism, realism promotes a scientific and objective approach to doing research. However, realists do not all adopt the same epistemology. Saunders et al. (2015) distinguish between two branches of realism based on how realist researchers collect data and make sense of those data. The first is direct realism, which proposes that what we see is what reality is. It shares an objectivist epistemology and holds that our senses (eyes, ears, hands, etc.) provide us with direct and accurate access to the natural and social worlds. Thus, this branch of philosophy sees the information collected by our senses as useful evidence which depicts reality. However, sometimes we are unable to see the whole truth. This is because we have insufficient information. Therefore, direct realists emphasise the collection of data from multiple sources in order to see the full picture of reality.

On the other hand, critical realism adopts a more subjectivist or social constructionist perspective of epistemology. Critical realists believe that our knowledge of reality is a result of social conditioning and cannot be understood independently of the social actors involved in the knowledge-derivation process (Bhaskar, 1978). In other words, what we see and feel about things may not reflect what things really are. Bhaskar (1989) argues that there exists a reality independent of our knowledge of it. But this reality and the way it behaves are, in important respects, not accessible to immediate observation. In other words, the reality and the 'representation of reality' operate in different domains – a transitive epistemological dimension and an intransitive ontological dimension. The task of the realist researcher is to unearth the real mechanisms and structures underlying perceived events. However, this is not an easy task. Critical realists recognise that societies are structures of social relations where people occupy different positions, have access to different resources and have different interests. Because of our social positions, we tend to see only some parts of reality and are blind to others.

A further difference pointed out by Saunders et al. (2015) is the degree to which direct and critical realists believe research can change reality. Direct realists believe that the social world is relatively stable and that we only study what it is to improve our understanding, whereas critical realists argue that the world is constantly changing due to the changing structures, procedures and processes within it. Our research may enhance our understanding of reality, as well as change it.

KEY CONCEPTS IN CHINESE: REALISM

现实主义承认客观的存在论，所以现实主义者做研究的主要目的是为了寻找客观的，独立于人的认知能力以外的真理。但现实主义者对认识论没有统一的看法。主要有两种观点，直接现实主义和批判现实主义。直接现实主义者认为应该持有客观的认识论。但与实证论不同，现实主义讨论的重点是究竟通过人们感官（如眼睛，鼻子，耳朵，手）收集的信息能不能代表现实或真相。直接现实主义认为现实就是我们直接看到，听到，和感受到的事物。即所谓的'眼见为实'。而批判现实主义者则倾向于主观的认识论。批判的意思是看问题不能光看表面现象。认为人作为社会的个体都是有局限性的。我们对社会现象的看法往往受我们自己成长过程和所处的社会角度的影响。我们认识的事物都是片面的，带有个人偏见的。所以'眼见的不一定就是现实'。

例如很多企业采用员工弹性上班时间，即有需要的员工可以经上级同意自行安排上下班时间。享受过该项政策的员工觉得这项措施好，因为这使他们达到工作与生活的更大平衡。而不采用该项政策的员工觉得这项措施造成管理混乱。批判现实主义者认为虽然有客观的现实（弹性上班时间的后果），但我们对它的认识只能是主观的（不同的人有不同的体会）。做研究的目的是为了发现那些更深层的，无形的社会结构和机制。因为这些结构和机制经常左右人们的想法和行为规范。在对社会科学的研究上，因为大部分的概念（如企业文化）都没有物理的形态，所以研究员大多采纳批判现实主义。

3.2.3 Interpretivism （解释主义）

Interpretivism is often presented as a competing philosophy against positivism. Indeed, interpretivists believe that positivist methods are unable to capture the rich experience of human actors and argue that the social world is too complex to be reduced to a series of definite 'laws'. Denzin (1983), for example, notes, critically, that 'references to the social world that [can] not be verified under quantifiable, observable, scientifically controlled conditions must – following Wittgenstein's dictum – "be passed over in silence"' (p. 132). In a nutshell, this branch of philosophy sees human interpretation as the starting point for knowledge development in the social world (Prasad, 2005). Most interpretivists assume a subjectivist ontology which entails that reality and the individual who observe it cannot be separated (Weber, 2004). How we perceive reality and act on it are inextricably influenced by our life experience. In epistemology, interpretivists have a strong commitment to *verstehen* (the German word for understanding) and emphasise the role of humans as social actors in constructing meaning in the world. It is argued that we intentionally form our understanding by making sense of the world we live and work in. Interpretivists believe that the knowledge we develop is contextualised (Halldén et al., 2008), as it bears the mark of our particular culture, experience, history, and so on. The same information can be interpreted by different individuals in different ways, and assume different meanings depending on the context in which the information is explored.

Moreover, interpretivism recognises the role of the researcher within the knowledge construction framework. Researchers are social actors themselves, with a pre-understanding of the phenomenon (Alvesson and Sköldberg, 2000). As frequently the aim of interpretivist research is to increase understanding or seek an explanation for some social phenomenon, the challenge of researchers is to keep an open mind and see the world from the research subjects' point of view. However, this is by no means easy. Scholars from symbolic interactionism suggest that we, as humans, are constantly interpreting the world around us and we adjust our views and actions as a result of our interaction with others in our socialising process. In this case, knowledge produced in a piece of research is co-constructed by the researcher and the researched.

Just as positivism is often associated with quantitative methods, interpretivism is linked to qualitative research (Denzin and Lincoln, 1995). With a view to producing 'thick description', interpretivist studies are conducted at a micro level to develop detailed and contextualised descriptions of certain social phenomena. This insightful understanding of a small part of society is used as a window to look into wider social issues. However, as interpretivist inquiries operate within a small number of observations to acquire in-depth knowledge, they are limited in their ability to generalise. Many interpretivists reject generalisation as a research goal. Guba and Lincoln (1982: 238) maintain that 'The aim of inquiry is to develop an idiographic body of knowledge. This knowledge is best encapsulated in a series of "working hypotheses" that describe the individual case. Generalisations are impossible since phenomena are neither time- nor context-free'. Scholars have since developed new criteria to assess interpretivist and qualitative research (see, for example, Symon and Cassell, 2012). We will elaborate on the issues of sampling and assessing research quality in the next two chapters.

KEY CONCEPTS IN CHINESE: INTERPRETIVISM

解释主义提出很多与实证主义不同甚至相反的理论。解释主义的提倡者认为研究社会科学不应该用研究自然科学同样的方法。社会科学（包括管理学）在很大程度上是研究人们对事物的看法和观点，而不是一个事物本身。解释主义者大多接纳主观的存在论，认为社会上的事物存在于人们认知的层面。一些社会现象（如歧视）的存在是因人而异的。感受到其后果的人认为它存在，而感受不到的人则认为它不存在。所以'真理'产生的过程跟认知这个事物的人有很大关联。解释主义同意主观的认识论，认为人们对事物的看法，解释跟个人的背景分不开。知识和理论的产生其实是我们对社会现象的解释。而这种解释，或我们对事情的感受与看法，总受到我们自身的文化、背景、生长的社会环境，历史环境的影响。这些都是唯心的。

解释主义者关心的是对社会现象进行深入的调查，了解事情的来龙去脉：现象为什么会产生，如何产生，对人们有何影响，人们的感受如何等。解释主义常从微观的角度研究，采用定性研究法，通过面谈，长期深入的观察等方法收集数据，提供解释。解释主义认为研究者在调研的过程不是被动、中立的。研究员本身对某件事物的看法是知识产生的一部分。

3.2.4 Pragmatism （实用主义）

After reading the above discussions, you may find it very difficult to completely agree with either an objective or a subjective ontology and either an objective or a subjective epistemology. This is exactly the argument of pragmatism. Some pragmatist researchers believe that it is futile to engage in endless debate between the positivists and the anti-positivists. The term pragmatism comes from the same Greek word which means action. It was also developed into other English words we use frequently, words such as 'practice' or 'practical'. This branch of philosophy originates in the work of some American philosophers, such as William James and John Dewey, as a way to escape the epistemological deadlock between the realist view and the relativist view. Pragmatists do not always have the same ontological perspective. Some, for example Peirce (1878/1992), appear to adopt a more realist stance, while others, such as Rorty (1980) and James (1975), reject any attempt to represent a world independent of possible human experience. In epistemology, or the theory of knowledge, pragmatists place an emphasis on practice. Pragmatists accept a view that our practical knowledge is greater than our theoretical knowledge, as any theory must arise out of practice and individual experience (Mounce, 2000). James (1975) argues that the truth of a belief lies in its consequences for experience. A belief can be seen as true if it enables us to anticipate further experience. However, when experience is insufficient to distinguish between two competing views of the world, we tend to accept the one that is more persuasive (Rorty et al., 2004).

In terms of doing research, pragmatists reject the notion that there are predetermined theories that depict reality. Nor do they believe people can construct meaning out of nothing (Rorty et al., 2004). Instead, pragmatists suggest that our research question determines the method we adopt. A researcher can have both objectivist and subjectivist epistemologies depending on what is being studied. In other words, there is no need to stick to one perspective, and it is perfectly acceptable to adopt variations in ontological and epistemological issues in different projects and sometime even in the same project. For example, some researchers use mixed methods – both quantitative and qualitative methods in one piece of research. We will return to the discussion of mixed methods in Chapter 4.

KEY CONCEPTS IN CHINESE: PRAGMATISM

实用主义起源于19世纪后期和20世纪初期几位美国哲学家的著作，主要倡议人包括查尔斯皮尔士，威廉詹姆士和约翰杜威。实用主义打破了唯物论或唯心论的对立，认为这些争议都是次要的。有的实用主义者甚至认为哲学家们争论不休的存在论和认识论都是没有意义的。实用主义被认为是唯物，唯心论之间的折中或妥协的办法。实用主义既否定了实证主义的很多基本前提，即任何事物都有不受人思想控制的规律，做

(Continued)

研究就是要找出这些规律。但实用主义也否定了极端唯心主义，即真理只存在于每人的意识形态里。实用主义者在存在观上接受多元论，即社会上有些概念是客观存在的，有些是主观存在。但哪些是主观，哪些是客观的其实我们也不一定知道。因此，他们的认识论也接受主，客两种观点。

在学术研究上，实用主义强调两点。第一，研究的问题或对象决定研究的方式。如果你研究的是客观存在的事物，那可以用客观，中立的方法，如做试验，发问卷等。但如果你研究的是意识形态上的问题，如人的情感，对事物的态度等，就要用感性的方法，如通过深入的访谈，研究个人背后的故事或其感想等。第二，实用主义认为即便有客观真理的存在，这些真理也必定来源于人们实践的经验。杜威提倡的现实主义提别强调抽象的理论和个人经验，反思之间达成平衡。要判断一种理论的'好'与'不好'，就要看其是否有实用价值。对于某种知识，不管它是用哪种方法论发展出来的，只要是有用的就是'真理'。这有如中文里常说的'不管黑猫还是白猫，能抓老鼠的就是好猫'。

因为实用主义强调理论的实践价值，所以对管理科学的研究起了重要的贡献。实用主义也受到一定的批评。反对者认为实用主义太过讲究实际效果，其实是功利主义。有些理论可能短期内不一定有很强的实用效果，但不见得是没用的。而且，有用与否有时是因人而异。我们不能否定一些真理的存在，只因为它们对我们没用。

3.3 RESEARCH APPROACHES

As we suggest in Chapter 2 and throughout this book, your research should be underpinned by a body of existing knowledge and involve a set of theories. Although you may learn your theories and methods from separate courses, there is interplay between theory and method (Dubois and Gibbert, 2010). Van Maanen et al. (2007) make this explicit when they suggest that 'it is our stand that theory and method are – or should be – highly interrelated in practice. Theories without methodological implications are likely to be little more than idle speculation with minimal empirical import. And methods without theoretical substance can be sterile, representing technical sophistication in isolation' (pp. 1145–6). While the links between theory, method and empirical phenomena are crucial, in practice not every piece of research draws on the same amount of theories at the design stage of research. The amount of existing knowledge and theories available in your topic and the extent to which you are clear about the theories at the beginning often inform the choice of your research approaches. In this section, we explain three research approaches, namely deduction (演绎法), induction (归纳法) and abduction (溯因法), and the implications of adopting each approach in relation to developing context-related knowledge. (See Table 3.1.)

3.3.1 Deduction

The deductive approach (or top-down approach) owes much to positivism and Popper's (1959) falsificationism. As you may have guessed, it is related to the use of quantitative methods. Some researchers also adopt a case study method – see, for example, Yin (2014). Popper famously

Table 3.1 Comparison of research approaches

Research approach	Philosophy	Knowledge in relation to context
Deduction	Positivism Realism	Context-free knowledge, context-embedded knowledge
Induction	Interpretivism	Context-specific knowledge
Abduction	Critical realism Pragmatism	Context-embedded knowledge, context-specific knowledge

proposes his hypothetico-deductive method, in which he argues that researchers should try to disprove (rather than prove) their theories. He suggests that no matter how many instances we observe that could confirm our theory, it is always possible that the next observation could contradict the theory. In other words, we can never be sure that our past experience would be adequate to predict future instances of the phenomenon we are interested in. As such, we might probably never be able to prove our theory to be true. What we could do, instead, is to falsify it. Science advances as we get closer to the truth by removing the errors.

Popper further suggests that in order to make this process operationalised, we should develop hypotheses – a set of unproven assertions about the relationship between the concepts (Gill and Johnson, 2010) – and test them. The process of deductive logic is presented in Gill and Johnson (2010), where they outline five steps: (1) theory – deduction starts from the development of a conceptual and theoretical framework or model; (2) hypothesis formulation and operationalisation – following the deductive logic and review of literature, researchers formulate speculative statements that make precise predictions about what should happen. Theoretical concepts are tested through a set of measurements; (3) data are collected to test the hypotheses and by implication the underlying theory; (4) if the theory survives empirical testing, it becomes facts of reality; (5) otherwise, the theory should be adjusted. Details of developing and testing hypotheses will be presented in Chapters 4 and 8.

The deductive approach has been highly popular among scholars conducting research related to China. Quer and colleagues' review of 180 empirical articles in leading international journals in the areas of business and management in China show that an overwhelming 82.2% of the articles adopted a deductive/quantitative approach (Quer et al., 2007). In a similar vein, but more specific to the HRM discipline, Cooke (2009) analyses 230 China-related papers and concludes that quantitative methods, typically in the form of a questionnaire survey, dominate data collection. In developing global management knowledge, the deductive approach might be particularly useful in context-embedded research, i.e. research that uses a nation's social, cultural, legal and economic variables as predictors and organisational attributes as dependent variables (Cheng, 1994). Context-embedded research starts with Western theories and models and incorporates contextual factors of China, such as collectivism or *guanxi*, in an attempt to modify or extend existing theoretical predictions in relation to the dependent variables. This type of research generates context-bounded models (Tsui, 2004). If the findings show that the theories are insensitive to the context, this research could also generate context-free or universal knowledge.

KEY CONCEPTS IN CHINESE: DEDUCTION

演绎法和归纳法是西方研究方法论里最普遍的两种方法。演绎法遵循实证主义和证伪论的原则，其目的是要找出事物之间的因果关系。采取演绎研究方法的人一般也采用定量研究法。但也有一部分人采用案例分析法。演绎法推理的过程是先提出理论，再用实例或数据来验证该理论。具体操作包含几个重要的步骤：第一是从现有理论为出发点，逐步推论并提出一些假设（即新理论），如提高工资会提高员工的积极性。第二是找出测量主要概念的方法。第三是收集和分析数据。第四是用结果证实或否定该假设。演绎法经常被认为是前半段难，后半段易。做研究时，开始要大量阅读文献，参考前人的理论从而提出自己的理论框架，所以前期工作量较大。演绎法强调研究过程必须很严谨，数据必须有效和可靠，这样得出的结果才能够作出科学预见。

　　演绎法有一定的局限性。第一，研究的过程不够灵活。由于在前半段已经提出了理论框架和假设，后半段就很难再加进新的东西。即便研究人员后来有新的想法或发现更有趣的现象，也只能放弃。第二，演绎法有一定的风险。有人认为演绎法就跟钓鱼一样，提出的理论和假设'被证实最好，被否定了就拉倒'。如果所有的假设都被否定了，则浪费了时间和精力。

Example 3.1

DEDUCTIVE RESEARCH

An example of using deduction to conduct context-embedded research is the study of high-performance work systems (HPWS) and organisational performance in China by Zhang and Morris (2014). Their literature review starts from Western notions of HRM and performance, and then focuses on HPWS and employee outcomes, and their relevance in China. On this basis, six hypotheses were proposed. Data collection involved a survey of HR directors/managers of firms in Beijing. Measurements were adopted from existing research from the West. Data analysis shows that five hypotheses are supported, which thus confirms that these Western theories are applicable to the Chinese firms.

3.3.2 Induction

While deduction starts from theory and later uses empirical data to prove or disprove the theory, the logic of induction is almost the reverse. To put it simply, the inductive (or bottom-up) approach attempts to build theory based on empirical observations in the world. Historically, the debates between supporters of the two camps have been longstanding and often involve natural science pitted against social science researchers. Research using an inductive approach in social science shares at least three characteristics.

First, many inductive researchers challenge the idea of establishing a theory upfront (Gill and Johnson, 2010). They argue that it is pointless to give explanations of social phenomena based on speculation. Instead, theories developed out of real-life experience are more useful and accessible to practice. They also oppose relying too much on literature, because existing theories limit our imagination and negatively affect the novelty of research. Researchers should conduct research without a priori constructs, as this allows them to let concepts emerge from the data rather than being constrained by previous theory (Randall and Mello, 2012). Perhaps the most famous method developed out of the inductive tradition is grounded theory, which is designed to allow theories to emerge from the data (Glaser and Strauss, 1967), as will be discussed in Chapter 4.

Second, proponents of induction reject the deductive approach of attempting to uncover the causal relationships between variables. Researchers following this tradition often subscribe to an interpretivist philosophy and see human interpretation of the social world as a crucial step in developing knowledge. Thus, they argue that an inductive approach allows them to establish insightful understanding about those situations leading to human actions, and the subjective dimension of human action, such as people's intentions, motives, attitudes and beliefs.

The third characteristic lies in the methods that researchers use for data collection and analysis. Proponents of induction are critical of deduction, which tends to follow a rigid methodology that leaves little room for alternative explanations. They argue that, at best, researchers using a deductive approach can only find what they seek (to prove or reject a hypothesis). The inductive approach that relies on the qualitative method of data collection and analysis, on the contrary, enables a more flexible structure to allow a potential change of research emphasis as the study progresses. However, every piece of research should have a focus. To solve this problem, research adopting induction usually forms research questions at the beginning and uses them to guide the process.

The inductive approach has gained increasing recognition in the researching-China community since the mid-1990s, as many researchers quickly realise that general knowledge developed in the West provides limited or little explanation of local concepts that are deeply embedded in Chinese culture and society. Chinese culture is fundamentally different to that of the USA or Europe. The search for a theoretical framework to research phenomena unique to the Chinese context (guanxi, Confucius ethics, yin-yang, job allocation in state-owned enterprises, etc.) in the literature often proves fruitless. In their article on the methodological challenges of researching in China, Stening and Zhang (2007) point out that 'Western conceptualisations and measurements of Chinese culture are inadequate and flawed insofar as they take, among other things, a rational perspective rather than one based on contradictions and process' (p. 123). Thus, there have been a number of calls for context-specific or indigenous Chinese research that leads to context-bound knowledge (Meyer, 2006; Quer et al., 2007; Tsui, 2004). Tsui (2004: 501) defines indigenous research as that which 'involves the highest degree of contextualisation or research that does not aim to test an existing theory but to derive new theories of the phenomena in their specific contexts'. Developing such highly contextualised knowledge is certainly the strength of inductive research. While it is considered good practice to start with a review of the literature, researchers generally go beyond the boundary of existing conceptual frameworks. Western theories are treated as preliminary and their limited explanatory power is indicated right at the beginning. Most of this type of research focuses on a unique social phenomenon and uses a small sample with unique attributes to build new theories based on observations.

KEY CONCEPTS IN CHINESE: INDUCTION

归纳法的推理逻辑与演绎法相反。提倡归纳法的人认为理论的发展应该从社会现象为出发点，通过深入的观察，用各种研究方法收集数据，最后归纳总结出理论。由于理论来源于经验和实际操作，这样研究出来的理论知识才有实际意义，而且可行性较高。大部分采用归纳法的人倾向于接受解释主义的哲学思想，认为社会概念跟物理概念不同，人有思想，而物体没有，所以不能用同样的方法研究。社会概念存在于人们的主观意识中。人们对这些概念的认识很多时候是既模糊又复杂。因此社会概念不能简化为测量，并采用数学的方式分析。支持归纳法的人一般采用定性研究法，虽然他们刚开始也参考文献，以增加对该研究课题的了解，但不会提出一个完整的理论模型。归纳研究法是上半段易，下半段难。前期对文献的回顾是点到为止，提出研究的问题即可。后期收集数据（通常采用访谈，观察，去现场亲身体会等方式），分析数据（如逐字逐句地分析访谈的文字稿），到最后归纳出理论的工作量较大。

归纳法也有局限性。首先，归纳法强调质量而非数量。追求对现象进行深入的调查，所以只能研究较少数的样本或人。因此很多人质疑归纳法提出的理论，认为这种理论没有合法性和广泛性。其次，归纳法也有风险。由于研究的过程较灵活，涉及的面广，有时容易迷失方向，失去重心。所谓面面俱到，其实是面面不到。

Example 3.2

INDUCTIVE RESEARCH

One such indigenous study conducted in the Chinese context using an inductive approach is Woodhams et al. (2015), who examined female managers' careers. After discussing the distinctive social and cultural environments in which Chinese women develop their careers, the authors question the suitability of applying Western theories in China. To obtain authentic understanding, the authors conducted 20 interviews with female managers who held senior and executive positions. Data were analysed using two culture-specific factors: the system of gender relations and the culture of collectivism. Using this framework, the authors developed a four-fold taxonomy that captures Chinese women's career orientations.

3.3.3 Abduction

Both inductive and deductive approaches assume that the relationship between theory and empirical data, or vice versa, is one-directional. One apparent issue when conducting research is that there is interplay between theory and the empirical world. Abduction has been presented as an approach that could combine the advantages of both deduction and induction. Originating from the philosophical position of pragmatism, the abductive approach has also become popular with critical realists and moderate constructionists. Järvensivu and Törnroos (2010: 102) discuss the use of research approaches in relation to researchers' ontological and epistemological positions:

> Naïve realists usually adopt a deductive research process, wherein researchers begin with theoretical argumentation and test these arguments with empirical observations. In contrast, naïve relativists often start with subjective accounts of lived experiences and from thereon build theory inductively. Critical realism and moderate constructionism are more in the middle and therefore adopt often a research logic based on abduction.

Proponents of this approach suggest a mutually dependent relationship between theory and empirical phenomena in research. The binary of theoretical insights and empirical observations should be treated simultaneously. It is argued that theoretical frameworks evolve as researchers examine data from the empirical world. As such, researchers should travel 'back-and-forth' (Dubois and Gibbert, 2010) to develop better understanding, so as to provide better explanations of the social phenomena as the research progresses. Typically, a study using abduction starts from social phenomena which lack applicable theories. A small number of core concepts are identified to set boundaries to the research (Friedrichs and Kratochwil, 2009). Researchers collect observations while applying concepts from existing knowledge. Instead of trying to impose a theoretical framework (deduction) or abstracting theories from observations (induction), researchers could synergise compatible theories or redefine the boundaries, such as changing core concepts, to create a better 'match' between theory and data. Using abduction is not completely risk-free. Setting core concepts at the beginning might suppress the generation of new theories. Moreover, researchers may unintentionally seek out theoretical frameworks that fit the empirical data and thus omit other perspectives (Järvensivu and Törnroos, 2010).

Abduction can be an important approach in developing context-embedded knowledge and even context-specific knowledge in China. The Chinese belief system is flexible and can synthesise what often appear to be competing, paradoxical or even contradictory notions (Warner, 2010). Arguably, this gives researchers the opportunity to 'abduct' Western theories and use them to provide theoretical depth for their studies in the Chinese context. Thus, abductive studies often take Western theory as a starting point, but go on to explore contextual factors in detail. These studies provide continuity between 'general knowledge' and contextualised knowledge and are seen as a middle way of developing global knowledge. Many scholars use it to expand Western theory and at the same time identify knowledge that is unique to the Chinese context.

KEY CONCEPTS IN CHINESE: ABDUCTION

溯因法被认为是演绎和归纳二法之间的中间途径。溯因法来源于皮尔斯提出的实用主义，认为社会科学研究的既不是事物之间的因果关系，也不是人们主观的意识。溯因法提出社会科学研究的目的应该是给社会概念和事件提供解释和说明原因。一件事情的发生有多种可能的原因。只要解释合理，这些原因都可以接受，所以没必要追求事物单一的'定律'。在研究方法上，溯因法强调理论和研究数据（包括文字，图像，等）之间的双向关系。具体操作灵活，研究员对某个社会现象产生兴趣，一般从现有文献开始，从现有的理论对其提出解释，然后从现实中收集数据看这个解释是否成立。采用溯因法的人大多用定性研究法，如用访谈或案例分析等收集数据资料，所以过程比演绎法灵活并容许新概念的出现。当研究员在研究的过程中发现之前提出的理论不足以完全解释所有的数据时，可以再去找别的理论甚至提出全新的理论来解释事件发生的原因。

溯因法有几个好处。第一，研究员可以以现有理论作出发点来研究新的课题，这样比较有的放矢，不容易跑题。第二，有些关于中国的课题只有很少的参考文献，所以从西方的理论着手可操作性较强。第三，溯因法比演绎法灵活，但比归纳法有章法。溯因法有一定的难度和风险。第一，因为研究员要不断地在理论和数据之间反复探讨，阅读量和工作量很大。第二，毕竟是从现有理论入手，有时很难发展出创新的理论。

──────────── **Example 3.3** ────────────

ABDUCTIVE RESEARCH

An example that utilises this approach is the study conducted by Yan and Gray (1994). The authors began with an interest in the issue of bargaining power in Sino-foreign joint ventures (the social phenomenon). The three core concepts (bargaining power, management control and performance) came from the existing literature (deduction). Through an abductive process, the study offers an expanded and revised model after four in-depth case studies. The newly proposed model includes several factors that are based on Chinese culture.

FURTHER READING

Easterby-Smith, M., Thorpe, R. and Jackson, P.R. (2015) *Management and Business Research*. London: Sage. Chapter 3 provides a useful overview and mapping for a range of major research philosophies and paradigms.

Johnson, P. and Duberley, J. (2000) *Understanding Management Research: An Introduction to Epistemology*. London: Sage. At PhD level, this book provides an excellent overview of different philosophical positions adopted in social science. Compared with other books about philosophy, this book is easy to read.

Saunders, M., Lewis, P. and Thornhill, A. (2015) *Research Methods for Business Students*. New York: Pearson Education. Chapter 4 provides a brief but accessible discussion on research philosophies and approaches.

REFERENCES

Alvesson, M. and Sköldberg, K. (2000) *Reflexive Methodology: New Vistas for Qualitative Research*. London: Sage.

Bhaskar, R. (1978) *A Realist Theory of Science*. New York: Harvester Press.

Bhaskar, R. (1989) *Reclaiming Reality: A Critical Introduction to Contemporary Philosophy*. London: Verso.

Cheng, L.C. (1994) On the concept of universal knowledge in organizational science: Implications for cross-national research. *Management Science* 40: 162–8.

Collins, H.M. (1983) An empirical relativist programme in the sociology of scientific knowledge. In K.D. Knorr-Cetina and M. Mulkay (eds) *Science Observed: Perspectives on the Social Study of Science*. London: Sage, 3–10.

Cooke, F. (2009) A decade of transformation of HRM in China: A review of literature and suggestions for future studies. *Asia Pacific Business Review* 47: 6–42.

Danermark, B., Ekstrom, M., Jakobsen, L., et al. (2002) *Explaining Society: Critical Realism in the Social Sciences*. London: Routledge.

Denzin, N. (1983) Interpretive interactionism. In G. Morgan (ed.) *Beyond Method: Strategies for Social Research*. Beverly Hills, CA: Sage, 408–24.

Denzin, N. and Lincoln, Y. (1995) Transforming qualitative research methods: Is it a revolution? *Journal of Contemporary Ethnography* 24: 349–58.

Duberley, J., Johnson, P. and Cassell, C. (2012) Philosophies underpinning qualitative research. In G. Symon and C. Cassell (eds) *Qualitative Organisational Research: Core Methods and Current Challenges*. London: Sage, 15–34.

Dubois, A. and Gibbert, M. (2010) From complexity to transparency: Managing the interplay between theory, method and empirical phenomena in IMM case studies. *Industrial Marketing Management* 39: 129–36.

Easterby-Smith, M. and Malina, D. (1999) Cross-cultural collaborative research: Toward reflexivity. *Academy of Management Journal* 42: 76–86.

Easterby-Smith, M., Thorpe, R. and Jackson, P.R. (2015) *Management and Business Research*. London: Sage.

Friedrichs, J. and Kratochwil, F. (2009) On acting and knowing: How pragmatism can advance international relations research and methodology. *International Organizations* 63: 701–31.

Gill, J. and Johnson, P. (2010) *Research Methods for Managers*. Los Angeles, CA: Sage.

Glaser, B.G. and Strauss, A.L. (1967) *The Discovery of Grounded Theory: Strategies for Qualitative Research*. New York: Aldine de Gruyter.

Guba, E. and Lincoln, Y. (1982) Epistemological and methodological bases of naturalistic inquiry. *Educational Communication and Technology*, 30: 233–52.

Halldén, O., Scheja, M. and Haglund, L. (2008) The contextuality of knowledge: An intentional approach to meaning making and conceptual change. In S. Vosniadou (ed.) *Handbook of Research on Conceptual Change*. London: Taylor & Francis, 507–32.

James, W. (1975) *Pragmatism*. Cambridge, MA: Harvard University Press.

Järvensivu, T. and Törnroos, J.-Å. (2010) Case study research with moderate constructionism: Conceptualization and practical illustration. *Industrial Marketing Management* 39: 100–8.

Johnson, P. and Duberley, J. (2000) *Understanding Management Research: An Introduction to Epistemology*. London: Sage.

Johnson, P., Buehring, A., Cassell, C., et al. (2006) Evaluating qualitative management research: Towards a contingent criteriology. *International Journal of Management Reviews* 8: 131–56.

Meyer, K. (2006) Asian management research needs more self-confidence. *Asia Pacific Journal of Management* 23: 119–37.

Mitroff, I. and Pondy, L. (1978) Afterthoughts on the leadership conference. In M. McCall and M. Lombardo (eds) *Leadership: Where Else Can We Go?* Durham, NC: Duke University Press, 145–9.

Mounce, H.O. (2000) Pragmatism. *Nursing Philosophy* 1: 80–1.

Peirce, C.S. (1878/1992) How to make our ideas clear. In N. Houser and C. Kloesel (eds) *The Essential Peirce*, Vol. 1. Bloomington, IN: Indiana University Press, 124–41.

Popper, K. (1959) *The Logic of Scientific Discovery*. London: Hutchinson.

Prasad, A. and Prasad, P. (2002) The coming age of interpretive organizational research. *Organizational Research Methods* 5: 4–11.

Prasad, P. (2005) *Crafting Qualitative Research: Working in the Postpositivist Traditions*. New York: M.E. Sharp.

Quer, D., Claver, E. and Rienda, L. (2007) Business and management in China: A review of empirical research in leading international journals. *Asia Pacific Journal of Management* 24: 359–84.

Randall, W.S. and Mello, J.E. (2012) Grounded theory: An inductive method for supply chain research. *International Journal of Physical Distribution & Logistics Management* 42: 863–80.

Rorty, R. (1980) Pragmatism, relativism, and irrationalism. *Proceedings and Addresses of the American Philosophical Association* 53: 717–38.

Rorty, R., Putnam, H., Conant, J., et al. (2004) What is pragmatism? *Think* 3: 71–88.

Saunders, M., Lewis, P. and Thornhill, A. (2015) *Research Methods for Business Students*. New York: Pearson Education.

Stening, B. and Zhang, M. (2007) Methodological challenges confronted when conducting management research in China. *International Journal of Cross Cultural Management* 7: 121–42.

Symon, G. and Cassell, C. (2012) Assessing qualitative research. In G. Symon and C. Cassell (eds) *Qualitative Organisational Research: Core Methods and Current Challenges*. London: Sage, 204–23.

Tsui, A. (2004) Contributing to global management knowledge: A case for high quality indigenous research. *Asia Pacific Journal of Management* 21: 491–513.

Van Maanen, J., Sørensen, J. and Mitchell, T. (2007) The interplay between theory and method. *Academy of Management Review* 32: 1145–54.

Warner, M. (2010) In search of Confucian HRM: Theory and practice in Greater China and beyond. *The International Journal of Human Resource Management* 21: 2053–78.

Weber, R. (2004) The rhetoric of positivism versus interpretivism: A personal view. *MIS Q.* 28: III–XII.

Woodhams, C., Xian, H. and Lupton, B. (2015) Women managers' careers in China: Theorizing the influence of gender and collectivism. *Human Resource Management* 54: 913–31.

Yan, A. and Gray, B. (1994) Bargaining power, management control, and performance in United States–China joint ventures: A comparative case study. *The Academy of Management Journal* 37: 1478–1517.

Yin, R.K. (2014) *Case Study Research: Design and Methods*. Los Angeles, CA: Sage.

Zhang, B. and Morris, J.L. (2014) High-performance work systems and organizational performance: Testing the mediation role of employee outcomes using evidence from PR China. *International Journal of Human Resource Management* 25: 68–90.

4
RESEARCH DESIGN

4.1 OVERVIEW

This chapter gives preliminary consideration to the complexities of different research designs in business and management research. In light of the increasing methodological diversity in the field, this chapter will start with some debate (Stake, 2000) between quantitative and qualitative research designs and introduce four of the most common research strategies (survey, experiment, case study and grounded theory). In some business research methods books, the qualitative approach is presented as an alternative strategy in a situation where quantitative approaches are not possible. Here, we want to emphasise that qualitative methodologies are gaining increasing acceptance as a means of undertaking business and management research (Symon and Cassell, 2012). Qualitative methodologies are not second-best options to quantitative business research, but are valuable on their own merit.

4.2 QUANTITATIVE, QUALITATIVE AND MIXED-METHOD RESEARCH

Three research strategies are often used in business and management research: quantitative, qualitative and mixed methods. In this book, we will introduce these concepts and make the distinction between different research methods as this will help in developing the discussion of a range of issues concerning a particular method.

4.2.1 Quantitative research

Quantitative research addresses research objectives through empirical assessments involving numerical measurement and statistical/mathematical analysis approaches. We use *quantitative data* in which numbers are used directly to represent the characteristics of the objects that we study. For example, the numbers of holidays taken by employees in a year, the number of sales of a new product, or the average income of UK university vice-chancellors – all of these are quantitative information.

Sometimes, the information is qualitative in nature, but you can present it in a quantitative manner. For instance, you may want to find out consumers' satisfaction level with a particular after-sales service by asking your respondents to score on a scale ranging from 1 (meaning 'very dissatisfied') to 7 (meaning 'very satisfied').

KEY CONCEPTS IN CHINESE: QUANTITATIVE RESEARCH

定量研究，也叫量化研究，是一种在社会科学（包括工商管理）常用的研究方法。它采用统计、数学等方法对商业现象进行系统性的经验考察（empirical assessments）。定量研究的目标是发展或验证与社会现象相关的数学、经济模型、理论和假设。这种研究关注的是大范围普遍的样本。

Quantitative research is often associated with positivism and a deductive approach. This research design starts off with existing theory, with the purpose of examining the relationship between theory and research. Its aim is to test *hypotheses* (假设) in quantitative research, particularly in an experimental design. A hypothesis is deduced from the theory and tested based on the data from your research. In a research paper or report, a hypothesis is a formal statement of some unproven supposition that tentatively explains certain facts or phenomena (Coolican, 2014). We need hypotheses to represent the meaning and purpose of our scientific investigation, especially when we are examining a quantitative relation between variables. For example, if we hypothesise that 'women have a lower level of career aspiration than men', the variables we want to examine are *gender* and *career aspiration*.

In a survey or experiment design, the researcher uses hypotheses rather than questions to predict whether or not a relationship will exist between the variables. A hypothesis can also go further by stating the direction of the relationship. For example, employees' job satisfaction is *positively* related to customers' satisfaction.

The focus of quantitative research is to use numerical data to test a theory. While there are a number of methods suitable for designing quantitative research, in this book we only focus on the two most common methods – survey and experimental research methods, which we discuss in sections 4.3 and 4.4. Due to space limitations, less common quantitative research methods (e.g. structured observation and content analysis) are not included.

--- **Example 4.1** ---

QUANTITATIVE RESEARCH

Whang et al. (2015) applied the concept of pop culture involvement (divided into situational and enduring involvement) to the tourism context and analysed the different impacts on formation and perception of destination image in China and Russia. A conceptual model and 10 hypotheses were proposed based on an extensive literature review. The study used a survey method including a self-administered questionnaire. Major constructs included involvement with pop culture, destination image, overall image of destination and intention to visit. All the measurement instruments were adopted from previous established research. The online survey resulted in 255 valid samples – 128 and 127 samples from China and Russia respectively. The empirical results indicate that situational involvement and enduring involvement have different effects on the proposed structural model in each country. The quantitative research design allowed the authors to build and test the research model and hypothesis, and draw conclusions with confidence using statistical findings based on large samples.

4.2.2 Qualitative research

Qualitative research addresses research objectives through techniques that allow the researcher to provide elaborate interpretations of the researched area without using numerical measurement. It attempts to 'discover true inner meanings and new insights' (Zikmund et al., 2009: 133). Arguably, qualitative research is less structured than most quantitative research, in that it is more research-dependent, requiring the researcher to extract and interpret meanings from those unstructured responses. Hennink et al. (2011) suggest that one of the main distinctive features of qualitative research is that it allows researchers to identify issues from the perspective of the participants, and to understand the meanings and interpretations that they give to behaviour, events or objects. Because of this participant focus, good qualitative researchers share some similar qualities, such as being open-minded, curious and empathic, flexible and able to listen to people who tell their own stories.

We will use qualitative research methods if our researched area is exploratory. In other words, there is little or no previous research in this area; and/or it is interpretive, that is, we want to investigate in-depth experiences and perceptions. Furthermore, arguably in qualitative research, participants interpret their own realities and researchers interpret participants' responses. As mentioned in Chapter 3, qualitative researchers often take the position of either an interpretivist or a critical realist paradigm, and qualitative methods usually engage with an inductive approach, i.e. the ideas and concepts emerge from participants' talk, rather than from existing literature (see Chapter 3 for further explanation of inductive research).

KEY CONCEPTS IN CHINESE: QUALITATIVE RESEARCH

定性研究，也叫质性研究，是另一种常用的研究方法。定性研究的目的是更深入的了解个别案例的特定行为、方式及其理由。它不同于定量研究方法，定性研究关注的是小范围集中的样本和个例。定性研究的主要特征如下：

(Continued)

- 研究员是研究过程不可分割的一部分，是开展定性研究的主要工具
- 有时需要收集、运用来自不同渠道的数据（注意：这里的数据不是数字。定性研究里数据具有广泛含义，可包括访谈文字稿，日记，观察笔记，录音，录像，图片，文献记录，等等各种各样的资料）
- 需要研究的是参与个体的故事，以及背后的意义、经历、感受和缘由
- 此类研究的课题通常是比较复杂、深入的，涵盖面也比较广
- 涉及到的理论和文献常常和社会、文化、政治、以及历史相关
- 研究结论要通过综合、全面、深入的理解和引申，去探寻现象的深层内涵

Commonly used methods for data collection are semi- or unstructured interviews, focus groups, ethnography, projective techniques, semiotics, and so on. In comparison with quantitative data, which are mainly numbers, *qualitative data* involve textual or visual descriptions. These types of data are represented by recorded words, phrases and sometimes pictures or videos.

Example 4.2

QUALITATIVE RESEARCH

Liu et al. (2015) explored the standardisation-localisation dilemma of brand communications for luxury fashion retailers' internationalisation and their movement into China. Using a phenomenological approach, the authors used interviews with senior marketing managers from 20 luxury fashion retail brands operating in China. For each brand, an average of two semi-structured, face-to-face interviews were conducted, of which at least one interview was at director level. Each interview lasted approximately 90 minutes. The qualitative data generated rich insights and allowed the authors to gain deep insights into the decision-making processes of industry experts responsible for negotiating those marketing challenges that result from internationalisation.

4.2.3 Choosing between quantitative and qualitative methods

In order to choose a research method that suits the purpose of your research, it is always beneficial to first consider your research question through a philosophical lens. Your philosophical assumptions will inform your methodological choice. Students may find it helpful to distinguish between quantitative and qualitative research. Table 4.1 outlines the key differences between the two research strategies. To summarise, quantitative research emphasises quantification in the collection and analysis of data, which employs a deductive approach with the purpose of testing a theory. By contrast, qualitative research usually emphasises words rather than quantification in data collection and analysis, which predominantly employs an inductive approach with the purpose of generating theories (Bryman and Bell, 2011).

Table 4.1 Quantitative versus qualitative approaches

	Quantitative	Qualitative
Objectives	Deductive; tend to be wide research; testing hypotheses or theory; tracking trends and making predictions	Inductive; tend to be small-scale research; exploring hidden motivations, values and behaviours; providing indications and explanations of a phenomenon or a small group of people
Epistemological orientation	Objective	Subjective
Type of research	Descriptive or causal	Exploratory
Type of questions asked	Non-probing	Probing
Sample size	Large	Small
Analysis	Objective; statistical	Subjective; sense-making
Results	Use numeric values; factual and clear	Use themes and quotes; results are open to interpretation
Replication	Easy(ier)	Difficult

4.2.4 Mixed-method research

In the previous sections, we talked about the nature of quantitative and qualitative research, and contrasted one with the other in terms of the role of theory, research objectives, data collection and analysis, and the presentation of results. However, it is important to know that the two research strategies can be combined within an overall research project. In fact, many management and business research projects adopt a *mixed-method research* design, using a mixture of quantitative and qualitative methods.

Johnson et al. (2007: 123) introduced their composite definition of mixed-method research as:

> The type of research in which a researcher ... combines elements of qualitative and quantitative research approaches (e.g. use of qualitative and quantitative viewpoints, data collection, analysis, inference techniques) for the purposes of breadth and depth of understanding and corroboration.

A mixed-method research design may use a deductive, inductive or abductive approach to theory development. A number of variations of mixed-method research designs have been identified, depending on how mixed-method research can be approached. For example, in Hammersley's (1996) classification, there are three approaches to mixed-method research:

- *Triangulation* (三角互证) refers to the use of more than one method or source of data within one study in order to cross-check findings. Webb et al. (1966) suggest that social scientist researchers are likely to exhibit greater confidence in their findings when they derive from more than one method of investigation, a strategy which has been referred to as *triangulation*. The idea of triangulation entails a need to employ more than one method of investigation and, within this context, qualitative and quantitative research may be perceived as different ways of examining the same research problem. For example, football fans' responses to questions in a questionnaire about how they support their team can be compared with ethnographic observation of how they behave when they are at a live match.

KEY CONCEPTS IN CHINESE: TRIANGULATION

三角互证，是指运用多种资料来源或者多种资料收集方法，对资料所做的定性的交互证实。三角互证研究方法在商业管理学科的研究里经常被使用。使用多种研究方法，运用来源于不同角度的数据，我们希望避免使用单一研究方法（单纯的质性或者量化研究）所带来的局限性和缺点，从而增强研究结果的可信度和有效性（reliability and validity）。

注意：Be careful with the use of the term triangulation! 在同一个研究项目中，运用多种研究方法并不一定就是 triangulation。

- *Facilitation* involves a situation where one research method used may lead to the discovery of new insights, which inform and are followed up through the use of a second method. For example, the findings of survey research may serve as a basis for the initial framing of research questions in qualitative work, or vice versa.
- *Complementarity* refers to the situation where two research methods are employed so that the information gathered and the findings complement one another. Results from the different methods serve to elaborate, enhance, clarify, confirm and broaden the overall interpretations. For example, the quality of art education at school can be assessed from both students' and teachers' perspectives, using surveys, interviews or both for each perspective. Data from two streams can provide a more complete and comprehensive understanding of how art education is perceived.

Another way to classify approaches to mixed-method research is based on two criteria (Webb et al., 1966):

- *The priority decision.* To what extent will the qualitative or the quantitative method be the principle tool for data gathering? You may also give the two methods equal priority.
- *The sequence decision.* Which method comes first? Does the qualitative method precede the quantitative one or vice versa, or is the data collected simultaneously? For example, quantitative research may be conducted first, with the qualitative method used second to elaborate or explain the quantitative findings. But where the qualitative research is conducted first, the findings are often used to inform a quantitative design. *Concurrent mixed-method research* refers to gathering both forms of data at the same time and comparing findings.

—————————————— **Example 4.3** ——————————————

MIXED-METHOD RESEARCH DESIGN

Morgan (1998) examined Chinese KAM (key account management) from a Chinese supplier's perspective. Considering that very few empirical research studies have focused on the KAM activities of Chinese companies, the authors adopted a two-pronged research approach, consisting of both qualitative and quantitative data gathering. The qualitative data collection stage explored the reasons for Chinese firms engaging in KAM, the key activities involved and how they are adapting to serve Western KAs (key accounts). During this stage, in-depth interviews comprising open-ended questions were conducted with key personnel from a Chinese textile manufacturer and their Western KAs. Both phone interviews and email were used.

The quantitative stage aimed at developing an understanding of how organisational behaviour (OB) issues affect KAM success. The main constructs used were based on established Western OB theories, for example perceived supervisor effectiveness, job satisfaction and commitment. A questionnaire survey was used to collect data from 158 employees of the Chinese supplier and 513 employees of a Western MNC located at subsidiaries in the West. The research objective at this stage was to examine whether employee attitudes differ between Chinese and Western suppliers.

The use of a mixed-method approach, as stated above, allowed the author to explore Chinese KAM and OB issues (i.e. employee attitudes) associated with the pressures caused by rapid transformation to KAM platforms at Chinese supplier firms. Novel insights were generated through this investigation.

——————————————— FURTHER READING ———————————————

Two academic journals are recommended which publish peer-reviewed research using a mixed-method approach:

Journal of Mixed Methods Research

International Journal of Mixed Methods for Applied Business and Policy Research

4.2.5 Research strategy

A research strategy is an overall plan of action in order to achieve your research goals. In sections 4.3 to 4.6, we will outline four commonly used research strategies: survey, experiment, case study and grounded theory. Survey and experiment are mainly linked to a quantitative research design, while a case study design can adopt a qualitative, quantitative or mixed-method research design. Finally, a grounded theory approach is primarily linked to a qualitative research design.

KEY CONCEPTS IN CHINESE: RESEARCH STRATEGY

研究策略是一个总体计划，说明研究者将如何解答所提出的研究问题。它介于两者之间，充当了一个方法上的链接，即你的研究哲学 (research philosophy) 和下一步关于研究方法 (research methods) 和数据分析的选择。

4.3 SURVEY

The survey strategy is normally associated with a deductive research approach. The survey is widely used in society and in business and management research – for example, to measure public opinion on a new social or health policy, to measure how people in urban areas save and spend their money, or to carry out market research to understand consumer preferences or satisfaction level. Surveys are used in exploratory, descriptive and causal research to collect data about people, events or situations (Sekaran and Bougie, 2013).

KEY CONCEPTS IN CHINESE: SURVEY

调研，是指通过各种调查方式从人群中系统客观的收集信息，并通过研究分析描述、比较、或解释,研究群体的知识结构、态度和行为。

━━━━━━━━━━ **Example 4.4** ━━━━━━━━━━

LARGE-SCALE SURVEY IN CHINA

民政部政策研究中心于2015年7月启动实施"中国城乡困难家庭社会政策支持系统建设"和"社区治理动态监测平台及深度观察点网络建设"两大项目。两大项目将通过科学抽样，对全国29个省、148个区县、5000个村居开展入户或社区调查。调查内容包括基层社区治理状况和困难家庭基础性数据信息等。调查受访者将涉及社区或村居负责人、专业社会工作者、社会组织负责人、物业管理人员、业主委员会负责人、普通社区居民，以及低保户、低保边缘户、城市低收入流动家庭等城乡贫困群体。

Source: Ministry of Civil Affairs of the People's Republic of China (2015)

Example 4.4 demonstrates the main features of survey research, which is aimed at gathering the subjective opinions or feelings of the public/certain groups. The purpose of a survey is to produce statistics in order to describe, compare or explain certain aspects (such as knowledge, attitudes, behaviours) of the study population.

4.3.1 Collecting survey data

The main way to collect information is by using questionnaires, i.e. asking people questions. Their answers then constitute the data to be analysed. Nevertheless, it is impractical to collect information from every member of the population. Generally, we only collect information from a fraction of the population, that is, a *sample*. In a survey design, it is very important to ensure that your sample is representative. It is also crucial to design and pilot your questionnaire and try to ensure a good response rate (Sekaran and Bougie, 2013). (For more details on sampling, see Chapter 5.)

The majority of surveys created for dissertation projects are one-offs. There are continuing surveys, which allow the researcher to observe changes regarding a particular phenomenon or a group of people over time. *A self-administered questionnaire* is primarily used in surveys, which respondents are required to complete on their own, either on paper or via the computer. Chapter 6 provides details on questionnaire design and includes an example of a self-administered questionnaire.

KEY CONCEPTS IN CHINESE:
SELF-ADMINISTERED QUESTIONNAIRE

自填式问卷，是一种调查者将设计好的问卷，通过网络或者邮寄，发放给被调查者，由被调查者自己阅读并填写，然后再由调查者收回的一种调研方法。

Quantitative data can be collected through the survey strategy, which allows you to analyse the data using descriptive and inferential statistics (描述性和推论性统计). Moreover, particular relationships between variables can be tested (see Chapter 8).

4.3.2 Critiques of the survey method

There are a number of benefits of using the survey strategy. Surveys are relatively easy to administer and develop using the survey software available today (for example, Qualtrics, Snap, SurveyMonkey, Bristol Online Survey [BOS]). The method tends to be cost-effective, especially when online or mobile surveys are used. Moreover, a broad range of data regarding respondents' attitudes, opinions, beliefs, values, behaviours, and so on, can be collected amongst a large number of respondents.

However, it is necessary to also acknowledge the drawbacks of the survey strategy. First, in comparison with other research strategies such as grounded theory and ethnography, only a limited number of questions can be asked in a questionnaire. Second, answers to survey questions may reveal certain statistical relationships between variables, but it can be difficult to explain why there are such relationships when you have only asked a few closed-ended questions. Hence, a questionnaire survey may constrain the depth and scope of your research. Nevertheless, the questionnaire is not the only data collection method within the survey strategy. Other survey instruments are structured interviews (see section 6.3 for further details) and structured observations.

4.4 EXPERIMENT

The experiment strategy is widely used in the natural sciences, but also often seen in psychological and social science research. It is considered one of the most powerful ways of gathering evidence to support theories, because it can eliminate many alternative explanations, which can occur with other kinds of evidence. In an experiment, the researcher attempts to isolate cause and effect, and to eliminate alternative explanations for the observed relationships between variables (Saunders et al., 2016). Using an experiment strategy, the researcher makes predictions as to whether or not a relationship will exist between the variables (see Table 4.2), through hypothesis testing. A typical experiment will examine the effects of the independent variable on the dependent variable.

Table 4.2 Types of variable

Variable	Explanation	Example
Independent 自变量 (IV)	研究者主动操控，而引起因变量发生变化的因素或条件。数学函数模型 y=f(x) 中的x。	Students of different ages were given the same test to see how many car brands are recognised correctly. IV is the ages of the students
Dependent 因变量 (DV)	由于自变量变动而引起变动的量。数学函数模型 y=f(x) 中的y。	DV is the number of brands recognised
Control 控制变量	除了自变量以外的所有能使因变量发生变化而影响实验结果的变量。它们并不是本实验所要研究的变量，也称做无关变量。只有将这些变量控制住（保持恒定不变）才能避免它们对于实验中因果关系的影响。	Control variable here is the same recognition test – as it remains constant for all the participants
Mediator 中介变量	处于自变量和因变量之间的变量，即，y与x的关系受到第三个变量m的影响。自变量通过中介变量对因变量产生作用 。 X➔M➔Y	How much TV the students watch may be a mediator between age and level of brand recognition. One may assume that with an increase in age, the level of TV exposure increases and this leads to a higher level of brand recognition
Moderator 调节变量	解释的是自变量x在何种条件下会影响因变量y，调节变量影响因变量和自变量之间关系的方向（正或负）和强弱。 X Y	Gender may be a moderator in the relationship between the IV and the DV. For instance, male students may recognise more car brands than female students within the same age group

KEY CONCEPTS IN CHINESE: EXPERIMENT

实验研究方法，主要运用于自然科学学科里，但是在心理学和社会学领域也很常用。它是由研究者根据研究问题的本质内容设计实验，目的是研究自变量（independent variable）的变化给因变量（dependent variable）带来变化的可能性（probability）。实验研究方法需要用到假设检验（hypothesis testing）。

4.4.1 Types of experiments

Classical experiment

In a classical experiment, a sample of participants is selected and then *randomly* allocated to two groups. The participants in the *experimental group* will be exposed to planned intervention or manipulation, and the participants in the *control group* will not get any intervention. A random assignment of participants helps to eliminate any systematic differences that might result from the two groups consisting of different people with different characteristics, such as variations in age, income or educational level. The control group is subject to exactly the same external influences as the experimental group, except that they do not receive the planned intervention.

Between-groups

This is also known as 'between-subjects' or 'independent samples'. This type of experiment involves using different groups of participants for each level of the independent variable/planned intervention. For example, one participant belongs to either the experimental group or the control group but not both.

Within-groups or repeated measures

This is also sometimes known as 'related samples'. There will only be a single group and every participant experiences each and every level of the independent variable/planned intervention(s).

KEY CONCEPTS IN CHINESE: EXPERIMENTAL STIMULUS, BETWEEN-SUBJECTS DESIGN AND WITHIN-SUBJECTS DESIGN

实验 刺激 (Experimental stimulus)，在一个实验设计里，自变量(IV)通常是实验刺激。

被试间设计 (Between-subjects design)，每个实验参与者只参与一个实验变量的测试，可以简单理解为每一个参与者只参加一次实验。

被试内设计 (Within-subjects design)，每个被试者要接受所有实验变量的测试，也就是多次测试。

──────────── **Example 4.5** ────────────

EXPERIMENTAL DESIGN

Zhang (1996) examined how culture, product types and product presentation format influence Chinese consumers' evaluation of foreign products from different countries-of-origin (COOs). Three countries – the USA, Japan and South Korea (all major trading partners of China) – were selected. Using a quota sample of 300 shoppers in a shopping centre in Beijing, an experiment was carried out over a ten-day period. Adult shoppers were randomly recruited to participate in the study for about 15 minutes. They were invited to a booth where they were told what they needed to do and were subsequently presented with the experimental *stimuli*. The participants evaluated the product information and then answered questions contained in a questionnaire. A small cash incentive was offered for their participation.

The study had a *between-subject design* in the COO factor (the USA, Japan and South Korea) and the product information cue factor (single cue and multiple cue). It also had a *within-subject design* in the product type factor (non-durable product and durable product). Therefore, this study had a 3 × 2 × 2 *factorial design*.

The product stimuli used in the experiment included a shirt (a common non-durable product, easy to evaluate) and a 19-inch colour television set (a common durable product, more difficult to evaluate). Fictional brand names were given to these product stimuli to avoid a possible confounding of COO effects.

The COO product detail was presented to the participants in two different formats. For the single-cue condition, the product type, name and 'made in' label were printed on an 8 × 11-inch card and presented to the participants for evaluation. For the multiple-cue condition, the participants were presented with the physical product. The COO information was clearly displayed on the packaging of the products.

Dependent variables for the study included product evaluation, attitudes towards the brand and product choice – whether participants would purchase this product.

The findings revealed that COO information does influence Chinese consumers' reactions to foreign products, which is consistent with studies conducted in Western countries previously. Results also indicate that the COO effect may be subject to moderation by factors such as product type and presentation format. The impact of COO on Chinese consumers varied with different products. The single-cue condition was related to a stronger COO effect.

We formulate two types of hypotheses in a standard experiment design – the null hypothesis and the alternative hypothesis, which oppose each other.

KEY CONCEPTS IN CHINESE: NULL HYPOTHESIS AND ALTERNATIVE HYPOTHESIS

原假设或者零假设 Null hypothesis (H_0)，指进行统计检验时预先建立的假设。原假设说明总体参数等于某个值，一般是有意推翻的假设。原假设通常是初始声明，使用先前的研究或知识进行指定。但在商业管理研究中很少用。

备择假设 Alternative hypothesis (H$_1$)，备择假设说明总体参数不同于原假设中的总体参数的值。备择假设是可以相信为真实或有望证明为真实的内容。

　　原假设成立时，有关统计量应服从已知的某种概率分布。当统计量的计算值落入否定域时，可知发生了小概率事件，应否定原假设，接受备择假设。

4.4.2 Critiques of the experimental design

According to Forshaw et al. (2011), there are a number of strengths of experiments. First of all, an experiment tests cause and effect, so that it allows a conclusion to be drawn about the causal relationship between independent and dependent variables. Second, in an experimental design, we eliminate the alternative potential influences of other variables (apart from the independent variable) on the dependent variable by holding them constant. In essence, we further strengthen the ability to draw conclusions about cause and effect by manipulating the independent variable while trying to hold everything else at the same level. Third, the controlled nature of an experiment allows other researchers to replicate the process and potentially find the same results.

There are potential weaknesses with experiments. First, we conceptualise concepts in the way that we can manipulate or measure them in experimental settings and, hence, we may simplify or reduce the complexity of behaviours and phenomena into small and measurable 'bits'. Second, due to the artificial and laboratory nature of experiments, 'they might not provide a true reflection of the ways in which people behave in their everyday life' (Forshaw et al., 2011: 41). The criticism of a lack of *ecological validity* （效度） of experiments, however, does not reduce the validity of all experiments (see section 4.7 for further explanations).

--- FURTHER READING ---

Forshaw, M., Upton, D. and Jones, S. (2011) The basics of experimental design. In *Psychology Express: Research Methods in Psychology* (undergraduate revision guide). Upper Saddle River, NJ: Prentice Hall. This chapter (Chapter 3) provides both theoretical and practical suggestions for experiments and how to design them.

4.5 CASE STUDY

Unlike the first two designs we have discussed in this chapter, case study research is not about frequencies, incidence or generalisation. Rather, it is explanatory in nature and answers 'how' and 'why' research questions that deal with 'operational links needing to be traced over time' (Yin, 2014: 10). Researchers in business and management use this method to study firms and organisational behaviour (Mills et al., 2009). While the case study can be broadly classified as a kind of qualitative research, it has the potential to incorporate quantitative methods such as survey and experiment for data collection. In the view of Eriksson and Kovalainen (2016: 131), 'case studies are excellent in generating holistic and contextual in-depth knowledge through the use of multiple sources of data. Overall, case study research aims to make room for diversity and complexity and, therefore, avoids overly simplistic research design'. Taken together, Creswell (2012) offers a comprehensive definition, according to which a case study (1) is an exploration of 'a bounded system' which can be defined in terms of time and place (such as an event, an activity, an individual or an organisation); (2) takes place over time and through detailed, in-depth data collection; and (3) involves multiple sources of evidence.

Sometimes students confuse the case study research method with case studies they are presented with in lectures and tutorials. In general, a case study used to facilitate teaching is 'specifically created to direct students to a particular conclusion' (Amerson, 2011: 427). This is in contrast to the case study research method, which does not permit this type of manipulation but, instead, allows the researcher to 'report data from a real-life context in a truthful and unbiased manner' (Amerson, 2011: 427).

KEY CONCEPTS IN CHINESE: CASE STUDY

案例研究法是以个别案例为素材,对研究的问题进行深入的或多层的数据收集、分析,从而提炼出整体的、以现实现象为依据的理论知识。

4.5.1 Single-case design

A major decision of case study research before conducting any data collection is to choose between single- and multiple-case designs. In some research method books (e.g. Eriksson and Kovalainen, 2016), the distinction is also called intensive and extensive case study designs. In principle, the selection of a case or multiple cases should be related to the theory or theories that underpin your research. In a single-case research project, the job of the researcher is to develop a deep understanding of cultural meanings and sense-making processes within that particular context. Yin (2014) proposes five rationales (critical, unusual, common, revelatory, longitudinal) for using a single-case design. It should be noted that not all single-case research meets all five criteria. In fact, the second and third rationales are mutually exclusive.

The first rationale is to choose a case which would be *critical* to the theoretical development. The case should be able to provide explanations of new phenomena or alternative explanations of existing phenomena and answer the research questions. Thus, this single case can make 'a significant contribution to knowledge and theory building by confirming, challenging, or extending the theory' (Yin, 2014: 51). A second rationale is to choose a case which represents an *extreme* or *unusual* situation that differs from theoretical norms or everyday regularity. Findings from an unusual case might shed light on normal processes. Alternatively, a third option is to use a *common* case that reflects an everyday situation because it captures the social processes related to theoretical development. Fourth, a single-case design may use a *revelatory* case that allows the researcher 'to observe and analyse a phenomenon previously inaccessible to social science inquiry' (Yin, 2014: 52). This type of research can give the researcher the opportunity to uncover a phenomenon that it was not possible to study previously, and thus can make a significant contribution. The fifth rationale is the *longitudinal* case, in which the researcher collects data over an extended period of time, sometimes at pre-defined intervals. This research design focuses on how certain situations or processes change or develop over time.

Example 4.6

A SINGLE-CASE DESIGN

Yu (2008) examined the social impacts of labour-related corporate social responsibility (CSR) on upholding labour standards. The author selected a single case - Reebok's athletic footwear supplier factory in China, as this factory can be considered a critical and common case of many large multinational corporations from developed countries that adopted corporate codes of conduct to regulate the labour practices of their suppliers in developing countries. Data were collected through three channels - participant observation, in-depth interviews with managers, workers and unionists, and documentary review. The author used an analytical framework consisting of structural forces and agency-related factors at industrial, national and local levels. Analysis was focused on Reebok's strategy in human rights, manufacturing processes, HR practices, China's legal framework and the tension between labour standards and profitability. Despite drawing from the findings of a single case study, the study illustrated key determinants inhibiting the effectiveness of labour-related CSR policies and suggested two possible ways to overcome these inhibiting effects.

4.5.2 Multiple-case design

Many research projects contain more than a single case. Some researchers consider evidence from multiple cases to be more compelling and the overall study more robust (Yin, 2014). Others use multiple cases for theory development – for example, a comparison of each case offers more insight than simply investigating each case individually (Schwandt, 2001). In multiple-case research, the real-life context and detailed descriptions are not the focus per se (Eriksson and Kovalainen, 2016).

Cases are chosen instrumentally as a way to explore specific business-related phenomena and to develop propositions that can be tested in the study. It should be recognised that conducting multiple case studies can be time-consuming and it requires extensive resources and support. Therefore, it might not be practical for the dissertation of an undergraduate or masters student.

Multiple-case study or extensive case study (Eriksson and Kovalainen, 2016) is based on the assumption that the study of each individual case is less important than the comparison of cases. The focus of comparative case study (sometimes called cross-case analysis) is on the nature of the differences between cases. The selection of cases requires prior knowledge of the theories used and the levels of difference between the cases (Thomas, 2016). Interpretation is also made in the context of this knowledge. The simplest form of comparison is between two cases, whereby the researcher undertakes an analysis of the cultures of the two environments. You are likely to use a non-probability sample, thus the cases chosen are not representative samples of each phenomenon (Thomas, 2016).

--- **Example 4.7** ---

A COMPARATIVE CASE DESIGN

Gamble (2006) studied the employment practices of MNCs in China, with the aim of understanding how Western HRM practices have been transferred from Western to Chinese workplaces. The author selected 'UKStore', a Sino-British joint venture that replicated many of the HRM practices of its British parent company. To compare the adoption of Western practices with local practices, the author also used another store which is owned by the state. In order to explore employees' perceptions, data were collected both qualitatively and quantitatively. Qualitative data included interviews with employees and repeat visits to the stores. Quantitative data included a survey-based questionnaire with employees.

The author looked at issues such as motivation, job security, company rules and procedures, promotion, relationships with co-workers, relationships with supervisors, and favouritism. By contrasting employees' perceptions of these issues, the author was able to explore the degree of divergence or convergence between traditional Chinese HRM and Western-style HRM practices in joint ventures, thus making an important contribution to the study of international HRM.

4.5.3 Criticisms of the case study method

Despite the usefulness of this method in business and management research, it has been criticised, mostly by scholars from a positivist background, for its inability to meet the positivist criteria of construct validity, internal validity, external validity and reliability (see section 4.8). Perhaps the biggest criticism of the case study is its limitation in the generalisation of research findings. With 'a very small sample' it would be very difficult to extend findings from a few cases to a wider population; even more so when the study only involves a single case. Although some suggest that collecting a larger amount of data could increase generalisability (Yin, 2014), the findings from case studies remain unique.

A second issue is related to the presence of the researcher in the research process. Case study research often involves collecting data from multiple sources and using qualitative methods such as observation, interviews and documents (Chapter 5). Data analysis is subject to the researcher's theoretical background and interpretation, rather than to mathematics. It has been suggested that the researcher's involvement leaves room for registering false evidence or biased views and it would be impossible to ensure objectivity (Lee, 1989).

However, proponents of case study method argue that generalisation and objectivity should not be the goals in all research. The purpose of using the case study is to develop a deep understanding of one particular case; as Stake (1994: 245) suggests, 'the objective of the case study is not to represent the world, but to represent the case'. In defending the use of single cases, Stake (1994) further asserts that issues arising from the in-depth analysis of a single case allow for a better understanding of the circumstances of the phenomenon and thus could be more reliable.

FURTHER READING

Thomas, G. (2016) *How to Do Your Case Study*. London: Sage. This text provides easy-to-understand examples of various forms of case study research design.

Yin, R.K. (2014) *Case Study Research: Design and Methods*. Thousand Oaks, CA: Sage. While leaning towards a positivist standpoint, this book is a comprehensive guide for designing case studies.

4.6 GROUNDED THEORY

The grounded theory method was created by Glaser and Strauss (1967: 1), who defined it as 'the discovery of theory from data – systematically obtained and analysed in social research'. The central idea is that researchers should develop social theories *grounded* in their data. The aim of using grounded theory in the Chinese context is, thus, to generate theory rather than simply verify an existing theory developed in other contexts, or test a hypothesis. Subsequent definitions are in the same vein. Charmaz (2014: 1) considers grounded theory methods as:

Consist(ing) of systematic, yet flexible guidelines for collecting and analysing qualitative data to construct theories from the data themselves ... Grounded theory begins with inductive data, invokes iterative strategies of going back and forth between data and analysis, uses comparative methods, and keeps you interacting and involved with your data and emerging analysis.

Urquhart et al. (2010) identify four key characteristics of grounded theory. First, the main purpose of the method is theory building. Second, researchers should ensure that they have as few preconceived theoretical ideas as possible before conducting the research. Third, theoretical sampling should be followed, whereby researchers decide on, after some analysis, where to sample from next in order to generate more data in certain areas. Fourth, while analysing and conceptualising, the process of constant comparison should be followed, that is, every piece of data should be compared with all existing concepts and constructs, to see if it extends an existing theory, forms a new one or identifies a new relation.

KEY CONCEPTS IN CHINESE: GROUNDED THEORY

扎根理论最基本的主张是理论的建立和发展必须扎根在实际经验或社会现象上，所以经常被认为是一种归纳式的定性研究方法。扎根理论跟其它研究方法最主要的不同点是研究者在研究开始前不会回顾太多现有的理论。提倡者认为过分依赖现有文献会局限了研究者的思考角度，使得研究者对研究的问题产生理论上的偏见。这对新理论的建立是有害的。所以扎根理论者的文献回顾部分会写的比较笼统，只会概括大的研究方向。研究者在研究设计，数据收集和分析的过程中应该思想开放，不带任何的旧理论包袱。研究的过程是先采用定性方式（如访谈，观察等手段），较开放地收集资料，再从这些现实的资料中通过分析，归纳，从而提炼出自己的理论和概念。采用扎根理论可以打破旧的理论框架，提出开拓性的新理论。

但批评者认为使用扎根理论有一定的风险。第一，因为研究者开始没有大量的回顾现有的理论和文献，所以后面研究出来的结果有可能已经存在，或该理论早已有人提出过，最后有可能浪费了时间和精力。所以一定量的文献回顾还是有必要的。第二，由于研究的过程缺乏理论指导，收集的资料会比较散乱，分析时也无从下手。最后的结果有时会被认为较肤浅，没有重点。

4.6.1 Critiques of grounded theory

There are many benefits of using grounded theory. It has been suggested that grounded theory is a very useful method in areas where no previous theory exists (Glaser and Strauss, 1967). This can be particularly useful for researchers and students studying social phenomena unique in the Chinese context, where very few Western theories can be drawn on. It allows researchers to dig deep into data at a detailed level (Urquhart, 2013). It encourages researchers to analyse their data early, and a constant interplay between data collection and analysis (Myers, 2013). It is also good for studying processes (Myers, 2013), for example decision-making in organisations. It is flexible and can be used with various philosophical positions, including the positivist, interpretivist and constructivist perspectives (Urquhart, 2013).

However, first-time users, especially students, can find data analysis overwhelming, as its 'bottom-up' approach to coding (see Chapter 7) focuses on words and sentences. This attention to detail can make it difficult for inexperienced researchers to 'scale up' later to a more abstract level of concepts and themes (Myers, 2013). Moreover, theory building requires knowledge of how to conceptualise data (Hallberg, 2010), but many researchers lack such competence.

4.6.2 Two strands of grounded theory method

It should be noted that scholars (including the co-founders) of grounded theory do not always agree on what the method actually comprises and how it works. Following the disputes between Glaser and Strauss in the 1990s, the two scholars took grounded theory in two different directions – the Glaserian and the Straussian (Urquhart, 2013). The core of the disagreement lies in the different emphases on the meaning of prior theoretical knowledge for research. Glaser insists that grounded theory should be a method of discovery, and considered codes and categories emerging from the data. For Glaser, grounded theory is purely inductive. He rejects the idea of applying existing theory to data analysis, as it could force data and analysis into preconceived categories, supress emergence and turn data into a 'full conceptual description' of existing theory. He argues that '[with Strauss and Corbin's method, as discussed below] data is not allowed to speak for itself as in grounded theory, and to be heard from, infrequently it has to scream. Forcing by preconception constantly derails it from relevance' (Glaser, 1992: 123).

On the other hand, Strauss, while preserving the emphasis on inductive and iterative inquiry, takes a broader view of grounded theory and considers theoretical pre-knowledge as necessary in scientific research. He and co-author Corbin suggest that the development of new knowledge should be guided by prior knowledge, as 'every type of inquiry rests on the asking of effective questions' (Strauss and Corbin, 1990: 73). Moreover, prior theoretical knowledge should be allowed to flow into the interpretation of data to some degree, and researchers should be able to accept, modify or reject concepts as a result of research. Arguably, Strauss's version of grounded theory incorporates both abductive and inductive research (Reichertz, 2010). In addition, Strauss and Corbin propose technical procedures, i.e. breaking down the coding process into four prescriptive steps and using a coding paradigm, to systematically gather and order data, rather than relying only on constant comparison (Strauss and Corbin, 1990, 1998). However, their approach requires 'a good match' between categories and the research phenomenon (Urquhart, 2013).

Although there is a lack of systematic review of how scholars use grounded theory in the Chinese context, our observation is that Chinese scholars tend to adapt Strauss and Corbin's version of the method in the area of business and management (see, for example, Lockström et al., 2010; Wu et al., 2015). This may be for two reasons. First, their approach allows researchers to choose from a variety of analytical tools and 'make use of procedures in ways that best suit him or her' (Corbin and Strauss, 2008: x). This suits the pragmatic way of doing things in Chinese culture. Second, their version is more likely to provide continuity between existing (Western) and Chinese knowledge.

4.6.3 Literature review in grounded theory design

Users (especially students) of grounded theory often get confused about *how* and *when* the existing literature should be consulted. Some scholars, including Glaser, believe that reading the literature before conducting the study is problematic, as an early reading would inevitably create preconceptions and threaten the 'neutrality' of the researcher. He suggests that the review should be delayed to a later stage: 'when the grounded theory is nearly completed during the sorting and writing up, then the literature search in the substantive area can be accomplished and woven into the theory as more data for constant comparison' (Glaser, 1998: 67). This is in stark contrast with most other methodologies, which see an in-depth literature review as vital in understanding the field of investigation. However, Glaser's position has been criticised for its impracticality. For example, without prior knowledge, it would be difficult for a researcher to identify an appropriate research area and detect gaps in knowledge (McGhee et al., 2007). Coffey and Atkinson (1996) warn of the danger of 'rediscovering the wheel', if a researcher or a student is ignorant of the relevant literature.

On the other hand, Strauss and Corbin (1990) suggest five benefits of an early literature review:

1. It stimulates theoretical sensitivity.
2. It provides a secondary source of data.
3. It stimulates questions.
4. It directs theoretical sampling.
5. It provides supplementary validity.

Many other scholars are also in favour of engaging with literature at an early stage. For example, it can provide a justification for a research approach, ensure the proposed study has not been done before and help avoid conceptual and methodological pitfalls (McGhee et al., 2007). It can show how the phenomenon has been studied to date and thus contextualise the study (McCann and Clark, 2003). In line with these authors, Hallberg (2010) suggests that an early review of literature is necessary for students for three particular reasons. The first is to check if your proposed research has already been done and published. Second, the review may provide you with some background knowledge about the topic and identify gaps in the literature. Third, as a student, you are required to demonstrate that your research topic is worth doing.

Recently, a reflexive approach of the literature review has been proposed for users of grounded theory (Dunne, 2011; Ramalho et al., 2015). Rather than reviewing the literature as it is, this approach requires the researcher to constantly question presumptions, including the researcher's own. McCann and Clark (2003: 15) suggest the use of memos to 'reflect the researcher's internal dialogue with the data at a point in time'. Reflecting on her own doctoral study, Dunne (2011) postulates that a researcher can document their own thoughts, feelings and questions from reading the existing literature, while at the same time being aware that such thoughts, and so on, can be influenced by pre-existing conceptualisations. Later, at the analysis stage, the researcher can then compare the literature with data, codes, categories and memos to validate or reject the literature and develop new theories (Ramalho et al., 2015).

4.6.4 Theoretical sampling

Chapter 5 of this book is devoted to sampling issues in research. However, because of the uniqueness of theoretical sampling in grounded theory research, we feel it is necessary to discuss it here together with other issues around the method. Indeed, the importance of theoretical sampling is emphasised by Charmaz (2014: 192), who argues that 'the logic of theoretical sampling distinguishes grounded theory from other types of qualitative inquiry'.

Sampling strategies in a grounded theory research study comprise initial sampling and theoretical sampling. While initial sampling gives a point of departure for data collection, theoretical sampling guides theory building. At the initial sampling stage, you identify a sample based on your best knowledge of the people, cases, organisations or events that could help you to gather relevant information about the social phenomenon. For example, your research question is about how people with disability seek employment in China. You use a working definition of 'disability' to recruit participants. You carry out a few initial interviews about their experience of applying for jobs. After some analysis, you arrive at some preliminary and intriguing findings – people with certain types of disabilities find it more difficult to apply for jobs. However, the data is thin. You decide to investigate these problems more closely. Next, you particularly recruit people with the types of disabilities you have identified to further explore the issue. This sampling framework is called theoretical sampling, which, according to Charmaz (2014: 193), means 'seeking pertinent data to develop your emergent theory. The main purpose of theoretical sampling is to elaborate and refine the categories constituting your theory'. Thus, theoretical sampling is not concerned with representativeness of your sample to the overall population (see Chapter 5), but a technique to narrow down your focus.

KEY CONCEPTS IN CHINESE: THEORETICAL SAMPLING

理论抽样是扎根理论研究里常用的取样方法。与本书第五章里介绍的其它取样方法有很大区别。研究员首先通过现有知识寻找一些研究对象，如参加访谈的人，然后对收集的资料进行一定的整理和分析。之后再根据前期分析的结果，对感兴趣的内容和出现的问题，有目的地和有针对性地，进一步收集资料。这时，采访的对象是那些有某种特别经历的人而不是随机抽样的人。所以，使用理论抽样时，资料的收集与分析是个循环的过程。即前期的分析结果会影响下一步的资料收集。

Example 4.8

A GROUNDED THEORY DESIGN

Xiao et al. (2004) examined the role of the supervisory board in Chinese listed companies through the use of grounded theory methodology. First, the authors briefly reviewed the literature, focusing on the institutional background of the Chinese economy, the characteristics of list companies, issues around China's two-tier board structure, and contrasted it with other board systems such as the Anglo-Saxon style and Germanic style. The authors recognised that the existing research on the role of the supervisory board in the Chinese context is limited, both theoretically and empirically, and thus adopted a Strauss-style grounded theory approach. Data were collected through face-to-face semi-structured interviews with board directors, supervisors and senior executives in 21 Chinese listed companies. A short interview schedule consisting of open questions was flexibly applied to maintain broad consistency across all interviews. The length of the interviews varied from 1.5 to 3 hours. Based on their data and analysis, the authors developed an analytical framework to capture the various roles of the supervisory board.

FURTHER READING

Charmaz, K. (2014) *Constructing Grounded Theory*. London: Sage. This book offers excellent advice and guidelines for grounded theory research, including research design, data collection, memo writing, sampling and data analysis.

Urquhart, C. (2013) *Grounded Theory for Qualitative Research: A Practical Guide*. London: Sage. This is a short text, based on the author's own experience, with particular emphasis on coding, theory building and writing a grounded theory research report.

4.7 EVALUATING YOUR OWN RESEARCH

In this final section, we will consider issues surrounding the evaluation of the quality of your findings. It is very important for us to conduct such evaluation in order to know whether our research is 'good' or not. There are many evaluation criteria to help assess whether or not the research meets certain benchmarks. We will talk about how to evaluate the quality of quantitative and qualitative research in turn.

4.7.1 Evaluating quantitative research

- Generalisability（普遍性）— When you have made the decision to use quantitative methods, usually you will have the desire to *generalise* your findings. In other words, your research goal is to get results which can be said to apply generally. Generalisability is highly linked to the number of participants. In general, the more participants in the study the better; however, you also need to be aware of the characteristics of your participants and any potential bias from the sample. For example, the study cannot generalise to females of all ages if your participants were only college students. Recruiting participants with incentives may also create a bias in discerning the differences between those who participated and those who did not.

- Replicability（可复制性）— A valid and valuable piece of quantitative research will allow the results to be replicated in future studies. It is hence critical that quantitative studies follow a thorough procedural and statistical accounting to ensure *replicability*, making sure that you have rigorously designed research procedures to follow and do not miss any steps. When you conduct statistical analysis, you do not miss data from the results and report your results accurately.

- Reliability （信度）— reliability in general refers to whether your data collection techniques and analytic procedures would produce consistent and stable findings if they were repeated on another occasion or by other researchers. Reliability is particularly relevant to quantitative research as researchers are likely to be concerned with the question of whether a measure is stable or not (Bryman and Bell, 2011). When analysing quantitative data, reliability is the extent to which a measurement tool gives consistent results. For example, Lin conducted a survey of whether consumers of The Body Shop are satisfied with its products and services. If Lin uses the same questionnaire to test the same participants three times every three days, and gets totally different results, this would indicate that the reliability of the measure is low.

KEY CONCEPTS IN CHINESE: RELIABILITY

信度，指测量结果的一致性、稳定性及可靠性。 一般多以内部一致性来加以表示该测验信度的高低。信度系数愈高即表示该测验的结果越一致、稳定与可靠。

- Validity （效度）— Validity is concerned with whether the findings are really about what they appear to be about (Forshaw et al., 2011).

KEY CONCEPTS IN CHINESE: VALIDITY

效度，即有效性，它是指测量工具或手段能够准确测出所需测量的事物的程度。效度是指所测量到的结果反映所想要考察内容的程度，测量结果与要考察的内容越吻合，则效度越高；反之，则效度越低。

There are several types of validity that students need to distinguish between:

- *Measurement validity* （测量效度）, also often referred to as *construct validity* （建构效度）, is concerned with the extent to which a measurement tool measures what it is supposed to measure. For example, does the happiness test really measure variations in people's happiness? It is also important to know that a measure could be reliable but that does not necessarily mean it is valid.

For example, a set of items measuring job satisfaction on any individual from one day to the next may produce pretty much the same score. This is, therefore, a reliable measure. However, the obtained 'score' from the job satisfaction test could actually be measuring employees' mood, and then this measure would not be valid.

- ○ 建构效度是指你的测量工具（量表）是否真实衡量了你要测试的概念。注意，一个测量工具可能具备很高的信度，却同时不具备可接受的效度。

- *Internal validity* （内部效度）mainly relates to the issue of causality. For example, within an experimental setting, we would like to see whether a change in the independent variable would cause any change in the dependent variable. If the causal relationship (the link between independent and dependent variables) is a result of the manipulation of the independent variable (and not anything else), this experiment will achieve high internal validity. On the other hand, if the relationship is influenced by factors such as imbalanced groups or experiment effects, then the experiment will have low internal validity.

  - ○ 内部效度是指自变量和因变量之间存在因果关系的明确程度。如果自变量和因变量之间的因果关系并不被其他变量和因素影响，这项研究的内部效度就高。

- *External validity* （外部效度）is concerned with the question of whether the results of a study can be generalised to other samples and contexts. For example, we may want to see whether the findings of consumer ethnocentric tendency amongst the American population would be similar if the study was conducted within the Chinese population.

  - ○ 外部效度是指研究结果能够一般化和普遍适用到其他样本或者其他研究背景的程度。

- *Ecological validity* （生态效度）refers to the extent to which the findings of a social scientific study are applicable to our everyday life. For example, some business research is conducted within a laboratory setting using simulation, and we would be interested to see if these technically valid results would also apply in people's everyday lives.

  - ○ 生态效度是指将实验结果应用到实验情境以外、真实生活中的有效程度。

4.7.2 Evaluating qualitative research

Due to their positivist origin, the concepts of validity and reliability cannot be addressed in the same way in qualitative research. Instead, qualitative research emphasises the *trustworthiness* of a study. In order to be separated from the positivist paradigm, researchers such as Guba (1981) propose the following criteria to assess the quality of qualitative research, in pursuit of trustworthiness:

- Credibility （可信性）– credibility deals with the question of the congruence between the findings and social reality (Merriam, 1998). In other words, it refers to the extent to which the results of your research are believable. Credibility of the research is to do with the 'quality' of the data gathered and not the 'quantity'. Techniques such as *member checks* and *triangulation* can be used to ensure the accuracy of the findings.

- Transferability （可转移性）– due to the nature of qualitative research which tends to use small samples of particular environmental settings, it is difficult to conclude that the findings would be applicable to other contexts and populations (Shenton, 2004). Nevertheless, qualitative researchers are encouraged to provide sufficient contextual information about the fieldwork sites used to allow readers to make the transfer to their own situations. In addition, it is important to provide *thick description* of the phenomenon under investigation to enable readers to make comparisons between the present findings and those that they have discovered in other situations (Bryman, 2016).

KEY CONCEPTS IN CHINESE: THICK DESCRIPTION

指的是质性研究者需要提供对于研究现象的详尽、深入的描述，以便读者能判断其研究结果的真实性。

- Dependability （可靠性）– parallel to reliability in quantitative research, the dependability of qualitative research deals with the extent to which the research findings are consistent and could be repeated (Lincoln and Guba, 1985). It is suggested that the research process should be reported in detail, and completed records should be accessible from problem formulation, participant selection, fieldwork notes, interview transcripts, data analysis, and so on (Bryman, 2016). This would ensure that external researchers are able to repeat the study and achieve similar findings.
- Conformability （符合性）– conformability deals with the objectivity of the research. Although complete objectivity is impossible in qualitative research, research should provide findings that are 'the result of the experiences and ideas of the informants, rather than the characteristics and preferences of the researcher' (Shenton, 2004: 72). To enhance conformability, detailed methodological description would demonstrate how each research decision was made objectively.

FURTHER READING

Johnson, P., Buehring, A., Cassell, C. and Symon, G. (2006) Evaluating qualitative management research: Towards a contingent criteriology. *International Journal of Management Reviews* 8: 131–56. This article provides a comprehensive review of evaluating different kinds of qualitative research.

Saunders, M., Lewis, P. and Thornhill, A. (2016) *Research Methods for Business Students*, 7th edition. Harlow: Pearson. Section 5.6, 'The credibility of research findings', talks about a number of threats to reliability and validity. It would be very helpful to understand these threats and think about possible ways to reduce them. You may want to include this in your methodology chapter when writing up your dissertation.

REFERENCES

Amerson, R. (2011) Making a case for the case study method. *Journal of Nursing Education* 50: 427–8.

Bryman, A. (2016) *Social Research Methods*. Oxford: Oxford University Press.

Bryman, A. and Bell, E. (2011) *Business Research Methods*. Oxford: Oxford University Press.

Charmaz, K. (2014) *Constructing Grounded Theory*. London: Sage.

Coffey, A. and Atkinson, P. (1996) *Making Sense of Qualitative Data: Complementary Research Strategies*. Thousand Oaks, CA: Sage Publications.

Coolican, H. (2014) *Research Methods and Statistics in Psychology*, 6th edition. East Sussex and New York: Psychology Press.

Corbin, J.M. and Strauss, A. (2008) *Basics of Qualitative Research: Techniques and Procedures for Developing Grounded Theory*. London: Sage.

Creswell, J.W. (2012). Qualitative inquiry and research design: Choosing among five approaches, 3rd edition. Thousand Oaks, CA: Sage.

Dunne, C. (2011) The place of the literature review in grounded theory research. *International Journal of Social Research Methodology* 14: 111–24.

Eriksson, P. and Kovalainen, A. (2016) *Qualitative Methods in Business Research*. London: Sage.

Forshaw, M., Upton, D. and Jones, S. (2011) *Psychology Express: Research Methods in Psychology* (undergraduate revision guide). Upper Saddle River, NJ: Prentice Hall.

Gamble, J. (2006) Introducing Western-style HRM practices to China: Shopfloor perceptions in a British multinational. *Journal of World Business* 41: 328–43.

Glaser, B.G. (1992) *Basics of Grounded Theory Analysis: Emergence vs Forcing*. Mill Valley, CA: Sociology Press.

Glaser, B.G. (1998) *Doing Grounded Theory: Issues and Discussions*. Mill Valley, CA: Sociology Press.

Glaser, B.G. and Strauss, A.L. (1967) *The Discovery of Grounded Theory: Strategies for Qualitive Research*. Chicago, IL: Aldine.

Guba, E.G. (1981) Criteria for assessing the trustworthiness of naturalistic inquiries. *ECTJ* 29(2): 75–91.

Hallberg, L.R.M. (2010) Some thoughts about the literature review in grounded theory studies. *International Journal of Qualitative Studies in Health and Well-being* 5: 1.

Hammersley, M. (1996) The relationship between qualitative and quantitative research: Paradigm loyalty versus methodological eclecticism. In J.T.E. Richardson (ed.) *Handbook of Qualitative Research Methods for Psychology and the Social Sciences*. Leicester: BPS Books, 159–74.

Hennink, M., Hutter, I. and Bailey, A. (2011) *Qualitative Research Methods*. London: Sage.

Johnson, R.B., Onwuegbuzie, A.J. and Turne, L.A. (2007) Toward a definition of mixed methods research. *Journal of Mixed Methods Research* 1: 112–33.

Lee, A.S. (1989) A scientific methodology for MIS case studies. *MIS Quarterly* 13: 33–50.

Lincoln, Y. and Guba, E.G. (1985) *Naturalistic Inquiry*. Beverly Hills, CA: Sage.

Liu, S., Perry, P., Moore, C., et al. (2015) The standardization–localization dilemma of brand communications for luxury fashion retailers' internationalization into China. *Journal of Business Research* 69: 357–64.

Lockström, M., Schadel, J., Harrison, N., et al. (2010) Antecedents to supplier integration in the automotive industry: A multiple-case study of foreign subsidiaries in China. *Journal of Operations Management* 28: 240–56.

McCann, T.V. and Clark, E. (2003) Grounded theory in nursing research: Part 1 – Methodology. *Nurse Researcher* 11(2): 7–18.

McGhee, G., Marland, G.R. and Atkinson, J. (2007) Grounded theory research: Literature reviewing and reflexivity. *Journal of Advanced Nursing* 60: 334–42.

Merriam, S.B. (1998) *Qualitative Research and Case Study Applications in Education*. Chichester/New York: Wiley.

Mills, A.J., Durepos, G. and Wiebe, E. (2009) *Encyclopedia of Case Study Research*. Thousand Oaks, CA: Sage.

Ministry of Civil Affairs of the People's Republic of China (2015) Available at: www.mca.gov.cn/article/zwgk/gzdt/201508/20150800861945.shtml (accessed 20 November 2017).

Morgan, D.L. (1998) Practical strategies for combining qualitative and quantitative methods: Applications to health research. *Qualitative Health Research* 8: 362–76.

Myers, M.D. (2013) *Qualitative Research in Business and Management*. London: Sage.

Ramalho, R., Adams, P., Huggard, P., et al. (2015) Literature review and constructivist grounded theory methodology. *Forum Qualitative Sozialforschung* 16.

Reichertz, J. (2010) Abduction: The logic of discovery of grounded theory. *Forum: Qualitative Social Research* 11.

Saunders, M., Lewis, P. and Thornhill, A. (2016) *Research Methods for Business Students*. Harlow: Pearson.

Schwandt, T.A. (2001) *Dictionary of Qualitative Inquiry*. London: Sage.

Sekaran, U. and Bougie, R. (2013) *Research Methods for Business: A Skill-building Approach*. Chichester: Wiley.

Shenton, A.K. (2004) Strategies for ensuring trustworthiness in qualitative research projects. *Education for Information* 22(2): 63–75.

Stake, R.E. (1994) Case studies. In N.K. Denzin and Y.S. Lincoln (eds) *Handbook of Qualitative Research*. Thousand Oaks, CA: Sage, 236–47.

Strauss, A.L. and Corbin, J.M. (1990) *Basics of Qualitative Research: Grounded Theory Procedures and Techniques*. Newbury Park, CA: Sage.

Strauss, A.L. and Corbin, J.M. (1998) *Basics of Qualitative Research: Techniques and Procedures for Developing Grounded Theory*. Thousand Oaks, CA: Sage.

Symon, G. and Cassell, C. (2012) *Qualitative Organisational Research: Core Methods and Current Challenges*. London: Sage.

Thomas, G. (2016) *How to Do Your Case Study*. London: Sage.

Urquhart, C. (2013) *Grounded Theory for Qualitative Research: A Practical Guide*. London: Sage.

Urquhart, C., Lehmann, H. and Myers, M.D. (2010) Putting the 'theory' back into grounded theory: Guidelines for grounded theory studies in information systems. *Information Systems Journal* 20: 357–81.

Webb, E.J., Campbell, D.T., Schwartz, R.D., et al. (1966) *Unobtrusive Measures: Nonreactive Research in the Social Sciences*. Chicago: Rand McNally.

Whang, H., Yong, S. and Ko, E. (2015) Pop culture, destination images, and visit intentions: Theory and research on travel motivations of Chinese and Russian tourists. *Journal of Business Research* 69: 631–41.

Wu, C., Fang, D. and Li, N. (2015) Roles of owners' leadership in construction safety: The case of high-speed railway construction projects in China. *International Journal of Project Management* 33: 1665–79.

Xiao, J.Z., Dahya, J. and Lin, Z. (2004) A grounded theory exposition of the role of the supervisory board in China. *British Journal of Management* 15: 39–55.

Yin, R.K. (2014) *Case Study Research: Design and Methods*. Thousand Oaks, CA: Sage.

Yu, X. (2008) Impacts of corporate code of conduct on labor standards: A case study of Reebok's athletic footwear supplier factory in China. *Journal of Business Ethics* 81: 513–29.

Zhang, Y. (1996) Chinese consumers' evaluation of foreign products: The influence of culture, product types and product presentation format. *European Journal of Marketing* 30: 50–68.

Zikmund, W., Babin, B., Carr, J., et al. (2009) *Business Research Methods*. Mason, OH: South-Western, Cengage Learning.

5

SAMPLING

5.1 OVERVIEW

Sampling issues are crucial in data collection, as from whom the data will be acquired contributes to a better understanding of a theory. Sampling deals with some key questions of data collection: how many people will be involved; who will be the target population; what level of organisations will be targeted (individuals or teams); what sampling technique should be used to ensure the sample is relevant and representative. Ideally, researchers would collect and analyse data from every possible case or member in order to capture all the experience of the group. In reality, this is very rare due to restrictions in budget, time and access. Some empirical research investigates specific problems in a specific organisation. In this case, it is possible to access the entire population. For the majority of studies, it is only possible to collect data from a sub-group. Different research questions require different sampling techniques.

─────────────── **Example 5.1** ───────────────

DIFFERENT SAMPLING TECHNIQUES

For example, if a department store wants to know what customers think of its new TV advert, researchers from its marketing department might want to survey customers from different groups based on age, gender, income level, etc., so that they can generalise the results to all customers. On the other hand, if you want to understand how successful women juggle their career and family, you might interview women who have progressed to senior positions in their organisations to gain insights into their career barriers, their strategies and how they balance work and family. In this case, whether or not your results are statistically generalisable is less important.

This chapter will explore a range of sampling methods commonly used in business and management research. For the purpose of presentation, these methods will be divided into two types: probability sampling and non-probability sampling. We will then discuss issues related to sample size in the last section. Before we move on to detailed discussions of these techniques, it is useful to clarify some basic concepts which are used throughout this chapter. A *population* refers to the full set of cases or members in the entire group under study. A *sample* is a sub-group of cases or members selected from the population. Population and sample do not always mean people. Depending on the nature of your research subjects, they could be individuals, organisations, products, shares in the stock market, advertisements, and so on. *Sampling* refers to the methods or strategies you use to select your research participants (or sample). It is important for every piece of research to make this process clear and transparent in your dissertation or report, so that your supervisor or audience may assess the validity of your results. It should be emphasised here that there is no one best approach to sampling. Your choice of sampling technique depends (a) theoretically on your research objectives and (b) practically on issues such as whom and how many participants you have access to.

KEY CONCEPTS IN CHINESE: POPULATION, SAMPLE, SAMPLING

总体 (Population)，又称母体，是个集合名词，在研究术语里指的是考察对象的全体。

样本 (Sample)，是从总体中抽取的一部分个体（case）。取什么样的样本与所研究的问题有极大关联。有的样本需要有代表性，即研究员需要从样本推断出整体考察对象的特征。但有的样本需要提供广泛而深入的信息。如你要研究人的工作经历，那你要采访的人越多经验越好。这些人不一定有广泛的代表行。

取样方式 (Sampling)，是指你挑选样本的标准，手段和方式。在论文里，这些需要详细的记录并解释清楚。这样其他人才能判断你的结论是否有效。

5.2 PROBABILITY SAMPLING

Probability sampling is also called representative sampling and is widely used in survey-based research and experimental research. Within this sampling frame, the chance of each case being selected from the population is equal. The rationale is that by using this sampling method, you can make inferences from your sample about a population in order to answer the research questions. As such, a key point for consideration is how the sample represents the population. A perfect representative sample is ideal as it mirrors the exact composition of the population. For example, if you know that 60 per cent of your population is female and 25 per cent 40 years or older, your sample should also consist of 60 per cent female and 25 per cent aged 40 years or above. In order for probability sampling to work, you will need a complete list of all the cases in the population from which your sample is extracted. This, however, can be problematic, as you do not always have full knowledge of this population. In practice, it is extremely difficult to obtain probability samples that are representative of the whole of China (Roy et al., 2001), for several reasons: first, China's large size and the time and cost required to communicate with and access respondents in all regions; second, regional variances in culture, economic development and business practice are significant; third, researchers are frequently asked to obtain permission from the authorities when undertaking a large-scale survey or research that is deemed to be sensitive.

Therefore, nationwide probability sampling has been very rare in business and management research in China. Most researchers instead adopt local samples, for example within an organisation or within a list of companies provided by the Bureau of Industry and Trade in a city. As a result, most studies do not claim to be representative of China as a whole. For example, if your research aim is to investigate how performance-related pay affects the commitment of employees in state-owned enterprises (SOEs), potentially your population is all the employees working in all SOEs. But you do not have access to all SOEs. Nor can you obtain all the key information, such as how many employees there are, how old they are, what positions they hold, which industrial sectors they work in, and so on. In fact, you only have access to one SOE in one industry. In this case, your sampling frame is only all employees from that organisation. Strictly speaking, you can only generalise your findings to that organisation. You should not make claims that your results are generalisable to all employees in all SOEs. Moreover, you should acknowledge this limitation in your dissertation. After choosing the appropriate sampling frame, you could use the techniques presented below to achieve probability sampling locally.

KEY CONCEPTS IN CHINESE: PROBABILITY SAMPLING

概率抽样（Probability sampling）是定量研究（特别是问卷调查）中最常用的取样方法。其原则是通过随机抽样，使总体中的每一个个体被抽到的几率相等。目的是为了抽取出的样本在统计学上能一定程度代表总体所具有的特性。通常样本量越大，抽样误差越小。

5.2.1 Simple random sampling

Simple random sampling means that you select respondents at random from your sampling frame. To achieve this, you could first assign a unique number to each case in your sampling frame (for example, the first case is 1, the second case is 2, and so on) and then select cases randomly, either using a computer or an online program, until you reach your target sample size. There are several benefits of using simple random sampling. First, the technique ensures that each case of the population has an equal chance of being selected. Second, it allows you to choose your respondents without bias. Third, the sample selected can be considered representative of the entire population and therefore increase the generalisability of your results. A typical example of choosing at random is in a lottery, where numbers are marked on balls of the same weight. These balls are placed in a transparent container and whirled for each draw by a guest. However, there are also pitfalls of using this sampling approach. First, your selection of sample is more evenly dispersed throughout the population when your sample includes more than a few hundred cases. Otherwise, there is a risk that certain parts of a population could be either over- or under-represented. This increases the pressure to reach a good sample size. Second, if your population is located in various geographical regions, selecting participants randomly means that you might have to travel to all of these locations, should you need to conduct face-to-face interviews. This could increase the cost and time required for data collection. Thus, simple random sampling works best when data can be collected remotely, for example electronically or through the postal service. However, in China where personal connection is crucial for organisational access and data collection, collecting data remotely could mean a low response rate. Despite these difficulties, simple random sampling remains a popular choice for (especially quantitative) data collection. In a study about high-performance work systems and organisational performance, Zhang and Morris (2014: 77) mention that: 'Eight hundred and twenty companies were randomly selected from the list of firms in Beijing provided by the Statistics Bureau of the Beijing Government and were contacted in order to be invited to participate in this research'.

KEY CONCEPTS IN CHINESE: SIMPLE RANDOM SAMPLING

简单随机抽样，也称纯随机抽样，是指从总体抽样单位中任意抽取若干个单位作为样本。在简单随机抽样法下，每个样本可能被抽中的概率都相等。

5.2.2 Systematic sampling

Systematic sampling refers to the method of selecting your sample at pre-defined and regular intervals from your sampling frame. To use this approach, you could choose your first case randomly and then choose subsequent cases by selecting every nth case. The sampling interval n can be calculated by using the population size divided by the sample size. Systematic sampling is similar to random sampling, as it allows each case to have an equal chance of being selected. Moreover, it can be useful in situations where the cases in a population are not accessible at the same time (Ang, 2014). Occasionally, you might acquire a list of your population rather than constructing your own list. For example, you might get a list of all the suppliers of an organisation in order to send out your survey. However, to maintain randomness, you must ensure the chosen sample interval does not coincide with any existing periodic pattern on the list.

Example 5.2

SYSTEMATIC SAMPLING

Woodhams et al. (2009) provide an example to illustrate the use of systematic sampling in the Chinese context. In this study, the authors collected data from job adverts posted on a website to examine the discriminative elements required by some employers in China. The first job advert was chosen randomly on the website, and subsequently every 5th job advert was selected, until a sample size of 301 cases was reached.

KEY CONCEPTS IN CHINESE: SYSTEMATIC SAMPLING

系统抽样，也称等距抽样，首先将总体中的各个抽样单位按一定顺序排列，再根据样本容量要求确定抽取间隔，然后随机确定起点，每隔一定的间距抽取一个样本。

5.2.3 Stratified sampling

When using this sampling approach, you first divide your cases into strata based on one or a small number of attributes. In other words, you divide your population into sub-groups. Then, you select a certain number of cases from each sub-group randomly. The benefit of using stratified sampling is that you can ensure each sub-group is represented in your sample, thus achieving a higher level of representativeness compared with simple random sampling or systematic sampling. For example, if your research aims to understand how employees at different organisational levels respond to performance-related pay, you may want to send questionnaires to employees at all levels. You know that there are four levels of organisational hierarchy, therefore you divide your sampling frame into four sub-groups and randomly select respondents from each sub-group. It is common for some sub-groups to be bigger than others – for example, 60% workers, 15% team leaders, 15% managers and 10% senior managers. Your sample could be drawn in proportion to the percentage of employees at each level. Thus, if you want to achieve a sample of 300, your final sample will consist of 180 workers, 45 team leaders, 45 managers and 30 senior managers. Moreover, you could further stratify your sample using more than one attribute, such as age, gender, tenure, educational level, and so on, provided you have obtained all this information in advance. For instance, if you aim to understand whether gender is a factor, you could make sure you draw 50% of males and 50% of females at each organisational level. Although stratified sampling is useful in achieving representativeness, it also shares many disadvantages with simple random sampling and systematic sampling. Further, the more attributes you use to divide your population, the more complicated your sampling method becomes. The extra steps of stratifying your population mean that you may need to spend more time, effort and money during your sampling process. This can also be difficult to explain in your dissertation. In addition, Chinese people do not respond well to random sampling. Stratifying your sampling frame could further reduce your response rate. Thus, not surprisingly this method is less common for business and management research conducted in China, unless the research is supported by the authorities.

KEY CONCEPTS IN CHINESE: STRATIFIED SAMPLING

分层抽样，首先将抽样单位按照某种特征或某种规则划分为不同的层，然后从不同的层中独立随机的抽取样本。

5.2.4 Cluster sampling

Cluster sampling is similar to stratified sampling in the way that it involves you dividing your population into a number of sub-groups based on naturally occurring characteristics, such as industrial sector, geographical location, and so on. These sub-groups are called 'clusters'. Essentially, the actual process of cluster sampling includes two stages of random sampling. First, you randomly choose a few clusters. Then, at the second stage, you randomly select cases from each cluster. For example, you plan to survey 300 employees in an organisation which has offices in 10 cities. You could first select three cities randomly and then select 100 employees randomly from each city for your sample. There are advantages and disadvantages to this sampling method. If your data collection involves face-to-face contact with respondents, this method could reduce the time and costs required for travelling. However, cluster sampling also reduces the level of representativeness of your sample compared with simple random sampling, systematic sampling and stratified sampling. Thus, it is often considered a trade-off between representativeness and accessibility.

KEY CONCEPTS IN CHINESE: CLUSTER SAMPLING

整群抽样，又称聚类抽样， 是根据一些自然特征（如行业部门，地理位置等），将总体分割成若干个互不交叉，互不重复的群组，然后以群为抽样单位的样本抽取方法。

5.3 NON-PROBABILITY SAMPLING

The sampling techniques discussed in the last section emphasise the representativeness and statistical randomness of your sample. These methods are often problematic when researching in

China for three reasons. First, random sampling requires you to know your population. However, in much business and management research, this is often impossible and impractical. Second, in a relationship-driven society like China, recruiting randomly as recommended in Western methodologies without referrals might have a higher risk of receiving non-responsiveness or superficial feedback. Stening and Zhang (2007) argue that when researching in China, researchers often have to work with samples that are neither representative nor random. Third, some research questions do not require samples to be representative, as a small number of cases could provide far more insight into a particular issue than a large and random sample. This section will introduce a range of alternative sampling methods based on other concerns. Noticeably, not every researcher is in favour of these methods. These non-probability sampling strategies have been described by Patton (1990) as the least recommended approaches because they have 'low credibility' and are 'inappropriate for anything other than practice'.

KEY CONCEPTS IN CHINESE: NON-PROBABILITY SAMPLING

非概率抽样（Non-probability sampling）通常在定性研究中使用。但有时因为实际操作局限等原因，定量研究也采用该抽样方法。通过这一方式抽取的样本在统计学上很难代表总体的特征。

5.3.1 Convenience sampling

Convenience sampling is used when researchers do not have the luxury of having access to all cases in the population. When using convenience sampling, you choose those cases that are easy to access rather than those that are representative. Convenience sampling can be used in quantitative research, especially in pilot studies where there is little variation in the population. For example, in marketing research, if you want to obtain customers' feedback about the service quality of an airliner, you could go to a nearby airport and survey travellers who have experience with the airliner, have spare time and are willing to participate. You could continue surveying people until you reach your target sample size. But, predominantly, this approach is more widely used in qualitative research which emphasises an in-depth understanding of certain issues rather than generalisability. For example, if your research is about how executives make decisions, you may recruit a small number of general managers, directors and CEOs from your network and have some in-depth and semi-structured interviews with them to collect data. In this case, your sample is likely to be biased and non-representative of the total population of executives.

Convenience sampling is a very useful technique when conducting research in Chinese societies where people do not respond well to strangers. As noted by a number of scholars (Roy et al., 2001; Stening and Zhang, 2007), in a collectivist society like China, data collection often relies on *guanxi*, or the personal connections of the research team. Because of the problems associated with probability sampling, Roy et al. (2001) even argue that most management studies undertaken in China are, in effect, based on convenience samples. Convenience sampling has been widely used to collect quantitative data (particularly survey data) in China. For example, in a study of antecedents of collective organisational citizenship behaviour (Gong et al., 2010), the authors sent surveys to managers through two channels that they have a connection with: (a) senior executives attending training at a business school in Shanghai and (b) clients of a large HR consulting firm in Shenzhen. Convenience sampling can also be a useful technique to enhance the quality of data in qualitative research due to prior connections between the researcher and participants. Ng and Chakrabarty (2005), for example, successfully recruited three women managers in Hong Kong from their part-time MBA graduates and persuaded them to talk about sensitive subjects, including gender stereotypes, work–family stress, tokenism, sexual harassment, and so on.

KEY CONCEPTS IN CHINESE: CONVENIENCE SAMPLING

任意抽样，也称便利抽样，指调查人员本着方便、便捷的原则选择样本的抽样方式。任意抽样是非概率抽样中最简便、费用和时间最节省的一种抽样方法。但是抽取的样本并不具有代表性。

5.3.2 Snowball sampling

Snowball sampling is similar to convenience sampling in the sense that you start with a few cases that are easy to access. Then you ask these cases to introduce you to other cases from their contacts. You could further ask the new cases to identify new cases and repeat this process until you reach your target sample size. This method is efficient when researching a population (for example, people who experience domestic violence) that is otherwise hard to reach. On the other hand, this sampling approach is likely to create a very biased sample, as respondents tend to recommend new cases that are similar to them. This often results in a homogeneous sample. Moreover, if you recruit respondents from the same network, they are likely to know each other and thus leave out certain issues to avoid conflicts (Patton, 1990). This could potentially be a huge disadvantage in China, as Chinese people tend to maintain *mianzi* in their conversation if they know you have access to their network. Nevertheless, like convenience sampling, snowball sampling is particularly useful to identify respondents in Chinese society, especially for studies that target a small number of participants from hard-to-reach groups (Ng and Chakrabarty, 2005). When the researcher is referred to by an 'ingroup' member, it is easier to develop trust between the researcher and the researched (Tsang, 1998). Some qualitative researchers combine convenience sampling and snowball sampling techniques to maximise the number of respondents they can reach. Woodhams et al. (2015), for example, used these two approaches together to recruit 20 women managers who worked at very senior levels of their organisations. The rationale was that this elite group of women managers is rare and busy. Without referral from their friends, it would be almost impossible for the researchers to convince these women to participate in their study and have in-depth discussions about some personal issues.

KEY CONCEPTS IN CHINESE: SNOWBALL SAMPLING

滚雪球抽样，与便利抽样相似，也是通过少量样本单位来获取更多样本单位的抽样方式。研究人员通过人际关系相互引进介绍，类似滚雪球一般从开始的少量调查对象通过推荐找到越来越多的参与者。

5.3.3 Purposive sampling

Purposive sampling, also called judgemental sampling, refers to a sampling technique that allows the researcher to impose some selection criteria and use subjective judgement to recruit participants who meet such criteria. The aim of purposive sampling is for researchers to filter out cases that do not have the relevant knowledge and experience, and only select those who are most likely to be able to answer the research questions. Preparation is needed as researchers must understand the characteristics of the target population before collecting data. Such knowledge can be acquired from previous studies or the community under study (Tongco, 2007). One crucial point of purposive sampling is to define a good respondent or informant. Allen (1971) suggests that researchers should set very specific criteria of a good respondent by composing a list of qualifications, and select those who come as close as possible. For example, if you want to investigate the work–life balance of engineers working in the IT industry, you can write a list of the desired attributes you want your respondents to have: (1) undertake technical work; (2) hold an engineering degree; and (3) deal with information technology (you may want to define this term) on a daily basis. Although this sample is selected with a 'purpose', you also need to ensure that there is enough diversity in your sample. Thus, your final sample could include both male and female engineers who come from different age groups.

This sampling method can be applied to both quantitative and qualitative research. In quantitative research design, purposive sampling is often combined with random sampling to improve external validity. For example, in a study about how farmers managed their areas in China, Zhen et al. (2006) purposively chose four communes, and within each commune randomly select one village to distribute their questionnaires. In qualitative research design, this sampling method is effective in maximising the quality of data when only working with small samples. Recently, some researchers have also combined purposive sampling with internet recruitment to reach a 'hidden population' (Barratt et al., 2015). Online purposive sampling has become increasingly popular, as researchers can engage in large samples of people who are otherwise difficult to reach, such as illegal immigrants or drug users, at a relatively low cost (Barratt et al., 2015). An example is Fincher (2014), who used Sina Weibo (the Chinese equivalent of Twitter) to recruit 'leftover' women or *shengnü* (Chinese women who are over 30 years old and remain single). A drawback of online purposive sampling is that samples are self-selected. In other words, whether someone meets the criteria rests on the judgement of the respondent rather than that of the researcher.

KEY CONCEPTS IN CHINESE: PURPOSIVE SAMPLING

立意抽样，又称判断抽样，是指调查人员根据主观经验或某种标准从总体样本中选取那些被判定为最能代表总体的单位作为样本的抽样方法。

5.4 SAMPLE SIZE

A question frequently raised by students is 'how many cases are enough for my study?' The answer to this question is complicated. The sample size of a study is determined by many factors. First, there are different expectations and principles for judging sample size for quantitative and qualitative studies. Second, you are likely to face many practical restrictions that limit the size of your sample.

5.4.1 Practical constraints

Time

The majority of research projects have a time frame. Students normally have around three to four months to complete a dissertation for an undergraduate or a taught postgraduate degree in the UK. The actual time frame for data collection is only around three to four weeks. For doctoral students, data collection could last around six to nine mouths. However, most universities impose an ultimate deadline for submission. Academic staff also face tight deadlines, especially if the project is sponsored by a funder, who requires a final report to be produced within a certain period of time. Moreover, most journals set deadlines for articles invited for revise-and-resubmit. These time limits mean we have to be realistic about how many cases we can reach. Many projects have a cut-off date for data collection. When conducting research in a language other than English, you also need time to translate (and sometimes back-translate) questionnaires, interview questions and scripts.

Cost

Research often involves certain costs, especially when you collect primary data. It can be the cost of printing, posting and returning questionnaires, or setting up prizes to encourage participation.

Or it can be the cost of travelling and accommodation for conducting interviews. You might also need a budget to translate your questionnaires and interview scripts between English and Chinese if you are not able to do it all by yourself. For secondary data, you may be able to acquire some for free. For example, you can download data from stock markets or non-profit organisations, such as the World Bank or International Labour Organization, free of charge. However, in many cases, you need to pay to have access to databases.

Response rate

For whatever reason, not everyone would like to participate in your research. You are likely to encounter non-responsiveness, whether you are carrying out quantitative or qualitative studies. This will put extra pressure on reaching your desired sample size. Response rate is also an important criterion for assessing the soundness of a study, particularly one using the survey method (Mellahi and Harris, 2015). Currently, there is no 'golden rule' for what is an acceptable response rate in business and management research. However, low response rate is considered a threat to the external validity of quantitative studies. After reviewing 1,093 papers published in major international journals, Mellahi and Harris (2015) conclude that response rates vary across Chinese regions. For example, on average, research conducted in mainland China has a response rate of 56.93%, while in Hong Kong it is only 32.94%. There are a number of ways to enhance response rate – for example, by promising anonymity and confidentiality, writing a personalised cover letter or offering financial incentives. In the Chinese context, Cooke (2009) suggests that on-site surveys collected by researchers or designated research assistants yield a much higher response rate (well above 80%) than a postal survey (typically 15–30%). Moreover, in a relationship-driven society, conducting research with a small number of organisations, with which the researcher has personal connections, often enhances response rate and data quality for both quantitative and qualitative research (Cooke, 2009).

5.4.2 Sample size for quantitative research

For quantitative research, the general expectation seems to be that 'bigger is better'. Researchers tend to believe that a bigger sample size gives them more confidence in their results. Larger samples can reduce the likelihood of error and increase the generalisability of results. In reality, however, it is not always possible to derive your findings from large samples because of the restrictions mentioned earlier. The literature has suggested various techniques to calculate what sample size is appropriate. In the popular Saunders et al. (2015) book, the authors suggest that sample size should relate to the size of the population. In business and management research, researchers are normally expected to have at least a 95% level of certainty. This means that you are 95% confident that your sample is representative of the population. For example, if a company has 200 employees, you should survey at least 132 of them in order to reach a 95% confidence level. Detailed calculation can be found in Chapter 7 of Saunders et al. (2015). Other scholars suggest that your sample size depends on the number of predictor variables you use in the study (Ang, 2014). If you have three predictor variables or fewer, your sample size should be at least 100 (Nunnally, 1994). If you include 10 predictor variables in your research model, then a sample size of 400 is required. As a rule of thumb, Combs (2010) suggests that any quantitative research should have a sample of 100 in order for the result to be statistically meaningful.

5.4.3 Sample size for qualitative research

The bad news is that there is no magical formula to calculate sample size here. Sample size for qualitative research varies significantly, depending on the type of study you undertake. If you use a case study approach, you might only need one or two companies to be your typical cases. If you conduct interviews, Baker and Edwards (2012) suggest a sample size of between 12 and 60. If you use documents, you might have to review hundreds of pages of company files. But, in general, qualitative studies tend to have a smaller sample size than quantitative studies. Ritchie et al. (2014) give some reasons. First of all, whether the sample is representative of the population or not is not a major concern of qualitative researchers. Second, counting frequency is not the only analytical tool, as some phenomena need only appear once to be theoretically meaningful. Third, qualitative studies aim to produce rich and insightful understanding of a social phenomenon. Each interview, for example, contains many pages of information. To avoid being overwhelmed by data, qualitative researchers have to keep the sample size manageable. Many scholars, for example Morse (1994), suggest theoretical saturation as a guideline for sample size in qualitative research. For interviews, Guest et al. (2006) suggest that data saturation will occur by the time they have analysed 12 interviews, and after that new themes emerge infrequently. For focus group discussion, the suggested sample size is 6 to 12 groups (Saunders et al., 2015), with an optimum group size of 4–8 people in each group (Finch et al., 2014).

Having said this, it is important to make sure your sample size is not too small. A very small sample lacks diversity and you are likely to miss out on key information or experience. Moreover, you can add more cases to your sample at a later stage of your research, such as after you conduct preliminary analysis. This allows you to explore some themes more extensively.

TOP TIPS 小建议

- 中国学生为论文收集数据时，一般都会从身边的资源开始。很多人会联系父母的工作单位或自家以及亲戚朋友开的公司。还有同学联系以前工作过或实习过的公司。这些都是不错的办法。这样样本来源有保障。无论是发问卷还是做访谈，返还率和回应率（response rate）都会比在陌生的公司发的要高很多。

- 学生经常问的一个问题是：样本量究竟要有多大？如，要收多少问卷，要做几个访谈。一般来讲，收问卷的话，本科生论文大概要收 100 份以上，研究生论文要200份以上。要是做访谈，本科生要 5-8 个，研究生至少要8-10个。而且要30 分钟以上的深度访谈，不能是10分钟的泛泛而谈。
- 你要考虑你的样本（sample）是否有足够的知识，经验来回答你的问题。比如，你要研究一家公司的战略管理（strategic management），那你发问卷或访谈的对象应该是公司的高级管理层，而不是一般员工。因为员工不会接触到这些讨论。

FURTHER READING

Ritchie, J., Lewis, J., Elam, G., et al. (2014) Designing and selecting samples. In J. Ritchie, J. Lewis, C.M. Nicholls, et al. (eds) *Qualitative Research Practice: A Guide for Social Science Students and Researchers*, 2nd edition. London: Sage, 111–45. This chapter provides a comprehensive discussion of sampling issues in qualitative research.

Saunders, M., Lewis, P. and Thornhill, A. (2015) *Research Methods for Business Students*. New York: Pearson Education. Chapter 7 explores different sampling techniques commonly used in business and management, with a focus on quantitative research and other relevant issues such as representativeness and generalisability.

REFERENCES

Allen, H.B. (1971) Principles of informant selection. *American Speech* 46: 47–51.

Ang, S.H. (2014) *Research Design for Business and Management.* London: Sage.

Baker, S.E. and Edwards, R. (eds) (2012) How Many Qualitative Interviews is Enough? Expert Voices and Early Career Reflections on Sampling and Cases in Qualitative Research. Unpublished discussion paper for the National Centre for Research Methods. Available at: http://eprints.ncrm. ac.uk/2273 (accessed 4 January 2016).

Barratt, M., Ferris, J. and Lenton, S. (2015) Hidden populations, online purposive sampling, and external validity: Taking off the blindfold. *Field Methods* 27: 3–21.

Combs, J. (2010) Big samples and small effects: Let's not trade relevance and rigor for power. *Academy of Management Journal* 53: 9–13.

Cooke, F. (2009) A decade of transformation of HRM in China: A review of literature and suggestions for future studies. *Asia Pacific Business Review* 47: 6–42.

Finch, H., Lewis, J. and Turley, C. (2014) Focus groups. In J. Ritchie, J. Lewis, C.M. Nicholls, et al. (eds) *Qualitative Research Pracice: A Guide for Social Science Students and Researchers*, 2nd edition. London: Sage, 211–42.

Fincher, L.H. (2014) *Leftover Women: The Resurgence of Gender Inequality in China.* New York: Zed Books.

Gong, Y., Chang, S. and Cheung, S.Y. (2010) High performance work system and collective OCB: A collective social exchange perspective. *Human Resources Management Journal* 20(2): 119–37.

Guest, G., Bunce, A. and Johnson, L. (2006) How many interviews are enough? An experiment with data saturation and variability. *Field Methods* 18: 59–82.

Mellahi, K. and Harris, L.C. (2015) Response rates in business and management research: An overview of current practice and suggestions for future direction. *British Journal of Management* 27(2): 426–37.

Morse, J. (1994) Designing funded qualitative research. In N. Denzin and Y. Lincoln (eds) *Handbook for Qualitative Research*. Thousand Oaks, CA: Sage, 220–35.

Ng, C.W. and Chakrabarty, A.-S. (2005) Women managers in Hong Kong: Personal and political agendas. *Asia Pacific Business Review* 11: 163–78.

Nunnally, J.C. (1994) *Psychometric Theory*. New York: McGraw-Hill.

Patton, M.Q. (1990) *Qualitative Evaluation and Research Methods*. London: Sage.

Ritchie, J., Lewis, J., Elam, G., et al. (2014) Designing and selecting samples. In J. Ritchie, J. Lewis and C.M. Nicholls, et al. (eds) *Qualitative Research Practice: A Guide for Social Science Students and Researchers*, 2nd edition. London: Sage, 111–45.

Roy, A., Walters, P.G.P. and Luk, S.T.K. (2001) Chinese puzzles and paradoxes: Conducting business research in China. *Journal of Business Research* 52: 203–10.

Saunders, M., Lewis, P. and Thornhill, A. (2015) *Research Methods for Business Students*. New York: Pearson Education.

Stening, B. and Zhang, M. (2007) Methodological challenges confronted when conducting management research in China. *International Journal of Cross Cultural Management* 7: 121–42.

Tongco, M.D.C. (2007) Purposive sampling as a tool for informant selection. *Ethnobotany Research and Applications* 5: 147–58.

Tsang, E.W.K. (1998) Inside story: Mind your identity when conducting cross-national research. *Organization Studies* 19: 511–15.

Woodhams, C., Lupton, B. and Xian, H. (2009) The persistence of gender discrimination in China: Evidence from recruitment advertisements. *The International Journal of Human Resource Management* 20: 2084–109.

Woodhams, C., Xian, H. and Lupton, B. (2015) Women managers' careers in China: Theorizing the influence of gender and collectivism. *Human Resource Management* 54: 913–31.

Zhang, B. and Morris, J.L. (2014) High-performance work systems and organizational performance: Testing the mediation role of employee outcomes using evidence from PR China. *International Journal of Human Resource Management* 25: 68–90.

Zhen, L., Zoebisch, M.A., Chen, G., et al. (2006) Sustainability of farmers' soil fertility management practices: A case study in the North China Plain. *Journal of Environmental Management* 79: 409–19.

6
DATA COLLECTION

6.1 OVERVIEW

Data is important in any empirical research. Without robust data to support your claims, your theoretical model would not be meaningful. This means that your choice and process of data collection is a crucial and integral part of your research outcome. This chapter looks at the most common methods of data collection used in the Chinese context, namely questionnaire, interview, focus group and documents. We begin by distinguishing two different forms of data and move on to discuss the essence of each method. In particular, we will focus on applying each method within Chinese culture and society through the consideration of some examples. Attention will also be paid to using online tools to support these methods.

6.2 PRIMARY AND SECONDARY DATA

There are two kinds of data you can collect, depending on your research question(s). The first is primary data, which refers to the data you collect by yourself to suit your own purpose. This is the most common form of data in business and management research. Indeed, when being asked to collect data, most students will automatically think about collecting primary data. Ang (2014) further distinguishes self-reported data, i.e. those collected through interviews and questionnaires, and researcher-observed data, those collected through experiments and personal observations of the researcher. The first three methods (questionnaire, interview and focus group) that will be discussed later in this chapter are related to the collection of primary data. There are certainly some advantages of using primary data. First, you can have control over important issues, such as what methods you use, who you approach and how big your sample size is. As these data are 'tailor-made' for your research, they are most likely to help you to answer your research questions. Second, primary data are 'fresh' and up to date. When researchers and students analyse and write up their results shortly after collecting data, their findings are likely to contribute to the latest debates about the topic.

For example, after the financial crisis in 2007/2008, many research papers looking at the various consequences of the crisis (such as job losses, changes in consumer behaviour) were published. These timely papers are particularly useful for policy-makers when considering countering measures. However, collecting primary data is not risk-free. You might not have access to the organisation you would like to research. Or your response rate is too low to construct a reasonable sample, as discussed in Chapter 5. In summary, almost every step can go wrong in the process of collecting primary data.

KEY CONCEPTS IN CHINESE: PRIMARY AND SECONDARY DATA

数据的来源是多方面的，可分为第一手数据（primary data）和第二手数据（secondary data）。第一手数据是指由研究员根据特定研究项目收集的第一手信息，这些资料是由研究员通过现场实地调查而来的。而第二手数据的来源主要是依赖现有的数据资料。

Alternatively, you can use secondary data, which are data that have been collected previously by other researchers for other purposes. Secondary data can be raw data or published summaries. You can re-analyse such data according to the objectives of your own research. It is important to note that a literature review is *not* using secondary data, as a literature review does not require you to re-analyse the data. Albeit not as common as primary data, secondary data have been used in Chinese research. There are two main strategies to obtain secondary data in the Chinese context. The first is to look for existing databases. There are many international organisations that collect many kinds of data for many countries including China. Such organisations include the United Nations, the World Bank and the OECD. The Chinese National Bureau of Statistics also collects a large amount of data in the areas of industry and trade. As these are mainly not-for-profit organisations, they allow you free access to their online databases. Owners of commercial databases are likely to charge you for access. Your university may have paid a fee to some online databases (such as DataStream) which you can access through your library website or a few specified computers. Ye et al. (2010), for example, investigated the relationship between gender diversity and firm performance by drawing on the financial, stock return and corporate governance data of listed companies between 2001 and 2006, available from the Peking University Sinofin database. The authors also used another database, China Security Market Accounting Research (CSMAR), to test their results.

Second, many organisations nowadays collect a lot of information about their employees or customers to support their organisations' decision-making. These data include employee details, payroll information, sales and customer information and minutes of meetings. However, for reasons of data protection, most of this information and such documents are not available for public use. Negotiation is required to gain access. In a study of advertising media and cost-effectiveness in China, Hung et al. (2005) took data from the China National Readership Survey, which involved 48,000 participants. The original data were collected between 1999 and 2001 in 15 major cities by China Central Television (CCTV).

There are certainly advantages to using secondary data. First, researchers save the time and effort required for collecting primary data. Second, by using existing databases, you may access data that would otherwise not be possible for you to collect. These databases are particularly helpful if you are conducting research comparing multiple cities or countries. Cooke (2010) compared women's partic-ipation at work in four Asian countries (China, India, Japan and South Korea) mainly by combining secondary data from academic journal studies and statistical reports from national government and international bodies. Third, secondary data drawn from credible sources are sometimes more reliable than those collected by yourself, as large organisations such as the World Bank have greater finan-cial and human resources to conduct large-scale data collection. However, secondary data also have disadvantages. The first and biggest problem is that most secondary data are collected by someone else for other purposes. You may find that such data are not suitable for answering your research questions. Most researchers have to search a few databases and choose the most appropriate one. Second, access to secondary data might be difficult, as data collected for commercial purposes are often costly. Third, locating credible databases in China can be challenging, as there are very few available to the public. The quality of data obtained from the majority of databases on Chinese websites is difficult to control. Some Chinese databases might potentially have ethical issues (Resnik and Zeng, 2010). As most existing Chinese databases are more suitable for research in accounting and finance, we thus focus on the use of documents as secondary data in business and management research later in this chapter.

It is possible to combine both primary and secondary data in a research project for reasons of triangulation or supplementation. In their study of the innovation strategies of Chinese firms, Xiao et al. (2013) collected different forms of primary data, including 17 interviews and site observations conducted by one of the researchers. These are complemented by secondary data, including pub-lished statistical data on existing databases, the firms' internal documents and data from a published journal article.

6.3 QUESTIONNAIRES

The questionnaire is probably the most common method of data collection in Chinese business and management studies. Using questionnaires is considered a more effective method in terms of its accessibility to respondents, as well as time and cost-efficiency, compared with interviews

(Oppenheim, 2000). In addition, questionnaires enable researchers to analyse and explain the pattern of data statistically, while qualitative or ethnographic methods, for instance observation and unstructured interviews, tend to report data in descriptive ways (Bryman, 2012).

6.3.1 Questionnaire design

Saunders et al. (2015) suggest that the quality of collected data will depend on how valid the questions are. Questionnaire design and questionnaire structure are considered crucial factors in influencing how well the respondents understand the researcher's intention (Punch, 2003). A series of considerations for designing a questionnaire is discussed in this section.

Variables （变量）and measurements （测量度）

The conceptual framework offers the questionnaire a theoretical map (Punch, 2003). A list of variables is measured in the questionnaire, on the basis of the research questions and conceptual framework. During this stage, the researcher seeks existing measurement instruments from appropriate journal articles and applies them in whole, in part or in some combination to form a suitable questionnaire. The benefit of adopting established measurements is that they have been tested and verified in previous studies. For better reliability and validity, the quality of all these existing instruments must be assessed by comparing them with other measures in the relevant fields as well as investigating their applications over time. In particular, a careful assessment should be made to see if these instruments are suitable in the Chinese cultural and organisational context. Questionnaire design should also take into consideration the 'local differentiation', which refers to the wording and translation of the existing measures from English to Chinese (see Chapter 9 for more discussion about translating questionnaires). Therefore, your questionnaire is composed of existing measures adopted from the literature but is tailored to your research questions. In addition, you can also include demographical variables (sometimes called controlled variables) that can help you to understand the characteristics of your sample. These may include age, gender, occupation, income, marital status, industrial sector and managerial level.

Multi-item versus single-item measures （多重量化标准测量 和 单一量化标准测量）

For most variables, the form of a scale can be composed of multiple items or a single indicator. No matter whether a multi- or single-item measure is used, the main purpose of a scale is to collect information (Drolet and Morrison, 2001). The main variables or complex concepts, namely those important variables in your theoretical model, should usually have already been measured by multi-item scales.

--- **Example 6.1** ---

A 10-ITEM SCALE FOR MEASURING ORGANISATIONAL TRUSTWORTHINESS (DEVELOPED BY SEARLE ET AL., 2011)

1. This organisation is capable of meeting its responsibilities.
2. This organisation is known to be successful at what it tries to do.
3. This organisation does things competently.
4. This organisation is concerned about the welfare of its employees.
5. Employees' needs and desires are important to this organisation.
6. This organisation will go out of its way to help its employees.
7. This organisation would never deliberately take advantage of its employees.
8. This organisation is guided by sound moral principles and codes of conduct.
9. Power is not abused in this organisation.
10. This organisation does not exploit external stakeholders.

Source: Searle et al. (2011), reprinted by permission of the publisher Taylor & Francis Ltd, www.tandf online.com

However, some variables can be measured by a single item. It is not necessary to use a multi-item measure if the characteristic of the object can be conceptualised as concrete and singular (Bergkvist and Rossiter, 2009). It has also been asserted by practitioners that single-item measures can have advantages over multi-item measures in terms of cost, refusal rates and reliability (Bergkvist, 2015; Drolet and Morrison, 2001). In advertising and consumer research, Bergkvist and Rossiter (2009) demonstrate that a single-item measure can have equally high predictive validity as a multi-item measure. For example, using a single-item measure 'I would like to buy Product A' could adequately represent the notion of 'willingness to buy'.

Likert Scale （李克特量表）

For many attitudinal questions, you can measure the response by using a Likert-type scale. Many textbooks suggest an odd numbered scale, with a five- or seven-point scale the most common approach in the West, for example, (1) = strongly disagree; (2) = disagree; (3) = neutral; (4) = agree; and (5) = strongly agree. However, previous research in the Chinese context suggests that having a neutral point can be problematic, as Chinese samples tend to have a bias towards the central point. Some scholars (Hui et al., 2004; Roy et al., 2001) suggest using an even numbered scale (6-, 8- or 10-point) when researching in China, to shift the Chinese respondents' attention away from the scales' mid-point. There is also evidence that some 'lucky' numbers, such as 3, 8 and 9, are selected more frequently on a metric scale (Ang, 1996). One way to prevent this is to mark the intervals on a scale with only the end points indicating a specific number, for example 1 and 10.

Structure of questionnaire

Cover letter. A questionnaire usually begins with a covering letter, which is widely used to accompany a self-administered questionnaire, and explains the purpose of the survey (Saunders et al., 2015). Dillman (2000) indicates that the covering letter could affect the response rate. It should include: (1) your name; (2) a clear title for your questionnaire; (3) an introduction to the research topic; (4) a statement that data will purely be used for academic purposes; (5) an assurance of confidentiality and anonymity; and (6) a request for support. As suggested in Chapter 5, response rate varies in the Chinese context. Our experience suggests that including these elements will create a respectful image and increase respondents' willingness to fill in the questionnaire.

Instructions for completion. Another approach to increasing the response rate is to provide clear and unambiguous instructions on how to complete your questionnaire. You can start from an outline of the questionnaire structure and then give both general and question-specific instructions. Furthermore, in order to familiarise the respondents with the topic, a definition of important terms used in the questionnaire should be provided, to clarify and ensure that all respondents understand the terms and complete the questionnaire in the same way.

Main section. The appearance of a questionnaire is also an important element of achieving a greater response rate. You should leave plenty of space between questions. A consistent format should be used throughout the questionnaire. Questions should be asked in simple and clear language. You should avoid asking two questions in one. Previous research suggests that Chinese samples have problems in answering hypothetical questions, which should be avoided (Roy et al., 2001). Some students try to jam-pack as many questions as possible into one questionnaire. However, long questionnaires run the risk of incompletion. In general, the longer the questionnaire, the more likely people will drop out. Our recommendation is that when surveying Chinese samples, your questionnaire should have fewer than 45 questions and take less than 10 minutes to complete.

6.3.2 Internet-administered questionnaire

There are a few ways to distribute and manage your survey. If you are a student studying overseas, sending and receiving postal questionnaires individually to each respondent might be too costly to consider. Alternatively, your survey can be web-based. There are two options: email questionnaire and online questionnaire. If you obtain a list of email addresses for your respondents, you can send them a covering message (similar to a cover letter) and attach the questionnaire either as a Word document or a PDF file. They can reply by email. In this case, you are not limited by geography or time zones. Email questionnaires are also free and quick. However, it is difficult for respondents to maintain anonymity. As a result, the response rate can be low. Moreover, Word also potentially allows the respondents to modify the questionnaire.

The second option is to establish an online survey on a website. Web survey has all the benefits of email survey and protects the respondent's identity. Moreover, you can monitor the progress of the survey easily by checking the response rates and characteristics of your sample. Most websites now allow you to conduct basic descriptive statistical analysis. Once the survey is finished, you can download all your data straightaway, without the hassle of data input. However, there are also drawbacks, as identified by Hewson et al. (2016). First, people can get distracted by other internet activities, such as Facebook notifications, advertisements and emails. Second, unlike with email and printed questionnaires, people cannot flip through a web survey quickly to estimate the time required for completion at the beginning. This can result in a higher dropout rate, especially with lengthy questionnaires. Using a progress bar (a horizontal bar that indicates how much is completed and how much left) is considered good practice (Hewson et al., 2016). Third, it is tiring to read text on a computer screen for a long period of time. Thus, very lengthy questionnaires have a very low response rate. Tuten (2010) suggests that the completion time for a web survey should not exceed 10 minutes. Finally, it is difficult to detect multiple submissions. Thus, there are trade-offs and even tensions between the anonymity and reliability of data.

There is a lot of online survey software available, ranging from low-end packages that offer free access with limited functionality to high-end, expensive products that can be installed on the customer's computer. Many software companies offer package deals in a multi-tiered pricing system, depending on the functions and features required. Popular survey software includes SurveyMonkey, Kwiksurveys and Google Forms. Hewson et al. (2016) suggest two important criteria for evaluating online survey tools: flexibility (solutions to incorporate different design requirements) and robustness (reliability of the system). However, accessing overseas websites can be tricky for most China-based respondents. You may consider Chinese software and websites, such as www.sojump.com (问卷星), www.wenjuan.com (问卷网), www.diaochapai.com （调查派） and www.diaoyanbao.com (调研宝) which provide a similar service. Chinese software and websites have certain advantages, as they are compatible with (1) the Chinese language and (2) social networking sites like WeChat.

Example 6.2

COVER LETTER

调查问卷

您好！

我叫李韵，是英国A大学管理系研究生。本次问卷调查的目的是为论文收集数据。这篇论文标题目是中国国有企业员工工作强度和员工的离职倾向的调查。本调查旨在分析员工工作强度，压力和工作满意度及离职倾向之间的关系。

您真实的意见将帮助我获得有效性的问卷从而深入了解以上主题之间的关系。所有问卷都是匿名的。您的名字也会保密。所有问卷都将由A大学独立分析。数据只用于完成我的毕业论文。大概需要10分钟完成。

非常感谢您的参与。

李韵

日期

Example 6.3

QUESTIONNAIRE

第一部分：个人资料 （选择题请只选**1**项）

1. 年龄:　　2. 性别：男 ☐　　女 ☐
3. 你所在企业的规模？　　50人以下 ☐　　50-199人 ☐　　200-499 人☐　　500-999人☐　　1000人以上 ☐
4. 你的最高学历为？

博士 ☐　　　　研究生 ☐　　本科☐　　专科 ☐　　高中 ☐

职中/技校 ☐　　其它（请注明）：

5. 你在本单位工作年限是　　年
6. 你目前的年薪（税前）是　　（人民币：元）

40,000 或 以下 ☐　　　　40,001-60,000 ☐　　　　60,001-100,000 ☐

100,001-180,000 ☐　　　　180,001-360,000 ☐　　　　360,001 或以上 ☐

7.　你是在哪个管理阶乘?

非管理人员/普通员工 □　　　　　初级经理 □　　　　　　　　中级经理 □

高级经理□　　　其它（请注明）：

第二部分：　你在本企业工作的个人经验

要求：请认真阅读以下每一项，然后选出你对该项的态度。每项请用✓选择一个答案。

调查项目	非常不同意		选择范围			非常同意
8. 本企业为员工提供稳定的工作（我能看到我职业的长期发展方向）	1	2	3	4	5	6
9. 本企业为员工及家属提供稳定的福利保障	1	2	3	4	5	6
10. 本企业关心我的个人利益	1	2	3	4	5	6
11. 本企业为了保护员工的利益会牺牲其本身的，短期的利益	1	2	3	4	5	6
12. 我可以指望本企业付给的工资生活	1	2	3	4	5	6
13. 本企业对员工的忧虑和福利会作出反应	1	2	3	4	5	6
14. 本企业在作决定时会考虑员工的利益	1	2	3	4	5	6
15. 本企业关心我长期的幸福	1	2	3	4	5	6
16. 本企业为员工提供的工作是有保障的（我不用担心会下岗）	1	2	3	4	5	6
17. 本企业一直以来都提供稳定的工资	1	2	3	4	5	6
18. 本企业只提供短期的工作	1	2	3	4	5	6
19. 本企业没有承诺要在将来留下我	1	2	3	4	5	6
20. 本企业只提供特定或有限时期内的工作	1	2	3	4	5	6
21. 本企业只要求我从事有限的职能，我的工作只限于老板聘请我做的事	1	2	3	4	5	6
22. 本企业支付的薪水只限于那些特定给我的任务	1	2	3	4	5	6
23. 本企业给我的工作只包括很固定的责任。	1	2	3	4	5	6
24. 本企业没有允诺会延续和我的雇佣关系	1	2	3	4	5	6
25. 本企业随时可以终止和我的雇佣关系	1	2	3	4	5	6
26. 本企业只提供和我目前工作相关的培训	1	2	3	4	5	6
27. 本企业只让我很有限地参与各项事务	1	2	3	4	5	6

(Continued)

第三部分：你和同事之**间的关系**

28. 我经常给同事帮忙	1	2	3	4	5	6
29. 我的同事有困难时可以指望我帮忙	1	2	3	4	5	6
30. 我认为被人帮了我，我也会帮他们的忙	1	2	3	4	5	6
31. 当我帮助了同事，他们会很感激	1	2	3	4	5	6
32. 帮助同事使得我们之间的关系更好了	1	2	3	4	5	6
33. 我宁愿依靠自己而不是其他人	1	2	3	4	5	6
34. 大部分时间我都靠我自己，我很少指望其他人相助	1	2	3	4	5	6
35. 我经常自我行事	1	2	3	4	5	6
36. 我要有自己的，与别不同的个性，这对我来说很重要	1	2	3	4	5	6
37. 我的工作要做得比被人好，这对我来说很重要	1	2	3	4	5	6
38. 胜利就是一切	1	2	3	4	5	6
39. 竞争是自然规律	1	2	3	4	5	6
40. 当其他人的工作做得比我好时，我会很紧张，不高兴	1	2	3	4	5	6
41. 如果同事获奖了，我也感到自豪	1	2	3	4	5	6
42. 同事生活幸福对我也很重要	1	2	3	4	5	6
43. 对我来说，快乐的是能和其他人在一起	1	2	3	4	5	6
44. 在工作中能和他人合作是很愉快的事	1	2	3	4	5	6
45. 父母和孩子应尽量住在一起	1	2	3	4	5	6
46. 照顾家庭是我的责任，即便有时我要牺牲我想要的东西	1	2	3	4	5	6
47. 不管付出什么样的牺牲，家庭成员应尽量在一起	1	2	3	4	5	6
48. 尊重集体的决定对我来说是重要的	1	2	3	4	5	6

TOP TIPS 小建议：设计问卷要讲究科学、简单、美观。
不妨参考以下建议：

- 很多刚学研究方法论的同学在设计问卷时总想自己编问题。这是不对的。大部分变量的测量度（measure）是可以从前人的研究上采纳过来。因为这些测量度被验证过，证实有效。而你自己编的因为没被科学测试过，是不准确的。
- 当然有个别问题你可以自己设计以适合你的研究目的。这一般适合于简单的问题，如：'你是否使用过A产品？'

- Likert Scale （李克特量表）最好给偶数选项（如6项）。中国人好中庸之道，如给奇数项选择（如5项），很多人会选中间。
- 一般先问简单的问题，如，年龄，性别，等。把难的或不好回答的问题放在后面。
- 问卷的措辞要简单，易懂，一目了然。不要让人猜你究竟问什么。
- 研究生论文的问卷一般40-45个问题就是上限了，太长了会出现很多废卷。
- 整个问卷要美观，字体要够大，不要把很多问题密密麻麻地堆砌在一、两页纸上。尽量多留些空白的地方让人填。但也不需要太花哨，美术字体就免了。
- 问卷做好了，最好找人试填，看需要多长时间完成，还可以找出是否有令人误解的地方。

6.4 INTERVIEW

In general, interview is a popular method of data collection in business and management research regardless of its national context. A classic definition describes this method as being a 'conversation with a purpose' (Webb and Webb, 1932: 130). However, the research interview is different from other types of interviews we encounter on a daily basis, such as job interviews or interviews in the media with celebrities. A key difference is that research interviews are conducted as part of a research project with an aim to produce data. Thus, Cassell (2015: 1) sees the research interview as 'a conversation where the researcher seeks information from an individual or group with the aim of using that information in order to progress their research'. Moreover, scholars acknowledge that a research interview is an actual interaction between the participant and the researcher, and this interaction will contribute to the form of data generated and the feature of knowledge produced (Yeo et al., 2014). Although there are various types of interviews, as will be discussed in sub-section 6.4.3, our discussion here will focus on in-depth qualitative interviews.

6.4.1 Advantages of the interview method

Qualitative interview as a means for understanding people's experience is well documented. In particular, there are a number of advantages of adopting this method. First, the interview is compatible with a range of philosophical positions outlined in Chapter 3. Notably, researchers from different philosophical traditions use the interview for different purposes. For example, neo-positivists use the interview as a modified oral survey instrument to discover 'softer' forms of objective and generalisable knowledge (Alvesson and Ashcraft, 2012). Critical realists see the interview as a way to access people's subjective experience so as to unearth the social structures that shape such experience. Interpretivists use interviews to locate the contextualised knowledge that is attached to individual experience.

The second advantage is that qualitative interviewing allows for an assessment of depth and complexity (Byrne, 2004). Open-ended and flexible questions allow researchers to access subjective issues such as values and experiences, which are less likely to be achieved in questionnaire or closed-question interviews (Byrne, 2004). Non-standardised interviews enable researchers to acknowledge interviewees' different positions and to respond accordingly, both at the time of interviewing and in the analysis stage. Open structure means research topics can be approached in a variety of ways. Issues of a sensitive nature (such as harassment at work) could be approached with opened-up dialogue to produce fuller accounts.

Third, qualitative interview offers the opportunity for researchers to establish rapport with and gain trust from participants (Yeo et al., 2014). Fontana and Frey (2003: 78) suggest that in qualitative research, 'the researcher must be able to take the role of the respondents and attempt to see the situation from their viewpoint, rather than superimpose his or her world of academia and preconceptions upon them'. In a collectivist society like China's, establishing rapport and trust with research participants is of paramount importance, as people rarely disclose sensitive information to strangers.

Fourth, Chinese scholar Yeung (1995) argues that this method performs its function as one of the best and most suitable methods in China. Often, researchers face serious social and cultural resistance to the questionnaire, as Chinese people do not tend to understand the aims and objectives of a study. Interviewing might overcome this problem via a face-to-face communication of the purpose of the research with the interviewees.

6.4.2 Critiques of the interview method

While qualitative interview is potentially a rich source of data, the use of such an approach is not without dispute. The core of the dispute lies in whether interviews can generate objective data which contribute to expanding social knowledge. Authors following a positivist position assert that interviews are not objective instruments designed primarily to collect 'pure' information. Silverman (2001) points out that this approach is 'seductive', and a significant problem lies in the question of whether the 'authentic accounts' produced are not simply the repetition of familiar cultural tales. As such, no knowledge about social reality is 'out there' waiting for the researcher to obtain from the interview. Miller and Glassner (2004) warn that interviews are interactions between interviewers and interviewees, and therefore any information obtained should be seen as context-specific or even invented.

Scholars including those taking a positivist stance, however, gradually recognise that knowledge exists and can be understood through the richness stemming from the interview. Silverman (2001: 87) notes that interview participants construct not just narratives, but social worlds, because 'the primary issue is to generate data which give an authentic insight into people's experiences'. Although 'research cannot provide the mirror reflection of the social world that positivists strive for', it 'may provide access to the meanings people attribute to their experiences and social worlds' (Miller and Glassner, 2004: 126). The recognition that interviews are symbolic interaction does not discount the possibility that knowledge of the social world beyond the interaction can be obtained (Miller and Glassner, 2004).

Moreover, constructionists hold the belief that people create and maintain meaningful worlds through social discourse. Interview data provide a better understanding of other people's lives and have merit beyond the immediate context of the interview itself (Yeo et al., 2014). Miller and Glassner (2004) argue that a strength of qualitative interviewing is the opportunity it provides to collect and rigorously examine narrative accounts of social worlds. While coding, categorisation and typologising of stories in the research process result in telling only parts of lives (Charmaz, 1995), researchers can describe truthfully segments of real persons' lives (Miller and Glassner, 2004).

6.4.3 Three types of interview structures

There are three ways to structure your interviews. Your choice of adopting a structure or not depends on your answers to a few important questions: What kind of questions do you want to ask? What kind of answer do you expect from your interviewees? Who else is involved? And how long do you expect the interview to last?

Structured and standardised interviews

Your interviews can be standardised. This means that you prepare a list of the questions in advance and stick to them during every interview you conduct in your project. This method is useful when you have limited time and money. It can also help to maintain consistency when there is more than one researcher conducting interviews. However, there are major limitations. The first is that this approach is suitable only when your research is about gathering 'facts' (e.g. what happened, who was involved, when and why). A highly structured interview becomes almost like a questionnaire. This leaves little room for your respondents to elaborate on the issues they believe are important. The second problem is that it gives the researcher little flexibility in the wording or order of questions. This makes it difficult for you to prompt further answers. Finally, for untrained interviewers or students, it is easy to just go through the list of questions and receive superficial answers. This could potentially be a big problem in China when you interview a stranger. Thus, arguably, fully structured interviews are too strict for most qualitative research (Eriksson and Kovalainen, 2016).

Semi-structured interviews

The majority of qualitative interviews fall into this category, as this type of interview can be used to study not only 'what' but also 'how and 'why' questions. When conducting semi-structured interviews, you still prepare a list of topics, issues, themes or questions in advance. However, you only use them as a guide rather than following them strictly word by word. A major advantage is that you could be both systematic and flexible at the same time during the interview process. For example, you could ask the question differently in each interview depending on how the conversation flows. You could even skip a question when you feel it has been covered in previous discussions. Yet, a challenge is to keep a balance between the number of topics you want to cover and, at the same time, the depth of answers you strive to achieve within your time limit. Thus, the approach would suit the more experienced researcher. Moreover, as interviewees are allowed more freedom to say what they want to say, you could end up with a large number of themes in your data and find it hard to identify 'patterns'.

Unstructured and open interviews

Some qualitative interviews are unstructured and open. While you may still prepare some topics and themes related to your research questions, the conversation can be driven in any direction of interest (Eriksson and Kovalainen, 2016), depending largely on what the interviewee talks about. Typically, this type of interview is used for exploring people's life experience and subjectivity from their point of view, thus each interview is highly individualised and contextualised. The narrative interview is one of such kind of interviews, where the researcher is interested in the 'plot' of people's life stories and how they felt at different points. This method can be very time-consuming and thus only suitable if you have a very small sample. Moreover, students and unexperienced researchers could find it hard to control the flow of the conversation.

6.4.4 Different ways to conduct your interviews

Your interviews can be carried out in a number of ways, depending on the time and budget constraints that you and your participants face. As illustrated below, each approach has its advantages and disadvantages. Thus, for each study, the appropriateness of interview modes should be considered on their own merit (Yeo et al., 2014).

Face-to-face interview has traditionally been the preferred approach, as it helps to establish a good rapport between the researcher and the interviewee. It allows the development of an environment 'where the interviewee can respond in a free-ranging and full way and where the researcher is able to take non-verbal communication into account' (Yeo et al., 2014: 182). For Chinese participants, the mode may help to develop *guanxi* and trust. However, this mode can be expensive and time-consuming as the researcher has to travel between locations. For the majority of Chinese students pursuing a degree overseas, this method might not be feasible.

Telephone interview is recommended as an alternative to reduce travel cost and time. It may also suit participants with a busy lifestyle. Calling China from overseas has previously been expensive, but there are now many telephone cards available at a more affordable price. However, recording interviews could be an issue, as the researcher has to use specialised equipment to do so. Another disadvantage is that body language or facial expression can be missed, which could be important indicators of the respondent's different point of view. Finally, poor signal or connection could reduce the interests of the participants and affect the quality of data. Thus, in traditional literature, this is only recognised as an additional option for qualitative researchers.

Online interview has become increasingly popular, as internet and wifi access are now common-place. Interview can be conducted synchronously by using real-time chat applications, such as Skype, WeChat, WhatsApp and Facebook Messenger. Many of these applications also support video chat, which helps to maintain some advantages of face-to-face interview while keeping the cost to a minimum. WeChat, an application that originated in China, has been particularly popular among Chinese users. Yet, most of these applications do not have the recording function themselves. Researchers have to install additional applications in order to record the video or the audio of the interview. Cassell (2015) thus suggests that researchers should check that the technology produces good results before starting the interview and have a back-up way of communicating (such as having a telephone number ready) should the technology fail.

6.4.5 Interview stages

Qualitative interviewing involves a number of stages. It is important to note that in order to produce quality data for your research project, the pre- and post-interview stages are as important as the actual interview itself. We present this sub-section with particular examples.

Stage 1: Pre-interview stage

A lot of preparation is needed in order for the interview process to be effective. The most pressing issue is the preparation of interview questions. Students are often confused about the difference between research questions and interview questions. Many students simply throw the research questions to their interviewees, hoping that the responses will be adequate to answer their research questions. This is in fact bad practice, as your research questions are often broad and theoretical. You should always break them down into simple and easy-to-answer questions. For example, if your research question is 'How do male managers maintain a work–life balance?', you should aim to generate data about male managers' experience of the interface between work and family. Your interview questions could be around what they do at work; what they do at home; whether they have experienced conflicts between work and family; if so, what their strategies are to maintain a balance.

In a qualitative interview, a range of different questions can be asked. You may prepare closed questions, such as 'what is your position in the company?' or open questions, such as 'can you tell me how you feel about working for this organisation?'. In preparing structured interviews, your aim is to gather 'facts', thus the majority of your questions could be 'what' questions.

In semi-structured interviews, you should combine 'what', 'how' and 'why' questions for the purpose of producing in-depth understanding about people's lives and experiences. In unstructured interviews, the majority of your questions should be open. You may want to gather some personal or background information about the interviewee as part of your data collection. This could include demographic questions about age, industrial sector, position, and so on. You should only ask those questions that are relevant to your research. For example, if your topic is work–life balance, it would make sense to ask questions about marital status and the number of children that your interviewee has. You may pilot your interview with someone to ensure the questions are understandable to Chinese participants. An example of an interview guide can be found below. The aim of the project is to understand why fewer women than men progress to senior management positions in Chinese organisations.

At this stage, you may contact your interviewees to schedule appointments. Fitting into the busy lifestyles of business people can be tricky. It is advised that you clarify the purpose of the research and the time required with your interviewees beforehand so as to make the interview process more productive. The length of the interview depends on the scope of your research and mostly the themes you plan to explore. At the pilot stage, the interviewer should have a rough idea about how long the interview will last. You may add or remove questions to make sure your interview fits the proposed time slot (normally 1 hour). Generally speaking, it will take 30 to 60 minutes to develop an in-depth discussion. The interviewing process is tiring for both the researcher and the interviewees. Some interviews start late or over-run. You may also want a break between interviews. Thus, it is not advised to arrange back-to-back interviews or more than three interviews per day (Cassell, 2015). Moreover, for telephone and online interviews, care should be taken over the different time zones between you and your participants. If you study in the UK, China is 8 hours ahead in the winter and 7 hours ahead in the summer. Finding a time that suits both parties could be a challenge.

You may consider where to conduct your interviews, although traditionally venues are decided by participants to increase their availability. Ideally, the interview should take place in an environment that is private, quiet and physically comfortable (Yeo et al., 2014). Most interviews take place in private locations, such as the participants' office, home or meeting room. Our experience is that Chinese people tend to be more open and talk more freely in private settings. Having said this, your own safety is important. Unless you feel safe, it would be better to have the interview in a neutral location. Some interviews are held in public places, such as at a café, restaurant or a community centre. It is important to agree on a location where both parties will feel safe and comfortable. On the other hand, you may have to tolerate the 'noise' in the background in many public venues. Sometimes, this makes the recording more difficult to transcribe and translate. Even if your interview is conducted online through Skype or WeChat, it is still helpful to be in a quiet room such as your office or study.

Example 6.4

INTERVIEW GUIDE

The following is a rough guide for conducting interviews:

1. Ask for demographic information about the interviewee, e.g. age, position, education, marital status, number of children, years of experience, industrial sector, current organisation.
2. Ask the interviewee for a brief discussion about how her career has developed since she graduated from university. (5 mins)

Recruitment and selection

3. What does she think about the company's policy in terms of equal opportunity for men and women?
4. What criteria does the company use to select candidates for a position? Are there any gender implications?
5. What kinds of questions are normally asked at the recruitment interviews? Are the same questions asked of men and women? Why/why not?

Promotion

6. What is the company's practice for promoting someone? Request specific examples.
7. What criteria are used to judge a candidate? Why? Prompt for gender-related answers.
8. How does the company evaluate a candidate's performance at work?

Maternity leave

9. When a woman is pregnant, how does this affect her career? Request specific examples.
10. What is the company's policy?

Other issues

11. Is there any special arrangement for women in terms of mentoring, training or flexible working?
12. Ask the interviewee's opinion on why there are so few women in top management roles in China, if not covered yet.
13. Is there anything else she would like to say?

Stage 2: During the interview

Your interview starts from the moment you meet your interviewee. You can spend the first few minutes introducing yourself and your project to establish rapport, regardless of whether you have done so previously. You can alert your interviewee at this point to any sensitive or private topics you plan to discuss with them. Consent for recording the interview should also be sought. Being interviewed for a research project is still not very common for Chinese people. In many cases, especially when interviews are recorded, Chinese people are keen to provide you with 'politically correct answers'. You can ease their concerns by telling them that their identities will be protected throughout the project and any information will be treated confidentially. You may also tell them that there is no 'right' or 'wrong' answer to most questions, and you are just interested in their experiences and opinions. In our experience, it is best to start with easy or factual questions (such as the demographic ones) to warm up the interviewee, while your interviewee also has a chance to 'practise' answering questions in a research interview. You can then move on to questions that require longer answers, for example questions about what they do in their jobs or how they developed their careers, to demonstrate the dynamics in an interview.

During the interview, you can guide your participant through the topics, according to your interview schedule, but explore the themes emerging from the participant's account to 'seek breadth and depth of coverage' (Yeo et al., 2014: 188). Your interviewee should be doing most of the talking at this stage, so you should interrupt as little as possible to let your interviewee work at a deep and focused level of thinking and discover ideas, thoughts and feelings. You should be an 'active' listener while your interviewee is taking: listening with interest, but also keeping in mind your overall research objectives and deciding whether to ask 'follow-up' questions or move on to a new question. Knowing when and where to ask prompt questions is an important skill for a qualitative interviewer. There are many ways of asking prompt questions. For example, you could ask for details by using 'why' and 'how' questions, or you can ask for examples. Another way is asking about their personal feelings or opinions, or using interpretive questions such as 'do you mean ...?' Care should be taken that your questions are non-leading. Leading questions are those that are constructed in a way that direct the interview in a certain direction. For example, instead of saying 'Did you feel very angry when the manager sacked you?', you could ask 'How did you feel when your manager sacked you?'

A common problem faced by most interviewers is that interviewees sometimes do not answer questions in the way you might hope they would. They might either misunderstand your questions or interpret them in a different way. As a result, the interview may drift into areas that are of little interest to you. In this case, you could paraphrase the question and ask it again. A challenge of conducting interviews in China is that people often assume that the answer is common sense, and that the researcher, an 'insider' who shares the same cultural background, knows the answer. They might say: 'you know ... things are like this in China'. Our suggestion is that you steer interviewees towards elaborating by asking further prompt questions, such as 'What things?', 'Can you give me an example?' and 'Like what?'. However, your interviewee might be reluctant to give sensitive information and become annoyed when you keep pushing and repeating probes like

'Tell me more about that'. If you sense that the interviewee does not want to further discuss an issue, you should move on to other topics. In our experience, challenging Chinese interviewees could make them feel like they are losing 'face', thus creating communicative difficulties between the two parties.

A final point is to finish the interview within the scheduled time and on a positive note (Cassell, 2015). You may appreciate the participants' help and tell them the conversation is interesting and useful for your research project. It is important for Chinese people to maintain harmony with others even at the end of the conversation. Thus, you may reassure them that their contribution will be used in confidence. If you are using snowball sampling, you can ask them to introduce other participants from their network who might be interested in taking part in the interviews.

Stage 3: Post-interview stage

Once you have conducted the interview, there are a number of issues to consider before you move on to data analysis. The first is data storage. If you have recorded the interview digitally, it is likely that you have a file of substantial size. It is very unlikely that your interviewee would agree to go through the interview process again should you lose your file. Thus, you should keep your file in a safe but easy-to-access location. Audio data can consume a lot of 'space' in the hard drive of your computer. A 1-hour interview can produce an MP3 file with a size of around 7.60 megabytes, if you use a digital recorder, or a 3GA file a size of 22 megabytes, if you use your mobile phone. It is worth uploading your interview data onto internet sites such as Dropbox, Google Drive or Microsoft's OneDrive, in case of equipment failure. These online platforms also facilitate file-sharing if you have a team of researchers or decide to outsource transcription and translation.

Transcription is a practice in which audio (sometimes video) recordings are transcribed into texts. There are two dominant approaches: naturalism and denaturalism (Oliver et al., 2005). In naturalism, every word or expression is transcribed in as much detail as possible to produce a full and faithful transcription, whereas in denaturalism, the idiosyncratic elements of speech (such as pauses, laughter, nonverbal gestures) are removed and grammar corrected. If your interviews are in Chinese, you will need to translate them into English. There is very little discussion in the research method literature about combining transcription and translation. Some scholars separate out the two processes. For example, they first transcribe the recordings into Chinese text and then translate the Chinese text into English text. Others transcribe and translate at the same time, i.e. listen to the Chinese recording and type the translated text in English. Given the time and budget constraints involved in completing a dissertation, it may be more reasonable to adopt a denaturalist approach and conduct the transcription and translation together. Further issues around translating interviews will be explored in Chapter 9.

TOP TIPS 小建议

在中国做研究访谈是很不容易的事情，因为大部分人不了解你访谈的目的。为了使你的访谈能产生更多有用的材料，不妨考虑以下建议

- 访谈前先聊个3到5分钟，让彼此有个了解。你可以介绍你的个人情况，如，你在国外读书，正在写论文，题目是...
- 尽量问具体的问题。如果你的问题太宽，太广，对方不好回答。比如，不要问'你对你们企业有何感想？'，因为'企业'包括很多方面。你需要把问题细化。你可以问'你对你们企业的管理（产品，人员，工资待遇，等）有何看法？'。这样对方才能有的放矢。
- 做访谈会遇到各种各样的人。有的人很健谈，你问一个问题，他能回答5分钟。有的人较沉默寡言，每个问题只回答'是'，'不是'，或'还好'。这种情况下，你要引导他多谈谈，比如你可以让他举个例子，描述一个具体事件，或把问题再问得具体些。还有的人也能谈，但是说半天总给你讲些国策，公司广告辞之类的话，而自己的真正想法却闭而不谈。这种情况下，你也要尽量鼓励他说具体的事件，例子，或让他谈谈个人的想法和经历。
- 不要满足于肤浅的，或路人皆知的回答。你可以把问题换个方法再问一次。
- 当然也不能总是刨根问底，这样会令人很烦。
- 问问题时要灵活。同一问题，不同的对象可以用不同的问法。有的人可以直接了当地问，而有的人却要婉转地问。
- 把容易的问题放在前面，难的问题放在最后。
- 访谈时间最好超过30 分钟， 以60 分钟最佳。时间太短，访谈没有效果。
- 如果面谈的话，可以准备个小礼品。

6.5 FOCUS GROUPS

Focus group research has its origins in market research of consumers' perceptions, opinions, beliefs and attitudes, but is now applied widely in other areas of business and management, including human resource management, accounting and entrepreneurship, among others. Eriksson and Kovalainen (2016: 181) define focus group research as research where 'a group of people is "focused" on discussing a selected topic or an issue'. However, a focus group interview is more than just 'interviewing a few people at the same time'. The emphasis here is on both the interaction between individuals and the content of what is discussed. This unique feature means that the focus group is one of the qualitative methods. It can be used either as a self-contained method in which it serves as the principal source of data, or as part of a multimethod in which it is combined with other means of gathering data (Morgan, 1997). In the Chinese context, recent years have seen an increase in the use of this method. An example is Leung and Chan (2012), who collected data through four expatriate focus groups to examine the stressors of Hong Kong construction professionals working in mainland China.

6.5.1 Advantages

Compared with the last two methods examined in this chapter, the focus group has a number of distinct advantages. First, group discussion is a 'quick and easy' way to produce concentrated amounts of data on topics that are directly related to the researcher's interests (Morgan, 1997). It is efficient in 'idea generation' and can save the researcher's time and reduce cost. Second, the interactive nature of a focus group provides access to forms of data that are not obtained easily by using a questionnaire or an interview. Similarities and differences in the participants' opinions and experiences can be gathered directly as opposed to comparing individual interview statements (Morgan, 1997). Moreover, the focus group provides a platform for the researcher to observe how individuals are influenced by and draw on others' opinions in a group situation (Eriksson and Kovalainen, 2016). This group synergy is used as data in its own right, as it allows the researcher to study how viewpoints are socially constructed and communicated (Puchta and Potter, 2004), albeit in a controlled situation. Third, participants can feel empowered as they are treated as experts. They can present their own views in their own words. They can also ask questions of each other and comment on what they have heard. As the discussion continues, 'individual response becomes sharpened and refined' (Finch et al., 2014: 212). Fourth, participants are not required to provide an immediate response. Rather, they can take time to think and reflect on their personal experience while listening to others. Finally, this method is considered to be particularly appropriate in China, in which Confucianism respects hierarchy and collectivism. Working in groups suits Chinese people, as they often do not appreciate being singled out or facing the researcher individually.

6.5.2 Critiques

Like other methods, the focus group also has its drawbacks. The first is that group discussions can suppress individuals with exceptional views or unusual experiences. They can be intimidating for shy members of the group or for people who are less confident at speaking in public. This can be a significant problem in the Chinese context where hierarchy, seniority and harmony are prioritised in the social encounter. In her field work in China, Watkins-Mathys (2006) noted that younger members are less likely to challenge the views of older members and that subordinates tend to agree with their managers in group discussions. She commented that a strong commitment to the collective discourages Chinese people from speaking their true thoughts and feelings. Second, focus group research is flexible and open-ended by nature. Sometimes, the researcher can find it difficult to control the direction of discussion when participants ask each other questions. Third, the interactions in group discussion can be seen as 'contaminated', as focus groups are controlled by the researcher. Thus, we can never be sure how natural the interactions are (Morgan, 1997). Finally, compared with individual interviews, group discussions do not allow the researcher to develop rapport with respondents. This can hinder the establishment of an interpersonal relationship or *guanxi* with key informants, who are often crucial to the success of your project in China. As such, focus group research is not suitable for many research situations or topics.

6.5.3 Group composition and size

Group composition is an important factor in determining the group dynamic and quality of discussion. Key questions to consider are whether you want heterogeneous or homogeneous groups; and whether you want group members to be strangers or acquaintances.

Homogeneity or heterogeneity

In homogeneous groups, members share similar experiences and characteristics, such as age, tenure and position, whereas in heterogeneous groups participants have mixed experiences and characteristics. Our experience is that Chinese participants tend to feel more relaxed and more likely to express their personal views in homogeneous groups where they feel safe. However, as pointed out by Finch et al. (2014), focus groups need diversity in order to tease out people's different views. It is difficult to facilitate discussion when members tend to agree on most points. Ideally, your groups should be constructed with some diversity in terms of age, gender and experience. On the other hand, a very heterogeneous group can also limit discussion, if participants feel threatened by other members. For example, if there is only one female member in a group which otherwise includes male participants, the female might feel reluctant to express a different opinion. Finch et al. (2014: 232) suggest that the

> socio-demographic make-up of the group can influence how open and full the discussion will be, particularly in relation to characteristics such as age, social class, educational attainment, gender and ethnicity. People are likely to feel more comfortable among others who they see as being from the same broad social milieu, and it is unhelpful if there are significant imbalances in social power or status within the group.

Therefore, extreme heterogeneity and homogeneity should be avoided. Moreover, in some cases, your research question (for example, how people in different groups shop online) requires you to compare people's experience between sub-groups in your sample. It is necessary to allocate participants into focus groups based on their age in order to draw out the differences in discussion.

Strangers or acquaintances

Generally, participants are usually more likely to express their views in a group of strangers whom they do not know and might not meet again. However, it is not always possible for researchers to recruit strangers. Students, in particular, often use convenience sampling and select participants from their personal network or through the connections of their family. This can lead to a situation in which Chinese participants are more interested in maintaining a harmonious atmosphere than challenging each other's views and perceptions. This is because protecting an acquaintance's *mianzi* (one's face or reputation) and exchanging *renqing* (a social norm that refers to both emotional and material support given to other in-group members) is seen as highly desirable in Chinese culture. Moreover, if the research is of a sensitive nature, people may feel uncomfortable sharing their experience for fear of subsequent gossip or repercussions (Finch et al., 2014). To overcome these problems, we suggest that researchers try to include strangers in focus groups where possible in the Chinese context.

6.5.4 The researcher's role

The researcher is typically a facilitator in focus group research with the aim of encouraging open and interactive discussion. Compared with other methods of data collection, focus group research requires more involvement and specific skills from the researcher. Overall, the researcher needs to have good interpersonal skills, though these skills can be improved with practice and experience. The role can be demanding and exhausting but also rewarding. Finch et al. (2014) highlight four techniques used by researchers to assist the progress of a discussion:

1. *Moderating the discussion.* This is to make sure the discussion is relevant and focused. It is necessary to prepare a list of themes or questions that you want to cover while allowing participants some freedom and flexibility of discussion. If the discussion diverts into topics that you see as irrelevant, you should draw participants' attention back to the purpose of the research.
2. *Probing for fuller responses.* Similar to conducting interviews, you can ask further questions to clarify an issue or to delve deeper into a subject rather than accepting a simple answer.
3. *Noting non-verbal language.* A focus group provides the opportunity to observe how the group interacts. You should be alert to participants' body language, for example nodding or shaking of the head, or looking bored. You can decide whether or not to ask further questions of the group or of an individual.
4. *Controlling the balance between individual contributions.* A very important task for the researcher is to ensure that every participant has a chance to contribute to the discussion, although in reality it is very rare that everyone has the same amount of time to speak. There are occasions when one or two members dominate the discussion. As a good facilitator, you should try to achieve a balance of contribution. You can invite others to speak by looking at others in the group or saying 'Let's hear some other opinions'. In contrast, there might be some members who are particularly silent for whatever reason (for example, they might be shy or believe their experience is not relevant). You should also draw them out. Moreover, you should step in when several participants try to speak at the same time, as it is difficult to transcribe simultaneous dialogue. Finally, you should maintain neutral in the debate and avoid expressing your personal views.

6.5.5 Online focus groups

As in interview, recent developments in technology makes it possible to conduct focus group research by using the internet, although this approach requires slightly different methodological considerations. It saves travel time and costs. It allows the researcher to include participants who are otherwise difficult to get together, for example those dispersed geographically or those with mobility problems. Participants can be more open and honest in their answers, as they can remain anonymous. Moreover, all text inputs are recorded automatically by the software and there is no need to transcribe. However, there are also limitations. First, the sample can potentially be biased, as online focus groups require participants to have computer literacy. Second, the researcher may find it more difficult to moderate the discussion than in person. Third, whether internet communication can provide adequate and reliable data to answer the research questions should be carefully assessed (Finch et al., 2014).

Online focus groups can be conducted synchronously （同步） or asynchronously （非同步） by using chat software, such as Skype or WeChat, both of which support typed messages and voice messages. In a synchronous group, both the researcher and participants can sign into a designated 'chat room' at the same time. Participants exchange views in a live group with the researcher asking questions and facilitating the discussion. A synchronous group usually contains four to eight participants and can last an hour. In an asynchronous online group, the discussion can last for several days. The researcher can post questions and probes on a 'bulletin board', and participants can sign in at a convenient time to read or listen to the messages and respond. In this case, the participants have more time to think about and reflect on the previous discussion before making their own comments.

TOP TIPS 小建议：FOCUS GROUPS

中文译为焦点小组访谈或专题小组讨论，是指把多名参与者组织起来，对某一主题进行深入的小组讨论。参考以下建议可以使你的讨论更深入，顺利：

- 讨论前事先要做好'功课'，把要概括的议题列好。
- 最好对参与者的个人背景有所了解。原来就有矛盾的人最好不放同一组。
- 对讨论话题保持中立态度，尽量不要同意或批评他人的观点。
- 对具体事件不要提供个人建议。
- 尽量不要打断他人发言，除非你觉得讨论跑题了。
- 当讨论进行得较激烈时，避免让多人同时发言。以免场面失控。
- 尽量照顾到在场的每一位参与者，让所有人都有机会发言。避免让一、两个人包揽所有的讨论，或影响其他人的观点。
- 需要察言观色，注意参与者的肢体语言。比如，有人一直想发言，但没机会。你可以点名让他发言。
- 鼓励深入的讨论，不要让重点话题一带而过。

6.6 USING DOCUMENTS

When studying overseas, some students find it difficult to collect primary data using questionnaires, interviews or focus groups, either because they have no access to organisations or because collecting data remotely becomes difficult to manage. One possible solution is to use documents. Documents in the sense of research can take many forms, including web pages, emails, blogs, newspapers, company records, photographs, government reports, and so on. In business and management research, researchers often combine a case study research design with using documents as a data collection method to build a rich picture of a particular organisation or industry. As such, students might have been familiar with this method already when completing coursework. Moreover, this method can be applied flexibly. Some researchers use documents as the only source of data while others use them as a supplement to other data such as interviews or personal observations.

6.6.1 Defining a document

A document has been traditionally defined as 'mute evidence' which can endure physically (Hodder, 2003: 703). It allows users to access information at a time and in a space that are different from those of the author or producer. This definition mainly recognises static forms of document such as written materials, pictures and diagrams. However, increasingly, many documents are no longer 'mute' or static, as advances in technology create new forms of documents including films, videos, television programmes, online discussion forums and interactive websites. Myers (2013: 153) thus sees a document as 'anything that can be stored in a digital file on a computer'. Altheide (1996: 2), on the other hand, offers a cultural perspective on documents, as he defines a document as 'any symbolic representation that can be recorded or retrieved for analysis'. Thus, music, audio and advertising are also considered to be a form of document. While most definitions see a document as 'what it should be', a small number of definitions take it as 'what it conveys'. Although documents can be seen as 'naturally occurring objects (i.e. not deliberately produced for the purpose of social research) with a concrete and semi-permanent existence which tell us indirectly about the social world of the people who created them' (Payne and Payne, 2004: 61), some scholars challenge the view that a document may be understood universally. Lee (2012: 391), for example, acknowledges that a document is subject to different interpretations, as he argues that '[a document] creates the possibility that the meanings of the representations may be interpreted differently – and employed accordingly – by the user'.

6.6.2 Advantages and disadvantages of using documents

Compared with other methods of data collection, the use of documents has some advantages. First, using documents is relatively cheap. As many documents are now available online, they are quick to access. Second, as Myers (2013) points out, sometimes documents can be the only empirical data available for a particular matter. For example, if someone has passed away, the researcher would not be able to interview him or her. But it is still possible to read the written materials someone leaves behind. Third, unlike questionnaires, interviews and focus groups, which tend to generate cross-sectional data (data collected from a population or a sample, at one specific point in time), documents allow researchers to take a longitudinal or historical view to study developmental trends across different periods of time or a life span. Fourth, some researchers use documents to triangulate or fill in gaps between data from other sources.

However, many documents are not available in the public domain. A major disadvantage is that some documents (e.g. private emails or personal diaries, minutes of meetings, investment plans, or historical documents in an archive) are difficult to obtain, either because you do not have organisational access or they are only available as hard copies. Yet, often these documents contain crucial information about an organisation or a person. A second problem is that the authenticity of a historical document can be difficult to assess. For online materials such as websites, videos or blogs, their reliability and credibility can be a concern.

6.6.3 Types of documents and where to find them

Lee (2012: 392–3) suggests that 'the collection of documents will depend in part on whether the chosen research question addresses the whole population that has to be surveyed, or considered a particular event, organisation or phenomenon that requires the study of one or more cases'. Either way, the first port of call should be the internet, as suggested by Myers (2013). Growth of the internet means that the number of documents (news, blogs, web pages, emails, etc.) created on the web has been rapidly increasing day by day (Heu et al., 2015). Smart multimedia devices (e.g. smart phones and tablet PCs) allow researchers to find information easily and quickly through diverse media (Heu et al., 2015). You can find many relevant documents by simply using general search engines such as Google, Bing or Baidu (a Chinese equivalent of Google, which provides information in Chinese). However, there are two major problems associated with using search engines (Lee, 2012). Using a single term may generate hundreds of thousands of results. For example, simply searching '淘宝（taobao）', the biggest online shopping platform in China, will yield nearly 2 million results in Baidu and 117 million results in Google. Clearly, more search terms are needed to narrow down the number of results to a more manageable level. In this case, you should include more key words, which are related to your research question(s). The second problem, as we repeatedly point out, is that the validity of some web pages may be difficult to determine. One approach is to use multiple sources to verify the authenticity of the information. Another approach is to focus on credible sources such as government-sponsored websites. For example, CIA: The World Factbook (www.cia.gov/library/publications/the-world-factbook/docs/profileguide.html) offers free access to information generally recorded for countries including China. Data and information are organised in categories, fields and subfields and thus are easy to browse.

Another useful website is the National Bureau of Statistics of China (www.stats.gov.cn) （国家统计局官网）. This is an online resource containing economic, development and census statistics freely available to the public.

Second, you may also access a range of digital databases through your university's library website. As with conducting your literature review, you can search China-related academic literature by using the e-resource provided by your library. Many UK universities subscribe to general databases, such as Web of Science, ScienceDirect, Business Source Premier and Scopus, as well as those that focus specifically on a certain subject or region. For example, China Academic Journals (also known as CNKI，中国学术文献网络出版总库) provides the largest collection of academic journals published in China. Coverage is from 1951 onwards and continuously updated. You can search in both Chinese and English. It should be noted that many articles are only available in the Chinese language. In addition, if there is anything that you are unable to find, you may contact your local librarians. In UK universities, librarians are subject-specific. They can provide useful advice about how to research a particular case or topic.

Your third port of search is the organisation or people that you are studying. Many important documents, such as minutes of meetings, personnel records, project reports, sales reports, are only available for internal circulation. To obtain those documents, you must have approval from senior management of the organisation or the person that your study focuses on. Sometimes, you will be asked to sign a confidentiality agreement.

Table 6.1 outlines the type of documents you may use and the potential approach to locate them. To simplify discussion, we follow Payne and Payne (2004: 61), who classify documents into three main categories: personal, private and public, 'depending on *who* wrote them, not the document's ownership or availability to the wider population'.

Table 6.1 Types of document and how to find them

Types of document	Forms of document	Where to find them
Personal	Individuals' letters, emails, diaries, notes, photos, files	The person you are studying
	Autobiographies, personal history	Bookshops, library, personal website, LinkedIn
Private	Minutes of meetings, personnel records, memos, employment policies, collective agreements with trade unions, marketing intelligence, budgets, organisational structure	The organisation you are studying
Public	Annual accounts and financial reports, corporate social responsibility reports, product range, strategic partners, history, goals, vision for the future, board of directors	Corporate website, online databases
	News reports, films, videos, photographs	News media, corporate website, internet

TOP TIPS 小建议：DOCUMENTS

可以广义地理解为档案，文献或根据事实材料所制作的纪实性的描述，记载。在研究方法论里经常同案例分析一起使用。很多人为了研究一个特定的对象如：人，公司或某个行业，经常会收集该对象的资料，文献以对起其进行进一步的了解和分析。收集和使用文献及资料时需注意以下几点：

- '文献'可以包括五花八门，各种各样的资料。如果你要研究一个公司，文献可包括该公司历史档案、照片、会议记录、人员记录、财务报表、对外宣传文件、网页、广告，还有媒体报道、记录片等。但不包括实物，如办公室、产品。
- 收集资料时需注意来源是否可靠。总体说来公司的官方网站、大的新闻媒体的报道，国家机关的报告、国际上知名的大机构（如世界银行，亚太经济合作组织）、已出版的书籍和文章都可以认为是可靠的。但很多网页是不被认可的，如百度百科、百度文库、百度知道、Wikipedia、YouTube、某些小公司的网上报道等。
- 资料最好来自多个渠道、来源。不要只听'一面之词'。如果你只从公司官网上收集材料，那你的材料只会说该公司多好，其产品多么有用。这样你的研究就有很强的偏见，很不客观。
- 很多公司的内部资料都不对外公开。所以你最好能联系到公司内部的人，得到公司负责人的允许才可使用这些材料。

有很多时候网上的资料总是不全。如果允许的话，你最好对公司关键人员进行访谈

FURTHER READING

Cassell, C. (2015) *Conducting Research Interviews*. London: Sage. This textbook provides in-depth and practical guidance on conducting interviews. It is written in concise and simple English and is accessible to students who are not native English speakers.

Punch, K. (2003) *Survey Research: The Basics*. London: Sage. This book focuses on small-scale quantitative surveys studying the relationships between variables. It takes a simple model of the survey, describes its elements and gives a set of steps and guidelines for implementing each element.

Ritchie, J., Lewis, J., Nicholls, C.M. and Ormston, R. (2014) (eds) *Qualitative Research Practice: A Guide for Social Science Students and Researchers*, 2nd edition. London: Sage. This textbook leads students through the entire process of doing qualitative research. It offers in-depth discussions about interview and focus group methods. It also covers observational research which is not included in this chapter.

REFERENCES

Altheide, D.L. (1996) *Qualitative Media Analysis*. Thousand Oaks, CA: Sage.

Alvesson, M. and Ashcraft, K.L. (2012) Interviews. In G. Symon and C. Cassell (eds) *Qualitative Organizational Research: Core Methods and Current Challenges*. London: Sage, 239–57.

Ang, S.H. (1996) Chinese consumers' perception of alpha-numeric brand names. *Asia Pacific Journal of Marketing and Logistics* 8: 31–47.

Ang, S.H. (2014) *Research Design for Business and Management*. London: Sage.

Bergkvist, L. (2015) Appropriate use of single-item measures is here to stay. *Marketing Letters* 26(3): 245–55.

Bergkvist, L. and Rossiter, J.R. (2009) Tailor-made single-item measures of doubly concrete constructs. *International Journal of Advertising* 28: 607–21.

Bryman, A. (2012) *Social Research Methods*. Oxford/New York: Oxford University Press.

Byrne, B. (2004) Qualitative interviewing. In C. Seale (ed.) *Researching Society and Culture*, 2nd edition. London: Sage, 179–92.

Cassell, C. (2015) *Conducting Research Interviews*. London: Sage.

Charmaz, K. (1995) Between positivism and postmodernism: Implications for methods. *Studies in Symbolic Interaction* 17: 43–72.

Cooke, F.L. (2010) Women's participation in employment in Asia: A comparative analysis of China, India, Japan and South Korea. *The International Journal of Human Resource Management* 21: 2249–70.

Dillman, D.A. (2000) *Mail and Internet Surveys: The Tailored Design Method*. New York/Chichester: John Wiley.

Drolet, A.L. and Morrison, D.G. (2001) Do we really need multiple-item measures in service research? *Journal of Service Research* 3: 196–204.

Eriksson, P. and Kovalainen, A. (2016) *Qualitative Methods in Business Research*. London: Sage.

Finch, H., Lewis, J. and Turley, C. (2014) Focus groups. In J. Ritchie, J. Lewis, C.M. Nicholls, et al. (eds) *Qualitative Research Practice: A Guide for Social Science Students and Researchers*, 2nd edition. London: Sage, 211–42.

Fontana, A. and Frey, J.H. (2003) The interview: From structured questions to negotiated text. In N. Denzin and Y. Lincoln (eds) *Collecting and Interpreting Qualitative Materials*, 2nd edition. London: Sage, 61–106.

Heu, J.-U., Qasim, I. and Lee, D.-H. (2015) FoDoSu: Multi-document summarization exploiting semantic analysis based on social Folksonomy. *Information Processing and Management* 51: 212–25.

Hewson, C., Vogel, C. and Laurent, D. (2016) *Internet Research Methods*. London: Sage.

Hodder, I. (2003) The interpretaion of documents and material culture. In N. Denzin and Y. Lincoln (eds) *Handbook of Qualitative Research*. London: Sage, 703–16.

Hui, C., Lee, C. and Rousseau, D. (2004) Psychological contract and organizational citizenship behavior in China: Investing generalizability and instrumentality. *Journal of Applied Psychology* 89: 311–21.

Hung, K., Gu, F.F. and Tse, D.K. (2005) Improving media decisions in China: A targetability and cost-benefit analysis. *Journal of Advertising* 34: 49–63.

Lee, B. (2012) Using documents in organisational research. In G. Symon and C. Cassell (eds) *Qualitative Organizationl Research: Core Methods and Current Challenges*. London: Sage, 389–407.

Leung, M. and Chan, I. (2012) Exploring stressors of Hong Kong expatriate construction professionals in mainland China: Focus group study. *Journal of Construction Engineering and Management* 138(1): 78–88.

Miller, J. and Glassner, B. (2004) The 'inside' and the 'outside': Finding realities in the interviews. In D. Silverman (ed.) *Qualitative Research: Theory, Method and Practice*, 2nd edition. London: Sage, 125–39.

Morgan, D.L. (1997) *Focus Groups as Qualitative Research*. Thousand Oaks, CA: Sage.

Myers, M.D. (2013) *Qualitative Research in Business and Management*. London: Sage.

Oliver, D.G., Serovich, J.M. and Mason, T.L. (2005) Constraints and opportunities with interview transcription: Towards reflection in qualitative research. *Social Forces* 84: 1273–89.

Oppenheim, A.N. (2000) *Questionnaire Design, Interviewing and Attitude Measurement*. London: Continuum.

Payne, G. and Payne, J. (2004) *Key Concepts in Social Research*. London: Sage.

Puchta, C. and Potter, J. (2004) *Focus Group Practice*. London: Sage.

Punch, K. (2003) *Survey Research: The Basics*. London: Sage.

Resnik, D. and Zeng, W. (2010) Research integrity in China: Problems and prospects. *Developing World Bioethics* 10: 164–71.

Roy, A., Walters, P.G.P. and Luk, S.T.K. (2001) Chinese puzzles and paradoxes: Conducting business research in China. *Journal of Business Research* 52: 203–10.

Saunders, M., Lewis, P. and Thornhill, A. (2015) *Research Methods for Business Students*. New York: Pearson Education.

Searle, R., Den Hartog, D.N., Weibel, A., et al. (2011) Trust in the employer: The role of high-involvement work practices and procedural justice in European organizations. *International Journal of Human Resource Management* 22: 1069–92.

Silverman, D. (2001) *Interpreting Qualitative Data: Methods for Analyzing Talk, Text and Interaction*. London: Sage.

Tuten, T.L. (2010) Conducting online surveys. In S.D. Gosling and J.A. Johnson (eds) *Advanced Methods for Conducting Online Behavioral Research*. New York: American Psychological Association, 179–92.

Watkins-Mathys, L. (2006) Focus group interviewing in China: Language, culture, and sensemaking. *Journal of International Entrepreneurship* 4: 209–26.

Webb, S. and Webb, B. (1932) *Methods of Social Study*. London: Longman.

Xiao, Y., Tylecote, A. and Liu, J. (2013) Why not greater catch-up by Chinese firms? The impact of IPR, corporate governance and technology intensity on late-comer strategies. *Research Policy* 42: 749–64.

Ye, K., Zhang, R. and Rezaee, Z. (2010) Does top executive gender diversity affect earnings quality? A large sample analysis of Chinese listed firms. *Advances in Accounting, Incorporating Advances in International Accounting* 26: 47–54.

Yeo, A., Legard, R., Keegan, J., et al. (2014) In-depth interviews. In J. Ritchie, J. Lewis, C.M. Nicholls, et al. (eds) *Qualitative Research Practice: A Guide for Social Science Students and Researchers*, 2nd edition. London: Sage, 177–210.

Yeung, H.W.-c. (1995) Qualitative personal interviews in international business research: Some lessons from a study of Hong Kong transnational corporations. *International Business Review* 4: 313–39.

7
ANALYSING QUALITATIVE DATA

7.1 OVERVIEW

The last chapter discussed various forms of methods used by scholars and students to collect qualitative data in Chinese society. However, after the data collection stage, students are often overwhelmed by a large amount of data, such as field notes, audio recordings, pictures, and so on, and are puzzled about how to use them. In this chapter, we will turn our attention to the issues of dealing with qualitative data. In the sections related to data collection, we have already mentioned that there is a repetitive interplay between the collection and analysis of qualitative data. Initial analysis often starts at the data collection stage. In a grounded theory design, earlier analysis can even help to later shape the data collected. This chapter, however, will focus on the analysis undertaken after all the data are collected. We will first understand the process of doing qualitative data analysis and then discuss in detail the different approaches to analysing and interpreting data. Given the vast variety of approaches, this chapter will only discuss the three approaches that are most commonly used in business and management research. Although each approach is presented separately in this chapter, it is sometimes rewarding to combine two approaches in your research, provided the data you have gathered support your strategy. The final sub-section will take a look at the computer-assisted qualitative data analysis software available on the market.

7.2 PROCESS OF QUALITATIVE DATA ANALYSIS

Qualitative data analysis can be aimed at building theory both deductively (taking into consideration concepts and issues in the research framework) and inductively (identifying themes emerging from the data). Ritchie and Spencer (1994) suggest five steps of qualitative data analysis: familiarisation with the data; identifying a thematic framework; indexing or coding; charting; and mapping and interpreting. First, it is recommended that data analysis proceeds initially through the researcher's reading of the scripts and notes to gain an in-depth understanding of how the data are related to the issues in the framework or key concepts. At this stage, you may look at your project document by document and reflect on their individual meanings. This early review can help to familiarise the researcher with the data and identify concepts and themes, which allows for a more systematic approach to the following stages of analysis.

Second, on the basis of this reading, an analytical framework can be identified. Data analysis requires researchers to see beyond individual scripts and to generate themes and ideas across the data (Richards, 2015). Miles and Huberman (1994) advise that researchers start with some general themes derived from a reading of the literature and add more themes and sub-themes as they go. Following this advice, data analysis can be conducted, first deductively in which pre-existing concerns and questions – themes within the research framework – are considered. Then, analysis can be conducted inductively from the data themselves – that is, to identify sub-themes that have emerged from the data.

The third stage is called coding, which 'involves placing like with like, so that patterns can be found' (Seale, 2004: 306). Coding is a kind of data reduction and retention. A code is a word or a short expression that captures or summarises the meaning of a chunk of data. It should be noted that coding in qualitative research is different from coding in quantitative research, which reduces everything to numbers (for example, male = 0, female = 1; see Chapter 8). Qualitative coding involves extracting meaning from raw data (e.g. sentences, paragraphs). Richards (2015) distinguishes three types of qualitative coding: descriptive, topic and analytical. Descriptive coding is similar to quantitative coding, in that it involves storing case information rather than interpreting texts, pictures or audio. The purpose is to sort data according to its attributes (e.g. gender: female; age: 45; position: marketing manager). Topic coding is labelling texts according to their subjects, which involves the researcher's interpretation of what is said (e.g. recruitment issues). Analytical coding is the most important but difficult step in qualitative analysis, as it requires the researcher to apply theoretical concepts to interpret data, and can lead to the development of theory. For example, you may code a paragraph as 'tension between work and family'. Most studies use all three coding methods. It is worth noting that other researchers categorise codes differently, but with similar principles. For example, Myers (2013) differentiates descriptive codes, interpretive codes, theoretical codes, pattern codes, and so on.

KEY CONCEPTS IN CHINESE: CODING AND CODE

定性研究里的分析主要靠编码 (coding) 完成。这里的编码并非把文字变成数字。所谓的编码是通过阅读理解了原始资料的意思后，找出跟我们研究课题相关的内容，通过理解，对某段文字进行编码归类，以便日后查询。编码过程主观因素较大。不同的人对同一段文字常常有不同的理解，因而编的 '码' (code) 也会不同。你编的'码'有可能是通过一个词或一句话概括了一段文字的意思。所以如果是一个小组进行编码，为了尽可能地公正和可信，编码过程进行之前，一般需要多位编码者对同一个文件或案例（case）内容进行编码。然后对编码不一致的地方一起讨论，达成共识，再继续对其他内容进行编码。另外，这些'码'也应该同你研究的课题息息相关，而不是毫无规律的概念或关键字。

Your codes can be hierarchical, i.e. you have different levels of codes. For example, for the paragraph which you code 'tension between work and family', you may continue to create lower level codes (or sub-codes), such as 'childcare', 'elderly care' or 'long working hours' to capture the different commitments. On the other hand, there could be free codes – standalone codes that do not belong to any hierarchy. These free codes are usually created by the researcher to represent concepts that do not belong to the framework yet can be linked to other concepts later. Some researchers import their Chinese scripts into computer software to assist in this process (see section 7.7 for a discussion around the tensions and advantages of such tools). Some researchers code in Chinese, as it is easy to remember, while others conduct their coding in English to establish a literal relationship between theory and data. After all scripts are coded, texts in each code and sub-code should then be read carefully to ensure each data item fits the intended definition of the code. Sometimes, similar codes can be combined so that texts in each code are not fragmented. This process of checking, developing clarity between similar codes and keeping coding as close to the original data as possible enables interviewees' views to emerge through the categorisation process (Seale, 2004). Moreover, it ensures an overall confidence in the coding process and a clear audit trail through the findings (Kumra and Vinnicombe, 2008).

Fourth, mapping is developing a complete codebook (note: a codebook is not an actual book). This is a set of codes you will use to analyse your data, thus it is sometimes called a coding framework to obtain a whole picture of the codes and data. Key themes should be linked with sample evidence, such as quotes from interviews. At this stage of data analysis, different sections of data should be compared and re-connected to establish a 'clue' (a holistic idea) of the overall findings. Richards (2015) warns against the 'coding trap' where researchers try to code everything and coding becomes a never-ending task. On the other hand, some researchers only focus on descriptive or topic coding as these are easier than analytical coding. Sadly, the theory does not seem to emerge from the data. Thus, mapping or constructing models is about identifying how the themes, concepts, beliefs and behaviours are connected to each other. Such mapping also helps to eliminate irrelevant themes.

The final step is to theoretically make sense of your findings. Based on an understanding of the major themes and concepts supported by the data, an interpretation of the research phenomenon should be developed. For example, your findings from the Chinese context should be compared with literature in the Western context in order to understand the similarities and differences between Chinese and Western values, practices and experiences. You can also revisit your research objectives and design and start constructing your own theory.

Example 7.1

A CODEBOOK

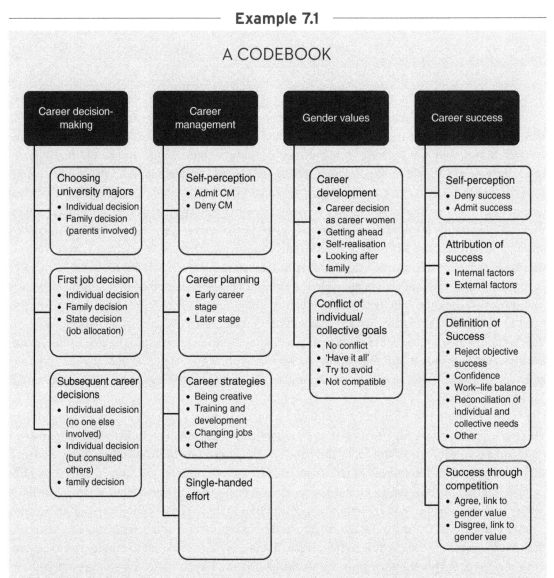

Figure 7.1 Codebook

Figure 7.1 is a codebook of a study about Chinese women's career decisions and values. After reading and coding, 52 hierarchical nodes were identified in 20 interviews. The first level of the codebook includes four overarching career themes (e.g. career decision-making, career management, gender values and career success) identified from existing theories. The second level of this codebook contains both codes from the literature (e.g. career planning, career strategies) and codes that have emerged from the data (e.g. first job decision, interviewees' self-perception about their success). The third level includes mainly codes derived from the data, as they represent the answers given by the participants. Moreover, all codes are either topic or analytical codes.

FURTHER READING

Saldaña, J. (2016) *The Coding Manual for Qualitative Researchers*. London: Sage. This book provides a useful manual for beginners; it guides you through the coding process and has detailed assessments of different coding types.

7.3 CONTENT ANALYSIS

7.3.1 Defining content analysis

In essence, content analysis is an interpretative and qualitative method, but its underlying positivist ontological assumption makes some believe that it is more suitable for researchers searching for forms of quantification in a qualitative study (Myers, 2013). For example, Neuendorf (2011: 277) suggests that 'content analysis is a summarising, quantitative analysis of messages that relies on the scientific method, including attention to objectivity/intersubjectivity, a priori design, reliability, validity, generalisability, replicability, and hypothesis testing'. This definition assumes a quantitative approach and codes are treated as variables that might be measured by counting the frequency of their appearances. Others, however, argue that content analysis is compatible with a range of philosophical positions including positivism, critical realism and pragmatism, and thus can be used for both hypothesis testing and theory building. In this sense, content analysis can be used in both inductive and deductive studies. Easterby-Smith et al. (2015: 188) see content analysis as

> an approach that aims at drawing systematic inferences from qualitative data that have been structured by a set of ideas or concepts. Researchers interrogate their data for the presence, meanings and relationships of these ideas or concepts, which are derived from a pre-existing theory or hypothesis, from the research questions or from the data themselves.

Regardless of researchers' preference of theory development, there is an agreement among researchers that content analysis should aim to discover patterns and regularities through qualitative data. The outcome of the analysis is to generate concepts or categories describing the social phenomenon under study.

KEY CONCEPTS IN CHINESE: CONTENT ANALYSIS

内容分析法是定性研究里最普遍的分析手段，也是中国学者，学生较容易掌握的一种方法。该方法是对被记载下来的资料进行研究、分析。原始资料可包括访谈记录、网页、演讲稿、信件、广告、观察记录、档案文献，等。其主要目的是分析各个记录或文件中存在的普遍主题（theme），从而找出共同规律，或潜在的社会结构（structure）。分析的过程，往往需要仔细地阅读所要分析的原始资料，对每个记录的内容进行详细编码。然后通过对比各个记录的编码，找出里面共同存在的，我们所关心的内容。编码的过程中可参考现有文献里的概念而制定预定的编码系统，或可以采用扎根理论方法，先对各个记录中内容进行编码归类，然后归纳出总体记录内的共同主题。

　　内容分析法关心的是每个记录或文件里包含的实质内容，而并非表现的手法。如分析访谈记录时，我们要研究的是'谁说/做了什么，对谁说/做的，为什么说，当时事情发生的背景如何，以及后来产生了什么影响'。但对某些事情怎么说的，叙事者用的语言修辞，或情节如何转变的不是太注重。

7.3.2 Benefits and criticisms

Content analysis offers a few benefits to researchers. First, unlike quantitative methods which reduce data to numbers, this method provides content-sensitive findings. The concepts and categories developed are supported by textual/visual evidence. Second, it gives researchers flexibility in terms of research design, as it works with various forms of data and coding can be conducted both inductively and deductively. Third, it can be used to develop in-depth understandings of the meaning of concepts in context or to identify critical processes in organisational studies. Despite its usefulness, content analysis has received criticism from both quantitative and qualitative scholars, both of whom consider it to be a simplistic technique. Scholars from the quantitative field believe this method does not lend itself to sophisticated statistical analysis, and the subjective nature of coding means that rigorous standards (such as reliability, validity and replicability) are unable to be met (Neuendorf, 2011). On the other hand, qualitative scholars warn that content analysis may result in a simplistic description of data and that inexperienced researchers can easily slip into a counting game – only counting the frequency of certain words – without a critical interpretation of their deep meaning (Elo and Kyngäs, 2008).

7.3.3 Doing content analysis

In business and management research, content analysis is most commonly used with textual data （文字型数据）, such as interview transcripts, company documents and observational notes. In some sub-disciplines (e.g. marketing), it has been used to analyse pictures and videos (e.g. advertisements). For researchers who adopt a positivist approach, content analysis is useful for looking at frequencies of words and monitoring their change in frequency over time. For example, in a study about brand recognition, the researcher can count how many times each brand is mentioned by participants in a focus group discussion. Recently, this method has also been used for conducting systematic literature reviews (Elo and Kyngäs, 2008).

Example 7.2

SYSTEMATIC LITERATURE REVIEW USING CONTENT ANALYSIS

Deng (2012) used content analysis to examine the theoretical development of the internationalisation of Chinese firms. After a literature search using various key words, including 'China', 'Chinese firms', 'international expansion' and 'internationalisation', the author identified 121 articles published in business, management and international business journals. Descriptive, topic and analytical coding techniques were employed. Three categories of analysis (antecedent, process and outcome) were developed and each of the three categories included several major themes. The author made within-theme and between-theme comparisons to draw out the theoretical perspectives. Eventually, matrices which consisted of six main themes (firm level, industry level, transaction-specific, institutional context, firm strategy and economic/financial performance) and a large number of sub-themes were proposed as the main framework for discussion. Based on such qualitative content analysis of the literature, theme-specific recommendations for the three categories as well as generic recommendations for directions for future research were made.

Elo and Kyngäs (2008) propose two approaches (inductive and deductive) to doing content analysis depending on the purpose of the study. In inductive content analysis, themes, concepts and categories emerge from the data, whereas in deductive content analysis, the structure of analysis is based on existing concepts and theories. However, before an analysis can be conducted, you need to decide your unit of analysis （分析单元）, which can consist of one word, one sentence or a paragraph. If the unit of analysis is too broad, for example a paragraph or a large chunk of text, the analysis process would be challenging as the unit contains several meanings. On the other hand, if the unit of analysis is too narrow, for example a word, the data may be fragmented. In principle, 'the unit of analysis should be large enough to be considered a whole and small enough to be kept in mind as a context for meaning unit' (Elo and Kyngäs, 2008: 109). In practice, many researchers choose a small paragraph or a bundle of sentences which provides enough contextual meaning for interpretation. While making sense of the data, Dey (1993) suggests that the following questions need to be considered:

- Who is speaking?
- Where is this happening?

- When did it happen?
- What is happening?
- Why?

Inductive content analysis is a bottom-up approach, which involves open coding （开放式编码）, creating categories and abstraction (Elo and Kyngäs, 2008). This is similar to the grounded analysis presented in Easterby-Smith et al. (2015). In open coding, the researcher codes data while reading the material. Codes and categories are generated spontaneously at this stage. After all data are coded, categories can be re-organised by, for example, creating higher levels of categories or grouping into similar categories, according to interpretations. Some data can be reclassified based on new interpretations. This process of creating categories involves a comparison between data and between the data and the literature. Dey (1993) points out that formulating categories relies on a researcher's decision regarding what to put into which category, through interpretation. This requires an in-depth understanding of the data and the theory-building capacity of the researcher. The final step is abstraction（从你的数据中提炼出概括性的概念或原理）, which involves generating a content-specific description of categories and subcategories. In so doing, the researcher conceptualises and develops theory. At this stage, the researcher aims to discover patterns and regularities among codes that are characterised by similarity, difference frequency, sequence, correspondence or causation (Saldaña, 2016). Inductive content analysis is particularly suitable for a grounded theory research design, as it allows the meaning of fragmented data to be understood within a specific context (Easterby-Smith et al., 2015). It prioritises the voices and views of research participants over existing theories.

Deductive content analysis, on the other hand, is a top-down approach. It can be used to re-test existing concepts, categories, models or hypotheses in a new context or to employ pre-supposed concepts and categories to create analytical frameworks. The researcher first creates a matrix of categories based on their literature review and codes the data according to this framework. In other words, the researcher systematically allocates data into a pre-defined set of codes. It could be argued that this approach only allows the researcher to look for data that fit the categorisation and therefore does not allow new themes to emerge. However, most qualitative researchers do not always strictly apply a very structured coding scheme. Instead, researchers create categories to accommodate aspects that do not fit into the pre-defined categorisation, by adopting the principle of inductive content analysis as described earlier. Indeed, many qualitative studies combine both deductive and inductive content analysis.

Example 7.3

CONTENT ANALYSIS WITH INTERVIEW TRANSCRIPTS

Woodhams et al. (2015) provided a useful example of applying Ritchie and Spencer's (1994) five-step data analysis process. Interview scripts were transcribed into Chinese texts and read by the Chinese-speaking researcher to identify initial themes. While developing a codebook, the authors took into consideration the presuppositions (e.g. feminine/masculine characteristics, individualist/collectivist framework) and themes emerging from the data, including, for example, critical influences on career, measures of career success, managerial skills and route to management. This framework was applied across all scripts and 37 nodes were established. The authors then mapped selected quotes to have an overview of the general distribution of the data. In order to make sense of the findings, the authors scoped the profile of each interviewee to capture the interviewees' career orientation.

7.4 DISCOURSE ANALYSIS

7.4.1 Defining discourse analysis

Unlike content analysis, which focuses on the 'content', discourse analysis emphasises language itself or how language is used in a particular context, for example in a conversation, an article, a report or on a web page (Cunliffe, 2008). All language can be under scrutiny. Language （指我们日常使用的语言或修辞） is not merely a channel through which people exchange information or facts about the world. Rather, language can be seen as a 'machine' that produces the social world (Jørgensen and Phillips, 2002). The understanding of language as a system helps us to understand our social identities and social relations.

The word 'discourse' refers to the communication between two parties (speaker/listener, writer/reader). With a priority in subjectivity, discourse analysis acknowledges that language contributes to the way we construct social and organisational realities. This approach is thus more suitable for scholars taking a subjective ontological standpoint (see section 3.1.1). Because of its philosophical focus, some even argue that discourse analysis is not merely an analytical technique, but a methodology of its own (Easterby-Smith et al., 2015). As a conceptual frame, discourse analysis is about acknowledging structures of understandings and meaning, questioning the politics of representation and exploring the role of language in the production of experience (Alvesson and Kärreman, 2011).

KEY CONCEPTS IN CHINESE: DISCOURSE ANALYSIS

内容分析法研究的是（谈话的）内容，即究竟说了什么。而谈论（discourse）分析法（有些书上也称其话语分析）研究的是话是怎么说的，着重点是语言本身。语言被认为是构成社会现实（social construction）不可缺少的因素。比如人们在讨论一件事情时用了什么语言，该语言体现了什么社会、文化状况、价值观。

(Continued)

谈论分析具体也分两种。第一种是通过研究人们在谈话、写文章中使用的语言、语气来研究人们如何从谈论，探讨中得出对事物的理解（sense-making）。如你偷听了两名员工之间的一段对话、他们谈论的焦点是关于企业里人员晋升新的规定。分析着重看的是双方讨论时用了什么语言、语气，双方究竟是赞成还是质疑该规定；一方如何提出观点，而另一方又如何反驳，双方如何使用论据和论点；谁先占有优势，而形势又可能会发生一定的变化；双方的态度，或强调点、措辞，通过谈论分析，最后达成什么一致的观点。所以人们对事物的认知不是自然形成的，其实是人们讨论的结果。

第二种方法研究的不光是谈话或一篇文章本身，还看其发生的社会背景，和其政治性。研究的是谁（如政府、某人、某机构）操控了言论的方向或舆论导向（rhetoric），其背后的动机是什么。关心的是权力（power）和说服力（persuasion）。如研究英国退出欧盟事件，各媒体报道时使用的措辞用句，标题配的照片，就能体现出各媒体本身的政治立场。而各媒体背后又有哪个政党支持。我们可以看出，谈论分析注重语言的使用、变化，目的是从语言的使用发现被研究的人和事所体现的社会价值。

7.4.2 Benefits and criticisms

Discourse analysis is useful in a number of ways. First, it offers a wide range of approaches to studying language use that can be in written, oral or symbolic form (Cunliffe, 2008). Second, the different perspectives within discourse analysis provide fruitful theories and methods for research in communication, culture and society (Jørgensen and Phillips, 2002). Third, it can be applied in the analysis of different social domains, including organisations (e.g. organisational culture), institutions (e.g. policy) and societies (e.g. national identity) (Jørgensen and Phillips, 2002). However, its emphasis on language (based on an interpretation of talk) has always exposed it to the criticism that there is much more to the world and to meaning than what is said in a conversation or an article (Cunliffe, 2008). In other words, social reality is more than just language and discourse. Indeed, even many social constructionists would admit that there are constraints and regularities in social life.

7.4.3 Doing critical analysis

Cunliffe (2008) observes that researchers in the business and management discipline tend to conduct two types of discourse analysis: critical discourse analysis and discourse analysis. In her view, discourse analysis draws on arguments of social constructionism（社会构成论）and examines the structures of meaning, expression, themes, routine ways of talking and the rhetorical devices used in the construction of reality. The focus is on subjective meaning and interpretations of utterance. In business and management research, data often include naturally occurring communications between people (e.g. organisational members) in the form of conversations, emails or other written documents. However, some researchers also employ quantitative methods in data collection and analysis.

Critical discourse analysis takes a more postmodern perspective and sees discourse as rhetoric (rhetoric 指有政治目的的舆论导向或社会辩论). According to Van Dijk (1996: 84), critical discourse analysis 'should describe and explain how power abuse is enacted, reproduced or legitimated by the talk and text of dominant groups and institutions'. In organisational studies, critical discourse analysis examines aspects of power and persuasion within relationships. It sees discourse from a broader context and interprets people's use of language from systems of thought, including social, economic, political, institutional and cultural discourse. The aim is to show how this context 'privileges some actors at the expense of others and how broad changes in the discourse result in different constellations of advantage and disadvantage' (Phillips and Hardy, 2002: 25). Some researchers find Fairclough's (1995) model of critical discourse analysis useful. The model consists of three integrated levels of analysis that, in turn, link to three integrated dimensions of discourse:

1. The object of analysis (including verbal, visual, or verbal and visual texts).
2. The processes by means of which the object is produced and received (writing/speaking/designing and reading/listening/viewing) by human subjects.
3. The socio-historical conditions which govern these processes.

Fairclough (1995) suggests that each of these dimensions requires a different kind of analysis:

1. Text analysis (description).
2. Processing analysis (interpretation).
3. Social analysis (explanation).

Example 7.4

DISCOURSE ANALYSIS

Zhu (2009) used discourse analysis to examine how the Confucian ethics of *qing* (emotion), *li* (reason), *guanxi* (connections), *renqing* (social relations or human interaction) and *mianzi* (face) were embedded in Chinese marketing communications. In order to understand the business practice, the author collected data from two main sources. First, the author selected 40 Expo promotion invitations from sales firms in six major Chinese cities. Second, the author collected 100 questionnaires and conducted two focus group interviews, both with Chinese managers. While analysing the first form of data, the author paid particular attention to the structure, processes and interaction of the discourse shown in the invitations.

(Continued)

In particular, four components were used to examine the specific ways of applying Confucian ethics to other marketing communications:

1. Purpose.
2. Overall structure of the Expo invitation text.
3. Motives and linguistic forms of inviting and advertising the products.
4. Managers' views on various levels of text.

The study concludes that elements of interdependence and harmony embedded in the invitations are compatible with Western advertising strategies but that the politeness principles are largely different from those used in Western practice.

7.5 NARRATIVE ANALYSIS

7.5.1 Defining narrative analysis

Narrative（叙述）refers to 'a spoken or written text that involves temporal sequences of events and actions' (Maitlis, 2012: 492). To some extent, narrative is similar to a story, as it traditionally involves a plot with a beginning, a middle and an end (Polkinghorne, 1988). If you are interested in doing narrative analysis, you should aim to collect 'stories' at the data collection stage. However, narrative is non-fictional as it contains real-life happenings. Narratives can be operated at two levels – the personal and the organisational. At the personal level, it is argued that humans often make sense of their life experience through telling narratives, since 'narrative descriptions exhibit human activity as purposeful engagement in the world' (Polkinghorne, 1995: 4). In social science research, empirical data can be collected through personal narratives, which may be taken from people's diaries, photographs, journals, tweets, blogs, web pages, emails or (open and unstructured) interviews. In this sense, narrative analysis examines a specific aspect of a narrator's life story, analyses how it is put together, considering its linguistic and cultural background, and sees how it persuades a reader or listener (Riessman, 1993).

Moreover, narratives can work at an organisational level. Czarniawska (2004) sees narrative as a main mode of knowing and communicating in organisational life, as telling stories in and about organisations is a way that people (including managers and workers) make sense of their working life. In this case, organisational narrative analysis is about inspecting how stories are made and offering explanations (Czarniawska, 2004). However, narrative analysis is open to different interpretations as people often organise events around different plots and come to different conclusions (e.g. managers' view vs workers' view) about organisational reality. Thus, organisational narrative analysis can open up organisational practice for negotiation. Researchers can consider 'how stories symbolise aspects or organisational culture or the role of story-telling in organisational sense-making' (Myers, 2013: 210).

KEY CONCEPTS IN CHINESE: NARRATIVE ANALYSIS

叙述分析跟内容分析和谈话分析都不同。叙述（narrative）是指一段文字或口述，其中包括一系列的人和事件，最后会有一结局。叙述分析的关注点不是某段话的内容或语言的使用，而是上下文的关联，故事中人物的出现和情节的转换，最后结局如何。比如，你研究安徒生童话就会发现其总体的故事情节一般是：男女主角（通常是王子和公主）偶然相遇，之后受到很多阻碍，有敌对势力（如白雪公主中的妖后）的出现，但这些都是铺垫，最后总是完美结局。当然，社会科学中的叙述主要指你收集的定性的数据，如访谈记录，而不是虚构的故事。

　　在管理研究中，具体是通过人们对事件的叙述（narrator　即叙述者）而了解他们对事物的认知和世界观。因为叙述也是一个人们　socially construct reality 的过程。叙述分析的对象主要是主观的认知，如人们的经验（experience）。比如研究一名大学毕业生在工作一段时间后对该企业的了解，对经理、同事的评价，对某事件的感受，对工作和社会的认识和改变，知识的增长。由此你可看出他的人生观的改变，他如何 construct 工作和社会这个 reality。叙述分析虽然也研究文字或谈话中的各个主题（theme），但更强调它们与总体结构的联系。

7.5.2 Benefits and criticisms

Perhaps the most useful aspect of narrative analysis is its focus on the 'plot'. Personal narrative analysis offers a holistic approach to looking at people's life history and 'preserves the complexity of human action with its interrelationship of temporal sequence, human motivation, chance happenings and changing interpersonal and environmental context' (Polkinghorne, 1995: 7). On the other hand, organisational narrative analysis is an avenue where we can engage in a dialogue with managers and workers (Czarniawska, 2004). For example, it can be applied to an investigation of organisational change, which may include the use of new technology, the development of new products, restructuring, or the resolution of a crisis. The process of change can be described as a sequence of unfolding events that constitute a historical narrative, and an explanation relies on the interconnections as to why something happened and how individuals understand these events (Stevenson and Greenberg, 1998). In this case, a case study research strategy is useful to facilitate such an investigation.

While narrative analysis provides in-depth understanding of personal experience and meaning in organisations, its process can be very time-consuming. For example, it may take hours to collect life histories through open interviews with an individual interviewee. Moreover, for masters and doctoral students, the vast amount of data collected could be overwhelming. Thus, narrative analysis can only work with a small number of interviews or cases.

7.5.3 Doing narrative analysis

A number of techniques have been suggested for conducting narrative analysis, albeit the technical terms used can sometimes be confusing for Chinese students. For example, Polkinghorne (1995) distinguishes between an analysis of narratives and narrative analysis. To simplify discussion, we broadly categorise them according to their philosophical positions and the level of investigation.

Realist versus constructivist

One way to classify different methods of narrative analysis is to distinguish between a realist approach and a constructivist approach. Inherited from a realist ontology, the *realist approach* is similar to what Polkinghorne (1995) describes as the 'analysis of narratives', in which the researcher collects stories told by people and then analyses their plots, structure or story types (Eriksson and Kovalainen, 2016) with the aim of finding patterns. The researcher assumes a one-to-one correspondence between the narrative and actual events/happenings (Myers, 2013). Narratives are treated as a form of representation or descriptive account of reality. If collective narratives are used in, for example, case study research, narratives are seen as being representative of the organisational reality. The researcher takes a neutral stance in the knowledge construction process and findings are sometimes reported in a chronological order and with an authoritative tone.

The *constructivist approach* takes a subjective ontological position and sees reality as constructed through the narrator's events and actions. Instead of taking an impartial view of reality, the researcher brings his or her personal experience to the knowledge construction process. Polkinghorne (1995) calls it 'narrative analysis', in which the researcher organises and interprets data (events, happenings and actions) in the way they construct narratives, which will be further interpreted and discussed. Thus, 'narrative' is a mode of analysis (Myers, 2013). In other words, the job of the researcher is to synthesise or configure data into an explanation of, for example, how individuals make career decisions or how an organisation handles change. A narrative report in this case can be written in non-chronological order.

Levels of analysis

Narrative analysis can be conducted at various levels. The researcher may analyse stories, structure and/or contexts. While we discuss them separately here, in practice many qualitative researchers use them in the same study. *Analysing stories* focuses on the meaning and content of the narrative, with the aim of answering the question of 'what is told' (Eriksson and Kovalainen, 2016). Data are organised according to themes, which can be concepts, trends, ideas or distributions emerging from the data. *Analysing structure* focuses on 'the plot' and answers the question of 'how the story is told'. This method puts more emphasis on structural and linguistic elements and gives insights into the storytelling (or not) in the narrative. For example, when examining communications, the method can analyse language differences between two speakers who come from different cultural backgrounds. *Analysing context* turns to the circumstances of narrative production and answers the question of 'how stories are related to various conditions of social life and location'. The purpose is to understand how the social and cultural context in which the narrator lives shapes their experience. Moreover, in an interview situation, it can also focus on the interaction between the interviewer and the interviewee.

Example 7.5

NARRATIVE ANALYSIS

Liang and Lin (2008) examined the impact of Western management education theories and pedagogies on China. They argued that while learning from the Western model, China may have imported some shortcomings of Western management education. The authors chose some MBA teaching cases used in Chinese business schools and the research question was whether Chinese MBA teaching cases, written following a large-scale infusion of Western management education models, more truthfully represent the multifaceted reality of organisational life. For this purpose, a realist approach was thus adopted.

The authors compared MBA cases written before and after 1994 and employed both content analysis and narrative analysis. First, the authors adopted content analysis and coded all cases by using natural paragraphs as the unit of analysis. Then they examined the narrative patterns of the cases by adopting a realist approach. The following questions were asked: who is the narrator, and from whose perspective is the story told? What are the issues discussed and what issues are left out? What are the implicit leadership roles and decision models? How is the social and historical context presented? How are ethical, moral and political issues dealt with in each of the cases? Finally, the authors compared the patterns with the literature to theorise their findings.

The authors concluded that the holistic approach seen in early cases has largely disappeared in post-1994 cases, which exhibit similar problems to those identified in the Western management education system. This study is a useful illustration of how researchers can combine different analytical approaches to qualitative research to develop in-depth understandings.

7.6 PRESENTING QUALITATIVE DATA

Reporting qualitative findings is very different from reporting quantitative findings, in that you have to get into detail rather quickly. Moreover, the way you present your findings should make sense to your readers. While there is no magical formula about what and how to present, many Chinese students find it helpful to follow the steps below.

First, you should identify a way of organising your findings. Some students broadly structure their findings chapter according to their research questions, and then report on the themes and concepts that have emerged from the data. Although qualitative research is not about quantity, some researchers do report frequency. For example, they may write 'the majority of interviewees believed (finding A)', or 'two thirds of the managers interviewed agreed that (finding B)'. Alternatively, empirical material can be written around a 'plot' that will guide the analysis. This is particularly important for reporting narratives. Eriksson and Kovalainen (2016) even liken a qualitative report to a novel. While we do not invent people or events, there should be a theme or an argument that links different sessions together.

Second, when writing about a particular theme, you could first summarise the general findings in each theme and then present details of each sub-theme. Moreover, your themes and sub-themes should be supported by empirical evidence or examples (e.g. quotations from interview scripts). When using quotes from your interviews, you should attribute each quote to the person who said it. The number of quotations used in a dissertation depends on your word limit, as they take up a lot of space. For a typical masters dissertation, you may have around 3,000 words for your findings chapter and may only include 15 to 20 quotes in total. Therefore, it is crucial to select examples that best illustrate your point.

Third, many qualitative researchers adopt a 'theory-guided presentation', whereby references to the literature are incorporated into the report of findings throughout the analysis. The advantage of such a method is that you can constantly compare your findings with previous research, which strengthens your argument. For masters students, this is a good approach to demonstrate your theoretical understanding.

Example 7.6

QUALITATIVE FINDINGS

Stories of female managers who developed a successful career in new industries and/or organisations dominated our findings. More than two-thirds of the female participants stated that market reform has created new types of industries and organisations which in turn have created chances for women to advance. The career histories of these women showed that they had entered these industries and organisations at an early stage and had helped to establish them. Most women showed a great degree of modesty and attributed their achievement to luck – the fact that they have been exposed to opportunities emerged from the reform. Like many Western women (Heatherington et al., 1993), these Chinese women saw themselves as someone 'doing right things at the right time'. This is typified by Kate's work history. Kate joined a famous machinery manufacturer as a human resources manager in 1998, when her company was in its infancy and employed only 36 workers. Within 10 years, this company has developed to be the biggest manufacturer in the market and currently employs over 2,000 people. Kate was also promoted to human resources director during this period. She said:

> My success is the by-product of the success of my company. If the company decided to stop somewhere, I wouldn't have had so many challenges. Because the company wanted to make China the 2nd biggest market in the world, they gave me a lot of opportunities. (Kate, 42-year-old HR director)

TOP TIPS 小建议

- 写定性研究结果的时候要小心措辞，不要用非常肯定地语气。因为你的样本太小，最好不要写 'this research proves …' 或 'this research confirms …' 之类的句子。一般最好用婉转的语气，如 'evidence in this research shows …' 或 'interviewee A's example suggests …'。
- 写的时候有点像写'故事'。从头到尾有个 argument，把每一部分串起来。不要仅仅把所有的themes 都罗列上去。你要有论点和论据，只说最相关的。不能光说你访谈的对象说了什么，要加上你自己的分析。
- 写的过程能整理你的思路，所以最好早点开始写你的 findings。

7.7 INTRODUCTION TO COMPUTER-ASSISTED QUALITATIVE DATA ANALYSIS SOFTWARE (CAQDAS)

A key challenge faced by qualitative researchers is the transformation of 'hundreds of pages of field notes to a final report' (Miles and Huberman, 1994: 281) through a rigorous and high quality research process, rather than 'a disorganised stumble through a mass of data, full of "insightful" observations of a mainly anecdotal nature' (Silverman, 1993: 43). Contemporary researchers often use CAQDAS to assist data organisation and analysis. Various programs are available that focus on different functions, and the most common ones include QSR NVivo, ATLAS.ti and MAXQDA. It should be emphasised that these programs do not replace human interpretation in coding and conceptualisation. Rather, they are used to increase the researcher's capacity in data management. Weitzman (2003) outlines four advantages of using CAQDAS: consistency, speed, representation and consolidation. First, researchers can possibly improve consistency by constantly reviewing all data assigned to a given conceptual category or theme to see if they address the same issue. Second, programs help to quickly re-sort a database, redefine codes and reassign chunks of text, and therefore enable and encourage researchers to revise their analysis and think about it whenever necessary. Third, software that provides a graphic map of relationships among code, text segments or cases can help researchers to visualise and extend their thinking about the data or theory at hand. Fourth, software can be a powerful support to the analysis process by allowing researchers to record field notes, interviews, codes, memos, annotation, reflective remarks, diagrams, demographic variables and structural maps of the data and theory all in one place. This function can be particularly helpful as researchers can immediately link codes, chunks of text, memos, thoughts, and so on, to existing theories or specific references. Recently, Sinkovics and Alfoldi (2012) suggested that CAQDAS helps to establish a 'dialogue with the computer', and thus to develop a greater degree of effectiveness and rigour during the research process.

Despite these advantages, the use of CAQDAS is not without debate among qualitative researchers. Two major criticisms are that this approach might be underpinned by a certain philosophical position, and that it might affect researchers' closeness to the data. Here we will deal with these issues separately. First, some commentators have raised concerns about whether the range of available software is dominated by a particular approach, methodology or epistemology (see, for example, Coffey et al., 1996). The assumption was made that CAQDAS was something that is relevant only to 'positivist' or 'quasi-positivist' perspectives in qualitative research (Weitzman, 2003). However, as Weitzman has repeatedly argued, although a program may facilitate researchers' organisation of data and development of theory, researchers need not, and should not, be trapped by the conceptual assumptions of software developers. In other words, software does not drive methodology. Like any other computer function, CAQDAS helps researchers to manage, shape and make sense of unstructured information. It provides a sophisticated workspace that enables researchers to work through the information, though program users are ultimately responsible for analysing the data and developing theory (Fielding and Lee, 1998; Macmillan and Koenig, 2004).

The second criticism of CAQDAS is that the use of software might have the effect of 'distancing' researchers from the data (Weitzman, 2003; Weitzman and Miles, 1995). It is argued that by using software, researchers could end up looking at only small chunks of text at a time, or maybe even just line-number references to where the text is (Weitzman, 2003). Some users fear that analysts would 'lose touch' with their data, if they cannot see the text and its codes clearly and easily on screen every time. This might be the case for earlier versions of CAQDAS, which have only limited functions and offer unfriendly ways of data access (see Weitzman, 2003 and Lewins and Silver, 2007 for different types and functions of software for qualitative data analysis).

However, in our experience, recent and more advanced software programs, such as QSR NVivo 11, minimise this effect and, at the same time, offer by far greater benefits and flexibility to the researcher. Such advanced software can be used to conduct a systematic literature review at the early stages of research design (Sinkovics and Alfoldi, 2012). These programs allow the researcher to access data in different ways. For example, texts can be displayed in the source document so that the researcher can see them in their full context, while they can still retrieve them from the node view to compare and to develop ideas. Moreover, such programs also allow the researcher to build links quickly between documents, nodes, memos, models and even external resources (e.g. web pages, online PDFs, Facebook posts, LinkedIn discussions and tweets from Twitter). Based on their own observations, a number of scholars even suggest that the program may actually help, rather than hinder, the researcher in getting closer to the data than he or she could with paper transcripts (Bazeley and Jackson, 2013; Weitzman, 2003). Having said this, learning to use this software takes time. Thus, we do not recommend the use of CAQDAS if you have fewer than five interviews.

Many Chinese scholars use computer-aided qualitative data analysis software to manage their data, report detailed findings and demonstrate the relationships between their data and their theoretical conclusion. For Chinese students completing a dissertation, the aim is to find software which is compatible with the Chinese language (as most of your scripts are in Chinese) and which may help organise your data and offer a flexibility that would assist your analysis method. QSR NVivo meets such requirements and is widely available at UK universities. Chinese scripts can be imported into NVivo for coding and theory building. It is worth noting that the English version of NVivo can display Chinese characters but does not support the Chinese language in its search function. There are Chinese versions of most CAQDAS, which are fully compatible with the Chinese language (both simplified and complex).

TOP TIPS 小建议

目前国际上流行的几种质性研究软件（CAQDAS），如 NVivo, ATLAS.ti 和 MAXQDA 都有中文版，并与繁体、简体中文兼容、而且发行时间基本上和英文版同步。有的软件还有中文的辅导书，淘宝上有卖，如：

郭玉霞，刘世闵，王为国黄世奇，何明轩，刘梓榆（2009），质性研究资料分析NVivo 8 活用宝典，高等教育文化事业有限公司出版

张奕华，许正妹（2010），质化资料分析 maxqda 软体的应用，台北：心理出版社

英文版的入门教材可从软件的官网下载，如：

NVivo 11 Pro for Windows: Getting Started Guide. Available at: http://download.qsrinternational.com/Document/NVivo11/11.0.0/NVivo11-Getting-Started-Guide-Pro-edition.pdf

---

FURTHER READING

Eriksson, P. and Kovalainen, A. (2016) *Qualitative Methods in Business Research*. London: Sage. Chapters 10, 16 and 17 in this text provide in-depth discussion of the three approaches of qualitative data analysis we mention in this chapter.

REFERENCES

Alvesson, M. and Kärreman, D. (2011) Organizational discourse analysis: Well done or too rare? A reply to our critics. *Human Relations* 64: 1193–1202.

Bazeley, P. and Jackson, K. (2013) *Qualitative Data Analysis with NVivo*. London: Sage.

Coffey, A., Holbrook, B. and Atkinson, P. (1996) Qualitative data analysis: Technologies and representations. *Sociological Research Online*, 1(1). Available at: www.socresonline.org.uk/1/1/4.html (accessed 20 February 2018).

Cunliffe, A.L. (2008) Discourse analysis. In R. Thorpe and R. Holt (eds) *The SAGE Dictionary of Qualitative Management Research*. London: Sage, 81–2.

Czarniawska, B. (2004) *Narratives in Social Science Research*. London: Sage.

Deng, P. (2012) The internationalization of Chinese firms: A critical review and future research. *International Journal of Management Reviews* 14: 408–27.

Dey, I. (1993) *Qualitative Data Analysis: A User-friendly Guide for Social Scientists*. London: Routledge.

Easterby-Smith, M., Thorpe, R. and Jackson, P.R. (2015) *Management and Business Research*. London: Sage.

Elo, S. and Kyngäs, H. (2008) The qualitative content analysis process. *Journal of Advanced Nursing* 62: 107–15.

Eriksson, P. and Kovalainen, A. (2016) *Qualitative Methods in Business Research*. London: Sage.

Fairclough, N. (1995) *Critical Discourse Analysis*. London: Longman.

Fielding, N.G. and Lee, R.M. (1998) *Computer Analysis and Qualitative Research*. London: Sage.

Heatherington, L., Daubman, K., Bates, C., et al. (1993) Two investigations of 'female modesty' in achievement situations. *A Journal of Research* 29: 739–54.

Jørgensen, M. and Phillips, L. (2002) *Discourse Analysis as Theory and Method*. London: Sage.

Kumra, S. and Vinnicombe, S. (2008) A study of the promotion to partner process in a professional services firm: How women are disadvantaged. *British Journal of Management* 19: 65–74.

Lewins, A. and Silver, C. (2007) *Using Software in Qualitative Research: A Step-by-step Guide*. Electronic resource. London: Sage.

Liang, N. and Lin, S. (2008) Erroneous learning from the West? A narrative analysis of Chinese MBA cases published in 1992, 1999 and 2003. *Management International Review* 48: 603–38.

Macmillan, K. and Koenig, T. (2004) The wow factor: Preconceptions and expectations for data analysis software in qualitative research. *Social Science Computer Review* 22: 179–86.

Maitlis, S. (2012) Narrative analysis. In G. Symon and C. Cassell (eds) *Qualitative Organisational Research: Core Methods and Current Challenges*. London: Sage, 492–511.

Miles, M.B. and Huberman, A.M. (1994) *Qualitative Data Analysis: An Expanded Sourcebook*. Thousand Oaks, CA: Sage.

Myers, M.D. (2013) *Qualitative Research in Business and Management*. London: Sage.

Neuendorf, K.A. (2011) Content analysis: A methodological primer for gender research. *Sex Roles* 64: 276–89.

Phillips, N. and Hardy, C. (2002) *Discourse Analysis*. London: Sage.

Polkinghorne, D.E. (1988) *Narrative Knowing and Human Sciences*. New York: SUNY Press.

Polkinghorne, D.E. (1995) Narrative configuration in qualitative analysis. In A. Hatch, Jr and R. Wisniewski (eds) *Life History and Narrative*. Washington, DC: Falmer Press, 5–23.

Richards, L. (2015) *Handling Qualitative Data: A Practical Guide*. Los Angeles, CA: Sage.

Riessman, C.K. (1993) *Narrative Analysis*. Newbury Park, CA: Sage.

Ritchie, J. and Spencer, L. (1994) Qualitative data analysis for applied policy research. In A. Bryman and R.G. Burgess (eds) *Analysing Qualitative Data*. London: Routledge, 173–94.

Saldaña, J. (2016) *The Coding Manual for Qualitative Researchers*. London: Sage.

Seale, C. (2004) *Social Research Methods: A Reader*. London: Routledge.

Silverman, D. (1993) *Interpreting Qualitative Data: Methods for Analyzing Talk, Text and Interaction*. London: Sage.

Sinkovics, R.R. and Alfoldi, E.A. (2012) Facilitating the interaction between theory and data in qualitative research using CAQDAS. In G. Symon and C. Cassell (eds) *Qualitative Organisational Research: Core Methods and Current Challenges*. London: Sage, 109–31.

Stevenson, W.B. and Greenberg, D.N. (1998) The formal analysis of narratives of organizational change. *Journal of Management* 24: 741–62.

Van Dijk, T.A. (1996) Discourse, power and access. In C.R. Caldas-Coulthard and M. Coulthard (eds) *Texts and Practices: Readings in Critical Discourse Analysis*. London: Routledge, 84–104.

Weitzman, E.A. (2003) Software and qualitative research. In N. Denzin and Y. Lincoln (eds) *Collecting and Interpreting Qualitative Materials*, 2nd edition. London: Sage, 310–39.

Weitzman, E.A. and Miles, M.B. (1995) *Computer Programs for Qualitative Data Analysis: A Software Sourcebook*. London: Sage.

Woodhams, C., Xian, H. and Lupton, B. (2015) Women managers' careers in China: Theorizing the influence of gender and collectivism. *Human Resource Management* 54: 913–31.

Zhu, Y. (2009) Confucian ethics exhibited in the discourse of Chinese business and marketing communication. *Journal of Business Ethics* 88: 517–28.

8

ANALYSING QUANTITATIVE DATA

8.1 OVERVIEW

The purpose of quantitative data analysis is to extract insightful findings from data and produce valid and reliable answers to the research questions. As we noted in Chapter 6, the data set you would get at the end of the data collection based on our sample questionnaire, would be in raw form – that is, the data do not speak for themselves. Our job of data analysis is to 'work through and with the data to draw out the findings and get at the "story"' (McGivern, 2009: 428). Quantitative data analysis requires the use of statistics.

8.2 PREPARING DATA

8.2.1 Scales of measurement

To produce valid and reliable findings, you need to understand the nature of the numbers you are dealing with. There are different types of quantitative data, depending on what the 'numbers' really mean. In the context of quantitative data analysis, it is important to understand the 'meaning' of data; and we use four *levels of measurement (scales)* to represent the different meaning of data.

KEY CONCEPTS IN CHINESE: MEASUREMENT AND LEVEL (SCALE) OF MEASUREMENT

We assign values to a variable following a set of rules, and this process is called measurement. 测量，指的是根据某种规则，将数值赋予到某个研究变量的过程。我们希望通过'测量'，使得变量的属性具有某种数字化的特质。

Level of measurement, or scale of measurement、测量水平或测量尺度，是统计和定量研究中，对于不同种类的数据，依据其尺度水平所划分的类别。

Nominal or categorical level of measurement

Nominal scales consist of names, labels or categories only, and the data cannot be arranged in an ordering scheme (such as from low to high). The purpose of using nominal scales is to identify and classify objects, individuals or events – for example, participants' political affiliation, gender, job title or position, brand names, companies, stores. We cannot perform mathematical operations on nominal data.

KEY CONCEPTS IN CHINESE: NOMINAL (CATEGORICAL) SCALES

名义、（类别）尺度标示分析对象的种类。

Ordinal level of measurement

Ordinal scales involve data that can be arranged in a certain order, but differences between data values either cannot be determined or are meaningless – for example, scales using names with an order such as: 'bad' (1), 'medium' (2) and 'good' (3); or 'very satisfied' (5), 'satisfied' (4), 'neutral' (3), 'unsatisfied' (2) and 'very unsatisfied' (1). In the latter case, you could reasonably say that a score of 5 indicates a greater level of satisfaction that a score of 2; however, you could not conclude that two 'unsatisfied' scores equate to one 'satisfied' score.

KEY CONCEPTS IN CHINESE: ORDINAL SCALES

次序尺度将信息进行排序，由高到低，或者由低到高。显示研究对象的特质为高、中、低；强或弱；喜欢、中立、或者厌恶等程度。要注意的是，每个刻度之间的距离是无法决定或者无意义去决定的。

Interval level of measurement

The interval level of measurement is similar to the ordinal level, with the additional property that the difference between any two data values is identical and meaningful. However, there is no natural zero starting point – in other words, the 'zero point' on an interval scale is arbitrary. For example, it makes sense to say that 35°C is 10 degrees hotter than 25°C, and that 15°C is 10 degrees hotter than 5°C. '10 degrees hotter' means the same in these two cases. However, you could not conclude that 15°C is three times as hot as 5°C. So, for interval data, you can add and subtract. Other examples include people's intelligence scores and years of birth (e.g. 1918, 2003).

KEY CONCEPTS IN CHINESE: INTERVAL SCALES

等距尺度假定每个刻度之间的距离相等。可以做加减运算。

Ratio level of measurement

The ratio level of measurement is just like the interval level with the additional property that there is also a natural zero starting point, where zero indicates that none of the quantity is present. For values at this level, differences and ratios are meaningful – for example, the price of shampoo brands, where £0 represents no cost and a £6 shampoo brand costs twice as much as a £3 shampoo brand. Other examples include incomes, distances and weights. You can perform add, subtract, multiply or divide functions on ratio data.

KEY CONCEPTS IN CHINESE: RATIO SCALES

等比尺度在自然科学中比较常见，与等距尺度唯一的区别是多了绝对的零。可以做各种数学运算。

Continuous or discrete variables 连续或离散变量

Another distinction between types of quantitative data is whether the scale is continuous or discrete. *Continuous data* result from an infinite number of possible values that correspond to the scale that covers a range of values without gaps, interruptions or jumps. For example, participants' height can be any value: 183.5, 168.7, 155.2, etc.

Discrete data are gathered when the number of possible values is either a finite number or a 'countable' number. For example, the number of visits that you made to the gym each month would be 0, 3 or 5. It would never be 2.5.

8.2.2 Reliability and validity of measurement

Reliability（信度）

As discussed in Chapter 4, the reliability of the measurement scale is established by examining both consistency and stability.

Internal reliability versus external reliability

Frequently, we see that many measures in business and management are made up of several elements (or items, or indicators). The participants are asked to respond to a series of items measuring a particular concept (or construct – for example, 'job satisfaction', 'brand loyalty', 'attitude towards an advert'; see Chapter 6) in the questionnaire. Researchers combine the scores of all the items to produce an overall score, which is then used to represent the measure of that concept.

Internal reliability is used in a situation where a multiple-item measure is used and to see whether the individual items of the measure are actually all measuring the same thing. In other words, internal reliability relates to the coherence of the measurement items. *Cronbach's alpha* can be used to test internal reliability. *External reliability* refers to how well the measure produces the same outcomes over time, when used on different occasions or if presented in different forms.

Students need to be aware of the trade-off between the internal and external reliability of the measure. On the one hand, to increase the internal reliability of a measure, you may intend to remove the 'bad' items. On the other hand, shorter scales tend to have lower external reliability over time. Therefore, researchers should seek a balance between increasing internal reliability while keeping sufficient items to ensure consistency over time (Bryman and Bell, 2011).

Cronbach's alpha is an internal consistency coefficient that indicates how well the items on a measurement scale are positively correlated to one another. The general rule is that a Cronbach's alpha lower than 0.60 is considered to be poor; above 0.70, acceptable; and over 0.80, good. For postgraduate dissertation projects, it is often required that students perform internal consistency tests through SPSS. (Further details on SPSS can be found in books discussing more advanced statistics such as Field (2017) and Pallant (2016).)

KEY CONCEPTS IN CHINESE: CRONBACH'S ALPHA

克隆巴赫（信度）系数，是内部一致性信度系数，它的数值在0～1之间，一般的准则是α> 0.7，是可以接受的内部一致性信度。如果α< 0.7，说明信度很低，问卷质量差。Cronbach's α 可以用SPSS计算。

——————————————————— **Example 8.1** ———————————————————

RELIABILITY CHECK

Meng-Lewis et al. (2013) used a 5-item, 7-point Likert scale modified from Klein et al.'s study (1998) to measure the construct of economic animosity. In this study, economic animosity measures the level of Chinese consumers' antipathy toward a foreign nation related to previous or ongoing economic conflicts.

Based on a sample of 811 Chinese consumers, internal consistency of the measurement scale was tested in SPSS. Cronbach's alpha value for the 5-item scale was .847, indicating good internal consistency. However, if we look into the items further (see Figure 8.1) and pay special attention to the 'Cronbach's alpha if item deleted' column, we would find that measurement reliability would be improved if the first item was removed. The Cronbach's alpha value for the remaining 4-item scale was .856.

	Scale mean if item deleted	Scale variance if item deleted	Corrected item-total correlation	Cronbach's alpha if item deleted
EA1- XX (country) is not a reliable trading partner	16.24	33.248	.502	.856
EA2- XX (country) wants to gain economic power over China	15.96	28.575	.698	.804
EA3- XX (country) is taking advantage of China	16.20	29.782	.701	.803
EA4- XX (country) has too much economic influence on China	16.04	30.758	.651	.817
EA5- XX (country) is doing business unfairly with China	16.11	29.427	.730	.795

Figure 8.1　SPSS output of item-total statistics

FURTHER READING

Leech, N.L., Barrett, K.C. and Morgan, G.A. (2011) *IBM SPSS for Intermediate Statistics: Use and Interpretation*. Hove: Routledge. Chapter 3 offers several methods for computing measurement reliability. In particular, Problem 3.1 illustrates how to compute Cronbach's alpha and gives a detailed interpretation of SPSS output.

Validity （效度）

In Chapter 4, we briefly introduced various types of validity, including measurement validity, internal validity, external validity and ecological validity. Here, we will further discuss measurement validity, that is, the validity of a measure. Measurement validity is concerned with whether or not a measure of a concept/construct actually measures that particular concept/construct. The different types of measurement validity can be seen in Table 8.1. Detailed discussion of how

Table 8.1 Different types of measurement validity

Face validity	Does the content of the measurement scale measure what it is supposed to measure? Face validity is an intuitive process, which is subjective and dependent on individual judgement	表面效度，是最基本的测量效度。它是最容易达成的，以及通过询问其他人（通常是有经验的学者或专家）来判断测量指标（indicators or items）是否真实的测量到所要测量的构念（construct）。
Content validity	This refers to the extent to which a measure represents all facets of a given concept/construct	内容效度，它与表面效度相似，但是更加深入、复杂。它关心的是测量指标是否全面的测量到所要测量的构念，没有遗漏的内容或含义。
Criterion validity	This is concerned with the extent to which a measure is related to an outcome	校标效度，是考查测量指标能够测量到我们想要测量特质的程度。
a. Concurrent validity	This refers to a comparison between the measure in question and an outcome assessed at the same time	a. 同时效度，测量指标与当前想要测量的特质之间的相关程度。
b. Predictive validity	This compares the measure in question with an outcome assessed at a later time	b. 预测效度，测量指标与将来想要测量的特质之间的相关程度。相关系数越高，测验工具的预测效度越高。
Construct validity	This tests whether the measure is actually measuring the underlying concept or construct in question	构念效度，关心的是研究者是否测量到了他想要研究的构念。
a. Convergent validity	This refers to the degree to which two measures of constructs that should be theoretically related are, in fact, observed to be related. In other words, if different types of measures are measuring the same concept, they should also correlate with each other	a. 聚合效度，当测量工具与其他理论上相似的构念的测量工具有相关性的时候，这种效度存在。
b. Discriminant validity	This looks at measures of constructs that theoretically should not be related to each other but are, in fact, observed to be unrelated. In other words, researchers should be able to discriminate between constructs that are dissimilar	b. 区别效度，当测量工具与其他理论上不同的构念的测量工具不相关的时候，这种效度存在。

these different types of validity can be established and tested is beyond the scope of this book. Students interested in knowing more can refer to the further reading recommended at the end of this section.

FURTHER READING

Burns, R.B. and Burns, R.A. (2008) *Business Research Methods and Statistics Using SPSS*. London: Sage. We recommend students read Chapter 17, 'Reliability and Validity', which introduces various types of reliability and validity, and, more importantly, how to use SPSS to assess reliability and validity.

8.2.3 Coding and inputting data

What is a concept?

A *concept* is 'an abstraction or idea formed by the perception of phenomena' (Hair Jr et al., 2016: 224). We use a combination of a number of similar characteristics (items or statements) to describe a concept. These characteristics are seen as variables in quantitative data analysis. Researchers often use *construct* (构念，抽象概念) as an interchangeable term with 'concept'.

Cases, variables and values

A *case* refers to a complete individual unit of analysis. One questionnaire is one case. Therefore, if you have a sample of 150 completed questionnaires, you will have 150 cases. In order to identify each of the cases, a series of unique numbers should be assigned. For example, you could number your 150 samples from 001 to 150.

As mentioned in Chapter 6, typically each of the questions in a questionnaire is a *variable*, and the answer that your respondent gives to this question is called a *value*. *Coding* is the process of assigning a number to a response. We use coding to transform non-computerised data into numeric values so that a computer analysis package (such as SPSS) can recognise and compute them.

Figure 8.2 presents a shortened sample questionnaire which we will use to demonstrate our coding strategy.

In real life, you would repeat the data input procedure for all your completed questionnaires. Figures 8.19 and 8.20 illustrate the data matrix for five questionnaires in SPSS 22.

第一部分：个人资料（选择题请只选<u>1</u>项）

年龄：<u>40</u> record age in years (0 if unknown)

性别：男 □　(1) 女 ✓　(2)

你的最高学历为?

博士 □　　　　　　　　　　　　(1)

研究生 □　　　　　　　　　　　(2)

本科 □　　　　　　　　　　　　(3)

专科 ✓　　　　　　　　　　　　(4)

高中 □　　　　　　　　　　　　(5)

职中/技校 □　　　　　　　　　　(6)

其它（请注明）：_____　　(7)

你在本单位工作年限是 <u>18</u> 年 input value (0 if unknown)

你目前的年薪（税前）是（人民币：元）

40,000 或 以下 □　　　　　　　(1)

40,001–60,000 □　　　　　　　(2)

60,001–100,000 ✓　　　　　　(3)

100,001–180,000 □　　　　　　(4)

180,001–360,000 □　　　　　　(5)

360,001 或 以上 □　　　　　　　(6)

你是在哪个管理阶乘?

非管理人员/普通员工 ✓　　　　　(1)

初级经理 □　　　　　　　　　　(2)

中级经理 □　　　　　　　　　　(3)

高级经理 □　　　　　　　　　　(4)

其它（请注明）：　　　　　　　(5)

第二部分：你在本企业工作的个人经验

要求：请认真阅读以下每一项，然后选出你对该项的态度。每项请用 ✓ 选择一个答案。

调查项目	选择范围					
	非常 不同意		← →			非常 同意
本企业为员工提供稳定的工作（我能看到我职业的长期发展方向）	1	2	3	4	5 ✓	6
本企业为员工及家属提供稳定的福利保障	1	2	3	4	5 ✓	6
本企业不关心我的个人利益	1	2	3 ✓	4	5	6

本企业为了保护员工的利益会牺牲其本身的，短期的利益	1	2 ✓	3	4	5	6
我可以指望本企业付给的工资生活	1	2	3	4 ✓	5	6

第三部分： 你和同事之间的关系

我经常给同事帮忙	1	2	3	4	5	6 ✓
我的同事有困难时可以指望我帮忙	1	2	3	4	5	6 ✓
我认为他人帮了我，我也会帮他们的忙	1	2	3	4	5	6 ✓
当我帮助了同事，他们会很感激	1	2	3	4	5 ✓	6
帮助同事使得我们之间的关系更好了	1	2	3	4	5 ✓	6

Figure 8.2   Sample questionnaire with answers

8.3 DESCRIBING AND EXPLORING DATA

8.3.1 Descriptive analysis

Descriptive analysis is perhaps the most basic statistical analysis. We use descriptive statistics to organise and describe the characteristics of data, such as central tendency, distribution and variability.

Measures of central tendency are often called *averages (均值)*, which contain three types of information – *mean (平均数)*, *median* （中位数） and *mode (众数)*. The mean is a type of average where all the numbers are added up and then divided by the number of numbers. For example, the mean of numbers 2, 4, 3, 5, 1 is 3. The calculation is (2+4+3+5+1)/5 = 3.

The median is the number that occurs at the middle point (or the mean of the two middle numbers) of the list of numbers. To find the median, you have to arrange the list in a numerical order, either in an increasing or decreasing magnitude. For example, the median of 1.10, 3.48, 4.50, 4.85, 6.23 is the middle number 4.50. If 6.23 was not included, the median of the list would be the average of 3.48 and 4.50, which is 3.99. Note that we have arranged the numbers in an increasing order to start with.

The mode is the value that occurs with the greatest frequency. One data set can have one, more than one, or no mode. For example, the modes of the list 1, 2, 2, 3, 5, 7, 7 are 2 and 7. Mode is the only measure of central tendency that can be used with nominal data – for example, the mode of colours 'red', 'yellow', 'yellow', 'blue' is 'yellow'.

Mean, median and mode as measures of central tendency offer information on the centre of the distribution of the data. Another way of looking at the distribution of data is to focus on its extent. *Range* （全距，极差）measures the distance between the greatest and the lowest value in a set of numbers. For example, the range of 1, 2, 2, 3, 5, 7, 7 is 7–1 = 6 (see also Figure 8.3).

Statistics

education

N	Valid	461
	Missing	0
Mean		2.32
Median		2.00
Mode		2
Std deviation		.905
Range		4

Education

		Frequency	Percentage	Valid percentage	Cumulative percentage
Valid	High school or less	83	18.0	18.0	18.0
	College	192	41.6	41.6	59.7
	Undergraduate bachelor	151	32.8	32.8	92.4
	Masters	25	5.4	5.4	97.8
	PhD	10	2.2	2.2	100.0
	Total	461	100.0	100.0	

Figure 8.3 An example of descriptive statistics in SPSS

KEY CONCEPTS IN CHINESE: STANDARD DEVIATION

标准差，也称均方差，反映一个数据集的离散程度 （dispersion）。平均数相同的一组数据，标准差不一定相同。标准差越小，这些值偏离平均值越少，反之亦然。我们通常接受 ∓1.96 以内的标准差。

8.3.2 Graphical representations

Graphs are helpful when you are trying to convey a lot of information to readers as they can visually represent any pattern in your results. In Figures 8.4 and 8.5, we asked our respondents (n = 461) how much money they had spent on sports in the last three years.

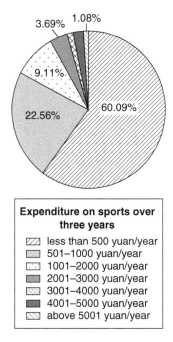

Figure 8.4 An example of a pie chart

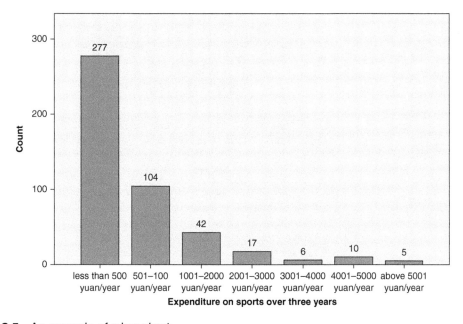

Figure 8.5 An example of a bar chart

TOP TIPS 小建议

- 饼状图常用来描述量、频率或者百分比之间的相对关系。
- 别忘记显示每个扇形的统计量。
- 避免出示 100% 或者 50% 对 50% 的饼图。

Likert scales are often used in dissertations and other research projects. To clearly represent the results, the two types of bar charts in Figures 8.6 and 8.7 are recommended. The measurement scale uses a 5-item, 6-point Likert scale to measure the construct of *guanxi* (see Figure 8.2, section 3 for the questions).

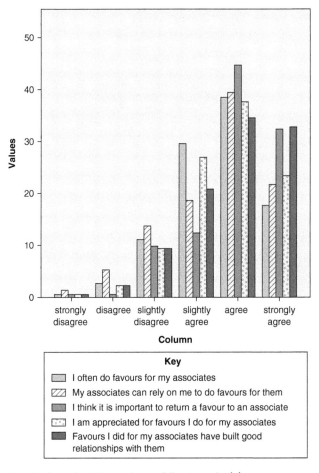

Figure 8.6   An example of a bar chart based on a Likert scale (a)

Note: The values on the y axis indicate percentages.

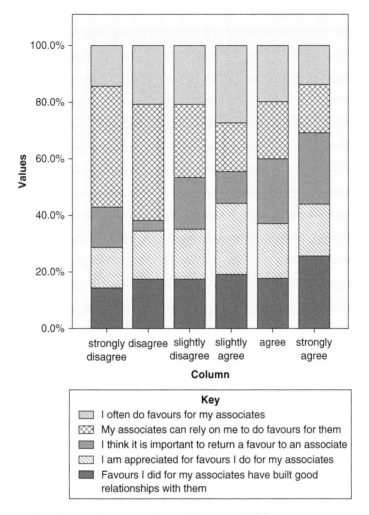

Figure 8.7 An example of a bar chart based on a Likert scale (b)

TOP TIPS 小建议

为了更清楚的展示Likert scales的测量结果，建议计算它每个测量指标的平均值（mean value）。如整个构念的，建议计算它每个测量指标的平均值（mean value）。如上例中的构念 Guanxi, 我们可以得到的各个测量指标均值分别为：

(Continued)

	I often do favours for my associates	My associates can rely on me to do favours for them	I think it is important to return a favour to an associate	I am appreciated for favours I do for my associates	Favours I did for my associates have built good relationships with them
N Valid	226	226	226	226	226
Missing	0	0	0	0	0
Mean	4.56	4.54	4.97	4.69	4.85
Std deviation	1.019	1.200	.975	1.028	1.077

Figure 8.8 SPSS output of mean and standard deviation of a Likert scale

进一步计算得出的整个构念的均值为：Mean guanxi = 4.72 (SD = .85)

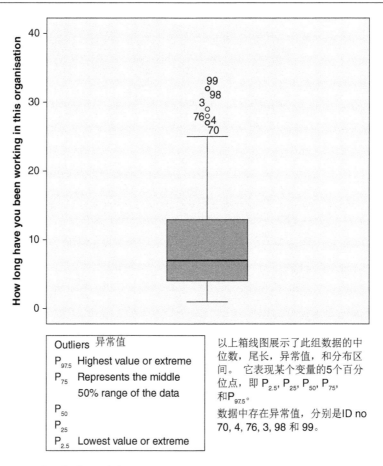

Outliers 异常值

$P_{97.5}$ Highest value or extreme

P_{75} Represents the middle
       50% range of the data

P_{50}

P_{25}

$P_{2.5}$ Lowest value or extreme

以上箱线图展示了此组数据的中位数，尾长，异常值，和分布区间。它表现某个变量的5个百分位点，即 $P_{2.5}$, P_{25}, P_{50}, P_{75}, 和 $P_{97.5}$。

数据中存在异常值，分别是ID no 70, 4, 76, 3, 98 和 99。

Figure 8.9 An example of a box plot

8.4. EXAMINING RELATIONSHIPS AND DIFFERENCES

8.4.1 Examining your hypotheses

In Chapter 4, we introduced the definition of *hypothesis*, including the concept of null and alternative hypotheses (H_0 and H_1). The general steps for hypothesis development and testing are:

1. Set up the null and alternative hypotheses (see Chapter 4).
2. Choose a **level of significance** (α) at 0.05 or 0.01.
3. Select the appropriate statistical test depending on the type of measurement scales used (i.e. nominal, ordinal, interval or ratio).
4. Use statistical software (e.g. SPSS) to analyse your data and judge whether the significance level is met, based on the ***p-value***.
5. Make the conclusion whether the null hypothesis is rejected, and the alternative one is accepted; or the other way around.

KEY CONCEPTS IN CHINESE: STATISTICAL SIGNIFICANCE, SIGNIFICANCE LEVEL AND *P*-VALUE

统计显著性，是指原假设 (null hypothesis) 为真的情况下拒绝原假设所要承担的风险。

显著性水平α，是指正确的原假设遭到拒绝的错误发生概率，它是一个概率值。一般取0.1，0.05或者 0.01 等数值。显著性水平的具体数值是由研究者根据研究目的，有关条件，假设检验量等具体情况主观确定的，是预先设定好的。总而言之，由于假设检验是根据样本提供的信息进行推断的，所以我们就有犯错误的可能。当原假设正确，而我们却把它当成错误的加以拒绝，犯这种错误的概率就是显著性水平 α，也就是决策中面临的风险。

*P*值。，要评估统计显著性，我们可以检查检验的 *p*-value，如果p值低于指定的显著性水平 α （通常为 0.1，0.05 或者 0.01)，则可作为'原假设不成立'的有力证据。

TOP TIPS 小建议: HOW TO PROPOSE A HYPOTHESIS

Note that, in practice, statistical inference can be done without a null hypothesis. In fact, most academic papers do not state the null hypotheses. Sample hypotheses are provided:

H_1: Consumer ethnocentrism will be negatively related to judgements of the foreign sponsor's products.

H_2: Consumer ethnocentrism will be positively related to judgements of the domestic sponsor's products.

(Continued)

From the above two examples, we can see that a hypothesis would include both independent and dependent variables and clearly state the direction (either negative or positive) of the relationship. Alternatively, you can hypothesise between groups:

H$_3$: Male employees have a higher level of work-life balance than female employees.

H$_4$: Male employees have a higher level of job satisfaction than female employees.

H$_3$ and H$_4$ are examples of hypotheses that compare group differences.

8.4.2 Statistical errors: Type I and Type II

Based on the previous discussion, we can see that we do not use statistics to 'prove' anything; instead, we use statistical tests to find out the *likelihood* (or *probability*) that our results come from random fluctuations in sampling. Statistical testing helps us to make a decision regarding whether we are confident enough to either reject or accept a hypothesis. However, it is possible that we will make some errors. Type I error happens when rejecting the null hypothesis when it is true. Type II error happens when accepting the null hypothesis when it is false. Table 8.2 describes the differences between Type I and Type II errors.

Table 8.2 Type I versus Type II errors 区分第一型及第二型错误

真实情况	根据研究结果得到的结论	
	拒绝H$_0$	接受H$_0$
H$_0$ 是正确的	第一型错误	正确判断
H$_0$是错误的	正确判断	第二型错误

8.4.3 Comparing group differences

The *independent samples t-test* is used to test whether there is a *statistically* significant difference between the means in two unrelated groups. The null hypothesis for the independent t-test is that the population means from the two independent groups are equal: H$_0$: $\mu_1 = \mu_2$. The alternative hypothesis is that the population means are not equal: H$_1$: $\mu_1 \neq \mu_2$. We then set a *significance level* (α) to allow us to either reject or accept the null hypothesis. The significance level (α) is often set at 0.05.

The reason for conducting t-tests is that when we are comparing the differences between scores for two groups, we have to take into consideration their means related to the spread of variability of their scores. In the three graphs in Figure 8.10, the mean difference is the same in all three scenarios. However, it is clear that the two groups in graph c (low variability) appear to have little overlap in their distributions. Hence, the difference between the groups is larger than those in graphs a and c. The two groups in graph b (high variability) appear to have the smallest difference as there is plenty of overlap in their distribution.

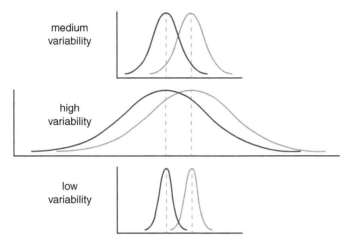

Figure 8.10 Three scenarios for differences between means

We demonstrate how to interpret t-test results in example 8.2.

Example 8.2

INTERPRETING T-TEST RESULTS

Based on a foreign country group (sample size 811) and a domestic country group (sample size 461), we attempt to examine whether there is a significant mean difference between the two unrelated Chinese sample groups regarding three constructs – *product judgement*, *attitudes towards the sponsor* and *purchase intention*. All three constructs are measured by 7-point Likert scales. For each construct, the significance of the F score is first checked to see if the variances are equal across the two respondent groups. The variances

Table 8.3 Comparing means across groups

Construct	Country group	N	Mean	Std deviation	Std error mean
AS	foreign	810	4.644	1.197	.0420
	domestic	460	5.742	1.215	.0567
PJ	foreign	811	4.476	1.142	.0401
	domestic	460	4.402	1.324	.0617
WBS	foreign	811	4.111	1.357	.0476
	domestic	461	4.918	1.562	.0728

Note: Cases with missing values are excluded from the t-tests

(Continued)

Table 8.4 Independent samples test

	Levene's test for equality of variances		t-test for equality of means					95% confidence interval of the difference	
	F	Sig.	t	df	Sig. (2-tailed)	Mean difference	Std error difference	Upper	Lower
AS Equal variances assumed	6.114	.014	-15.632	1268	.000	-1.098	.070	-1.236	-.960
Equal variances not assumed			-15.566	941.584	.000	-1.098	.071	-1.237	-.960
PJ Equal variances assumed	13.368	.000	1.046	1269	.296	.074	.071	-.065	.213
Equal variances not assumed			1.004	842.974	.316	.074	.074	-.071	.218
WBS Equal variances assumed	51.446	.000	-9.636	1270	.000	-.806	.084	-.971	-.642
Equal variances not assumed			-9.271	850.180	.000	-.806	.087	-.977	-.636

across two groups will be equal where a non-significant F score is observed. Otherwise, a significant F score indicates that the variances between groups are not equal. The t value is then checked in order to assess if the mean values are statistically different from each other, either under the situation of equal variance assumed or equal variance not assumed. The results are interpreted below (also see Tables 8.3 and 8.4).

Significant variance differences are found across the two respondent groups (the p-values for the F ratios are all below .05, which are statistically significant). Then, when the equal variances are not assumed, the significance of t values is checked. The findings are summarised as follows. In particular:

i.   Significant t values are found for the two variables, i.e. attitudes towards the sponsor and willingness to buy from the sponsor ($T_{AS} = -15.57$, $p_{AS} = .00$; $T_{WBS} = -9.27$, $p_{WBS} = .00$). Thus, significant mean differences on these three variables exist across the foreign and domestic country groups. It is clear that Chinese consumers have more positive attitudes towards the domestic sponsor than the foreign ones (M_{AS} for the foreign country group is 4.644 and for the domestic country group is 5.74). Also, Chinese consumers are more willing to buy domestic sponsors' products than those of foreign sponsors (M_{WBS} are 4.92 for the China group and 4.11 for the foreign country group).
ii.   Under the assumption of unequal variances, a non-significant t value is obtained for the variable product judgements ($T_{PJ} = 1.00$, $p_{PJ} = .32$). This means that Chinese consumers have equal judgements of domestic and foreign products.

8.4.4 Assessing the strength of association between two variables

Correlation is a statistical technique that shows whether and how strongly a pair of variables is related. For example, height and shoe size are related; taller people tend to have a bigger shoe size than shorter people. Correlation can tell you how much of the variation in people's shoe size is related to their height. In our case, there is a *positive correlation* as when one variable (height) increases, the other one (shoe size) also increases. *Negative correlation* happens when there is an inverse relationship between the pair of variables – that is, when one variable decreases, the other increases. For example, as a person does more exercise, their body weight decreases.

To quantify the strength of the association between a pair of variables, we use a *correlation coefficient* (usually represented by the letter *r*). The value of *r* must always fall between +1 (perfect positive correlation) and –1 (perfect negative correlation). In between, as *r* tends towards 0, means that the variables are uncorrelated.

KEY CONCEPTS IN CHINESE: CORRELATION COEFFICIENT (*r*)

相关系数，是衡量两个变量之间线性相关程度的指标。取值在 +1 与 -1 之间

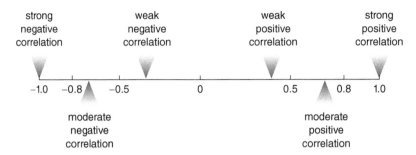

Figure 8.11 Values of the correlation coefficient

Source: adapted from Saunders et al. (2016)

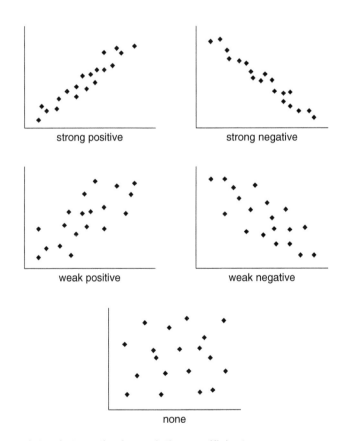

Figure 8.12 Scatter plots of strength of correlation coefficient

--- **Example 8.3** ---

CORRELATION COEFFICIENT

McLaren (2012) examined the correlation between someone's height (in inches) and shoe size (US sizes) based on a sample of 408 college students. First, a scatter diagram was generated to see visually if there was an association.

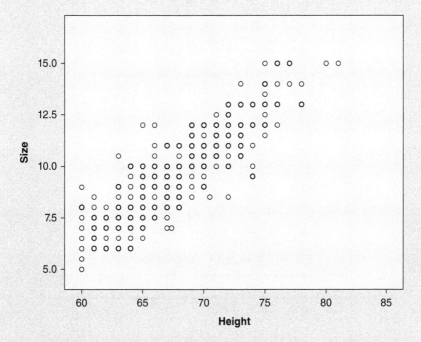

Figure 8.13   Scatter plot: height and shoe size

Figure 8.13 does suggest some positive correlations between height and shoe size.

Next, we calculated the correlation coefficient to show the strength of this association. **Pearson's r** (or **Pearsonian Correlation Coefficient**) is used in this case as it evaluates the linear relationship between two continuous variables.

A correlation coefficient of 0.871 indicates a very strong (but not perfect) positive correlation between height and shoe size. The correlation is statistically significant at $p < 0.01$ level. However, remember that although these two variables are strongly correlated, it does not necessarily indicate cause and effect.

(Continued)

		Size	Height
Size	Pearson correlation	1	.871**
	Sig. (2-tailed)		.000
	N	408	408
Height	Pearson correlation	.871**	1
	Sig. (2-tailed)	.000	
	N	408	408

Figure 8.14 SPSS output: correlation between height and shoe size

Note: ** Correlation is significant at the 0.01 level (2-tailed)

Example 8.4 shows the situation when we are analysing one or more ordinal variables.

— **Example 8.4** —

CORRELATION COEFFICIENT WITH ONE OR MORE ORDINAL VARIABLES

			CE	CA
Spearman's rho	CE	Correlation coefficient	1.000	.204**
		Sig. (2-tailed)	.	.000
		N	811	811
	CA	Correlation coefficient	.204**	1.000
		Sig. (2-tailed)	.000	.
		N	811	811

Figure 8.15 SPSS output: correlation between consumer ethnocentrism（消费者民族中心主义）and animosity（敌意）

Note: ** Correlation is significant at the 0.01 level (2-tailed)

We wish to examine the association between consumer ethnocentrism and consumer animosity based on a sample of 811. Note that both variables are ordinal variables (measured by multi-item Likert scales) and therefore Spearman's rho was used to assess the correlation (Figure 8.15).

A correlation coefficient of 0.204 indicates a weak positive correlation between levels of consumer ethnocentrism and animosity, although this correlation is statistically significant at $p < .01$ (McLaren, 2012). This is probably due to the large sample size.

ATTENTION!

Correlation does not mean causation! 两个变量相关不等于它们有因果关系。 不能用相关分析代替回归分析 (regression analysis)。相关分析的目的在于检验两个随机变量的共变趋势（即共同变化的程度），回归分析的目的则在于试图用自变量来预测因变量的值。

8.4.5 Assessing the strength of causal effect between dependent and independent variables

While correlation shows the strength of relationship between pairs of variables, it does not help us to forecast values for the dependent variable based on the values of the independent variable. *Regression* is useful in making predictions.

Line of best fit

A regression equation is represented in the following form:

$$y = a + bx$$

(where)

x = the independent variable

y = the dependent variable

a = the y-intercept (where the line crosses the y axis; the value of y when x = 0)

b = the slope of the line of best fit (**regression coefficient**).

─────── **Example 8.5** ───────

SIMPLE LINEAR REGRESSION

We still use McLaren's (2012) data set to illustrate an example of simple linear regression（线性回归）. It may be reasonable to assume that height predicts shoe size. Using all 408 observations, a scatter plot can be created. In order to illustrate the potential linear relationship between the two variables, the

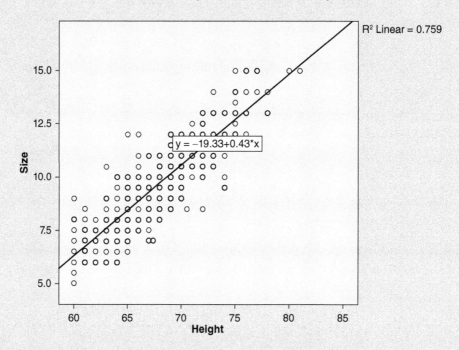

Figure 8.16   Scatter plot: height and shoe size with line of best fit

Coefficients[a]

Model		Unstandardised coefficients		Standardised coefficients		
		B	Std error	Beta	t	Sig.
1	(Constant)	-19.327	.820		-23.565	.000
	Height	.427	.012	.871	35.713	.000

Figure 8.17   SPSS output: regression table between height and shoe size

Note: a. Dependent variable: size

line of best fit is also generated (see Figure 8.16). The line helps us to make predictions of the likely values of the dependent variable for any specific values of the independent variable.

Figure 8.17 tells us the regression coefficient which is 0.427, statistically significant at the p < 0.01 level. We can also write out the linear regression equation as follows, based on the regression equation provided at the beginning of section 8.3.5:

$$y = -19.327 + 0.427 \times \text{shoe size} = -19.327 + 0.427 \text{ height}$$

This implies that for every inch of increase in one's height, shoe size will increase by 0.427. Therefore, we may conclude that if someone's height is 70 inches, then their shoe size will be:

$$y = -19.327 + 0.427 \times 70 = 10.563, \text{ i.e. a size of 10 and a half}$$

TOP TIPS 小建议: DISTINGUISHING BETWEEN CORRELATION AND REGRESSION

回归分析和相关分析是互相补充、密切联系的。相关分析需要回归分析来表明现象数量关系的具体形式，而回归分析则应该建立在相关分析的基础上。主要区别有：
一，在回归分析中，要根据变量的地位、作用不同区分出自变量和因变量，把因变量置于被解释，待预测的特殊地位。在相关分析中，变量间的地位是完全平等的，没有自变量和因变量之分。
二，相关分析只限于描述变量间相互依存关系的密切程度，至于相关变量间的定量联系关系则无法明确反映。而回归分析不仅可以定量揭示自变量对应变量的影响大小，还可以通过回归方程对变量值进行预测和控制。

FURTHER READING

Chikkodi, C.M. and Satyaprasad, B.G. (2009) *Business Statistics*. Delhi, Nagpur, Banglore, Hyderabad: Himalaya Publishing House. Chapter 12 introduces different types of correlation, methods of determining correlation and interpretation of results. Many examples and exercises are provided. Chapter 14 focuses on regression methods and provides details on regression equation and estimation. This book is recommended for students who want a good statistical background of the correlation and regression methods.

Taylor, R. (1990) Interpretation of the correlation coefficient: A basic review. *Journal of Diagnostic Medical Sonography* 6(1): 35-9. This article discusses the basic aspects of correlation analysis and provides interpretations and limitations of the correlation coefficient. Although the examples used are taken from medical journals, the insights can be applied in a wider context.

8.5 INTRODUCTION TO SPSS

8.5.1 Getting started in SPSS

SPSS (the name originally stood for Statistical Package for the Social Sciences) was introduced in the mid-1960s and over the last five decades has undergone many revisions. It is now known as IBM SPSS Statistics and the version that we have used for demonstration in this book is Version 22.

SPSS

原名为社会科学统计软件包，是一个大型通用的专业统计分析软件。它具有以下特点：

- 专业级的统计分析功能，能够进行基本简单和复杂经典的统计分析；
- 强大的数据管理能力，能够直观容易的输入，编辑，提取，转换绝大多数常用软件的数据文件类型；
- 强大的统计图形和制表功能；
- 可以采用简便直观的菜单操作或者先进强大的程序语言操作；
- 全部的分析结果和操作过程都可以在系统日志中完整的反映出来。

TOP TIPS 小建议: BASIC ANALYTICAL PROCEDURES IN SPSS

使用SPSS 进行数据分析的5个基本步骤：

1. 输入数据到SPSS （Data Editor 数据编辑窗口中的File 菜单）
2. 数据准备，包括数据核查，筛选，数据转换，编码等（Data 和 Transform 菜单）
3. 选择分析方法，分析过程和生成图标 （Analyse 和 Graphs 菜单）
4. 选择分析的变量和观察个体 （Data 菜单）
5. 运行分析过程和浏览分析结果（Viewer 结果浏览窗口）

Defining variables and entering data

Once SPSS is opened, you will see two workbooks: Data View and Variable View at the bottom left of the window.

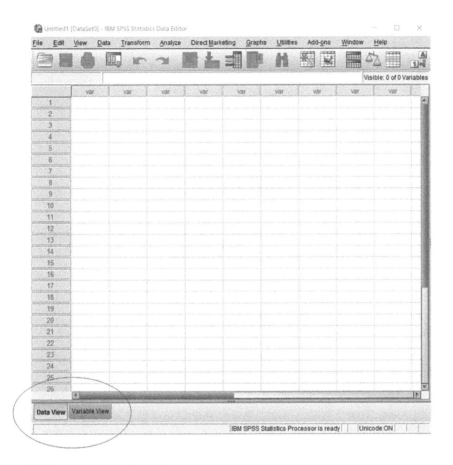

Figure 8.18   SPSS blank data editor window

Reprint Courtesy of International Business Machines Corporation, © International Business Machines Corporation.

Based on the questionnaire shown in Figure 8.2, a sample data matrix in SPSS is presented in Figure 8.18.

	ID	age	gender	education	tenure	salary	managerial_le vel	RC1steady_e mployment	RC2benefits	RC3concerns reversed	RC4interests	RC5wages_b enefits	Guanxi1	Guanxi2	Guanxi3	Guanxi4	Guanxi5
1		40	2	4	18	3	1	5	5	4	2	4	6	6	6	5	5
2	2	35	2	4	17	3	1	6	6	4	6	6	6	6	6	4	6
3	3	45	2	4	29	2	1	4	4	3	5	1	5	3	5	6	6
4	4	50	1	4	28	3	1	4	4	5	1	5	3	5	6	6	6
5	5	50	1	3	25	4	3	4	4	5	1	5	4	5	6	6	6

Figure 8.19   SPSS data view

Reprint Courtesy of International Business Machines Corporation, © International Business Machines Corporation.

In the Data View (Figure 8.19), you can browse, modify and edit values of your data. Every row indicates an observed case; and every column represents a variable.

	Name	Type	Width	Decimals	Label	Values
1	ID	Numeric	8	0	id	None
2	age	Numeric	8	0	age	None
3	gender	Numeric	6	0	gender	{1, male}...
4	education	Numeric	8	0	education	{1, PHD}...
5	tenure	Numeric	8	0	how long have been working in this organisation	None
6	salary	Numeric	8	0	what is your annual salary before tax	{1, < 40,000}...
7	managerial_level	Numeric	8	0	what is your managerial level	{1, non-managerial}...
8	RC1steady_employment	Numeric	8	0	my organization offers steady employment	{1, strongly disagree}...
9	RC2benefits	Numeric	8	0	my organization offers stable benefits to employee and their families	{1, strongly disagree}...
10	RC3concerns_reversed	Numeric	8	0	my organization is responsive to employee concerns and well-being	{1, strongly disagree}...
11	RC4interests	Numeric	8	0	my organization scrafices its short-term interests for employee interests	{1, strongly disagree}...
12	RC5wages_benefits	Numeric	8	0	my organization offers wages and benefits I can count on	{1, strongly disagree}...
13	Guanxi1	Numeric	8	0	i often do favors for my associates	{1, strongly disagree}...
14	Guanxi2	Numeric	8	0	my associates can rely on me to do favors for them	{1, strongly disagree}...
15	Guanxi3	Numeric	8	0	I think it is important to return a favor to an associate	{1, strongly disagree}...
16	Guanxi4	Numeric	8	0	I am appreciated for favors I do for my associates	{1, strongly disagree}...
17	Guanxi5	Numeric	8	0	favors I did for my associates have built good relationships with them	{1, strongly disagree}...

Figure 8.20 SPSS variable view

Reprint Courtesy of International Business Machines Corporation, © International Business Machines Corporation.

In the Variable View (Figure 8.20), you can define and name variables.

TOP TIPS 小建议: CODING SPECIAL CASES

- Missing data. 问卷调查中时常会遇到缺失的数据，在SPSS中输入这些缺失值时，只需要略过这一格即可 (leave any missing values as blank cells)。
- Reverse scoring. 要特别留意反向计分题，这些题目所表达的含义与其他题目相反，因此得分的方向和其他题目也是相反的。例如，Figure 8.2 中的第9个问题就属于反向题，需要反向计分。反向题可以通过SPSS的 '重新编码'的方法来处理。

Recoding variables 对变量进行重新编码

Transform → Recode into same/different variables, then choose the variables that you want to recode, then click on **Old and New Values** to input the new values (Figure 8.21).

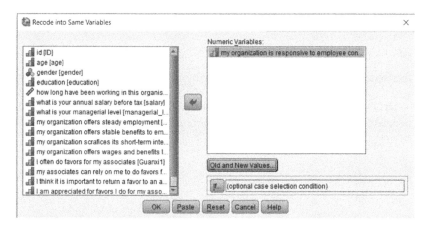

Figure 8.21   Recoding into same variables

Reprint Courtesy of International Business Machines Corporation, © International Business Machines Corporation.

Computing a new variable

Transform → **Compute Variable**, then you can create a new variable under **Target Variable** cell, and use the listed Numeric Expression and existing variables to create a new variable (Figure 8.22).

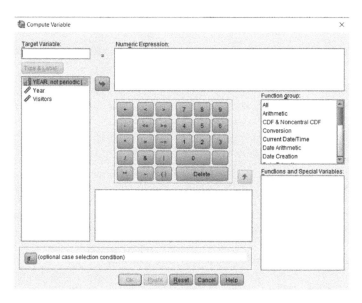

Figure 8.22   Computing variable

Reprint Courtesy of International Business Machines Corporation, © International Business Machines Corporation.

8.5.2 Data analysis with SPSS

Descriptive analysis

- Generating a frequency table

    Analyse → **Descriptive Statistics** → **Frequencies**, click on **Statistics** to choose the types of descriptive statistics that you want to perform on your data (Figure 8.23).

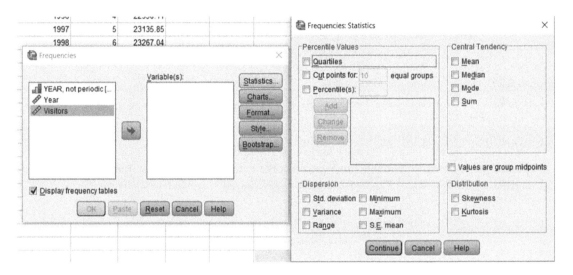

Figure 8.23   Generating a frequency table in SPSS

Reprint Courtesy of International Business Machines Corporation, © International Business Machines Corporation.

- Drawing graphs

    Graphs → **Chart Builder**

    Select **Pie/Polar (Bar, Histogram or Boxplot)** from the Gallery box on the bottom left and drag one type of chart to the blank area – 'chart preview' (top right)

    Drag and drop the relevant variable to the axis in 'chart preview'

    Click **OK** to execute (Figure 8.24).

Once you have a chart, you can edit it by double-clicking on the chart.

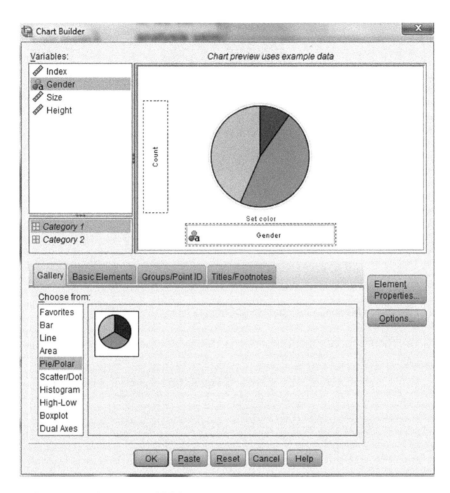

Figure 8.24 Drawing a pie chart in SPSS

Reprint Courtesy of International Business Machines Corporation, © International Business Machines Corporation.

TOP TIPS 小建议

When drawing a graph, try to select the option **Show Data Labels** in the **Element** drop-down box.

For example, the graph in Figure 8.25 shows both the percentages and counts of each of the segments.

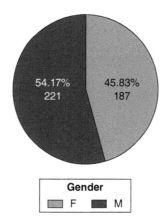

Figure 8.25   Showing data labels on graphs

Independent samples t-test

Analysis → Compare Means → Independent Samples t-test (Figure 8.26).

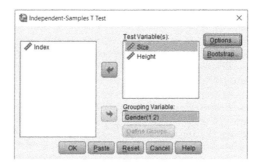

Figure 8.26   Independent samples t-test

Reprint Courtesy of International Business Machines Corporation, © International Business Machines Corporation.

Choose the variables that you want to test and use Define Groups to assign values to the grouping variable. In our case above, we want to see if there are significant differences between female (1) and male (2) groups regarding their shoe sizes and heights.

Correlation analysis

- Generating scatter diagrams

  Graphs → Chart Builder → Scatter/Dot

In Figure 8.27, we want to explore how height relates to shoe size visually by putting Height on the **X axis** and Shoe Size on the **Y axis**.

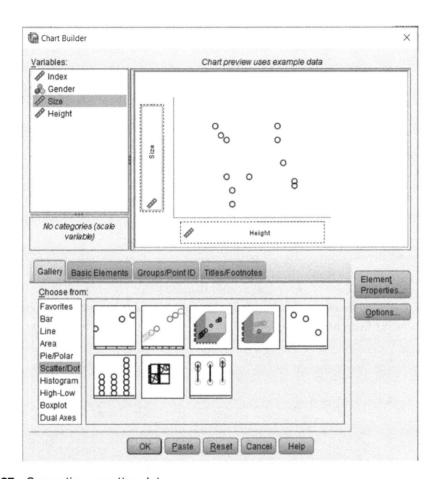

Figure 8.27   Generating a scatter plot

Reprint Courtesy of International Business Machines Corporation, © International Business Machines Corporation.

- Generating Pearson's r and Spearman's rho

    Analyse → Correlate → Bivariate

In Figure 8.28, both tested variables Shoe Size and Height are continuous, and hence **Pearson's r** is selected.

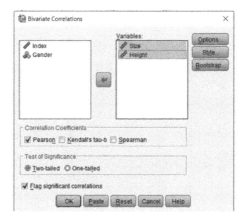

Figure 8.28 An example of bivariate correlations

Reprint Courtesy of International Business Machines Corporation, © International Business Machines Corporation.

Regression analysis

- Generating scatter diagrams and line of best fit

Repeat the general procedure of generating scatter diagrams (see Figure 8.27), and once the scatter graph is generated, double-click it to activate the **Chart Editor**. To show the regression line, click on **Elements → Fit Line at Total** (Figure 8.29).

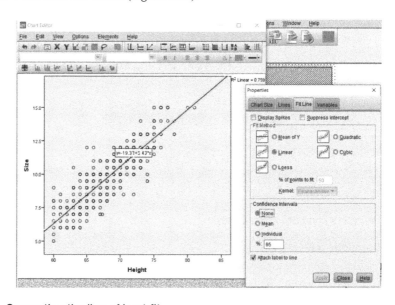

Figure 8.29 Generating the line of best fit

Reprint Courtesy of International Business Machines Corporation, © International Business Machines Corporation.

To calculate the regression coefficients, follow **Analyse → Regression → Linear**.

We intend to find out any cause–effect relationship between height (independent) and shoe size (dependent) in Figure 8.30.

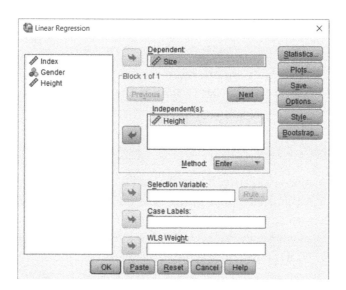

Figure 8.30　An example of linear regression

Reprint Courtesy of International Business Machines Corporation, © International Business Machines Corporation.

8.5.3 Frequently used operations in SPSS

- Reading data files

In addition to reading IBM SPSS Statistics data files, data can be imported from a number of different sources, including Excel, Stata, SAS and text files.

From the menus, choose: **File → Open → Data…** then choose a specific file type.

- Saving your data

From the menus, choose: **File → Save as…** to save data in the default IBM SPSS Statistics format: (.sav).

You can also save data in a wide variety of external formats, such as Excel, SAS and Stata.

The outputs of your analysis can be saved in the default format of SPSS Viewer Files: (.spv). From the menus, choose: **File → Save as…**

- Printing output

From the IBM SPSS Statistics Viewer window, choose **File → Print**.

FURTHER READING

Pallant, J. (2016) *SPSS Survival Manual: A Step-by-step Guide to Data Analysis Using IBM SPSS*, 6th edition. Basingstoke: Open University Press. This book is very easy to follow and understand. Key concepts are clearly defined and it is a useful book for someone who has little statistical knowledge.

For students who would like to learn more about statistics, we recommend:

Salkind, N.J. (2014) *Statistics for People Who (Think They) Hate Statistics*, 5th edition. London: Sage. This book introduces the fundamentals of basic statistics and is very clear and easy to follow.

8.6 REPORTING QUANTITATIVE RESULTS

At this stage, congratulations, you are half way through your research project. It means you have completed the research design, gone through data collection, run a number of statistic calculations and now you are faced with a huge amount of exciting results. Reporting your quantitative results is not easy, as the value of your research depends on how you communicate your results with your readers. As Abelson (1995) indicated, quantitative data analysis should 'make an interesting claim; it should tell a story that an informed audience will care about and it should do so by intelligent interpretation of appropriate evidence' (p. 2).

TOP TIPS 小建议： REPORTING YOUR QUANTITATIVE FINDINGS

- Use visual representation to display your results. However, do not put everything in the main text; use appendices wisely and only keep the most interesting graphs in the main body of your dissertation. For example, do not present the whole questionnaire and results for each of the questions in the main text.
- Distinguish between statistical and substantive significance. 区分统计上的显著性和实际上的显著性。我们通过样本统计、假设检验推断出的是 statistical significance, 而并没有证明 substantive significance。
- When interpreting the results, put them in your research context. The figures in graphs and tables do not speak for themselves and are subject to your interpretation within a specific research context.
- Try to use simple statistics and models where possible. Do not be over-ambitious and apply complex statistics and models when you have simpler options.
- Think about the generalisability of your findings. Are the findings also applicable in other contexts?
- Reflect on the credibility of your research. What are the limitations of your research, both methodologically and theoretically?

REFERENCES

Abelson, R.P. (1995) *Statistics as Principled Argument*. Hillsdale, NJ: Lawrence Erlbaum.

Bryman, A. and Bell, E. (2011) *Business Research Methods*, 3rd edition. Oxford: Oxford University Press.

Field, A. (2017) *Discovering Statitics Using SPSS*, 5th edition, London: Sage.

Hair, Jr J.F., Wolfinbarger, M., Money, A.H., et al. (2016) *Essentials of Business Research Methods*, 3rd edition. London: Routledge.

Klein, J., Ettenson, R. and Morris, M. (1998) The animosity model of foreign product purchase: An empirical test in the People's Republic of China. *The Journal of Marketing* 62(Jan.): 89–100.

McGivern, Y. (2009) *The Practice of Market Research: An Introduction*, 3rd edition. Upper Saddle River, NJ: Prentice Hall.

McLaren, C. (2012) Using the height and shoe size data to introduce correlation and regression. *Journal of Statistics Education* 20(3): 1–9.

Meng-Lewis, Y., Thwaites, D. and Pillai, K.G. (2013) Consumers' responses to sponsorship by foreign companies. *European Journal of Marketing* 47(11/12): 1910–30.

Pallant, J. (2016) *SPSS Survival Mannual*, 6th edition, Maidenhead: Open University Press.

Saunders, M., Lewis, P. and Thornhill, A. (2016) *Research Methods for Business Students*, 7th edition. Harlow: Pearson.

9
CULTURE, LANGUAGE AND TRANSLATION

9.1 INTERPLAY BETWEEN CULTURE AND LANGUAGE

As we mentioned in previous chapters, the majority of Chinese scholars and students collect data in the Chinese language (or, rather, family of languages, as we discuss below) and write up their work in English in the form of either a journal article or a dissertation. Regardless of the method we choose, we are inevitably confronted by matters of language, culture and translation during this process. Yet, surprisingly, these matters and even the problems are rarely discussed in conventional books about research methods, with the notable exception of Marschan-Piekkari and Welch (2004) who devoted a chapter in their book to language issues in cross-cultural interviews. From experience, we have discovered that these issues are highly problematic and contentious. Primarily, this chapter considers some essential problems, debates, strategies and techniques in relation to handling cross-cultural differences, language and translation.

Throughout this book, we have repeatedly suggested that Chinese culture and society have marked differences from their Western counterparts. Culturists Hofstede and Bond (1988) suggest that the Chinese culture, which is strongly influenced by Confucian teaching, emphasises the following four principles:

1. The stability of society is based on unequal relationships between people.
2. The family is the prototype of all social organisations.
3. Virtuous behaviour toward others consists of treating others as one would like to be treated oneself.
4. Virtue with regard to one's tasks in life consists of trying to acquire skills and education, working hard, not spending more than necessary, being patient and persevering.

A growing body of literature in the business and management discipline has highlighted the significance of Confucianism and neo-Confucianism in modern Chinese businesses and organisations (Warner, 2010; Zhu, 2009). However, culture cannot be separated from language and discourse (Wong and Poon, 2010). Linguistic anthropologist Sapir (1921) maintains that language is the symbolic guide to culture. He argues that grammatical structures are not just tools for communicating ideas but templates for thought itself, and thus help to construct meanings. Language and discourse, in the form of daily practice, define what is 'acceptable' and determine what people can do, say, feel and know. On the other hand, cultural meanings are not self-contained. They are constituted in and through social interaction, particularly in discourse. Appreciating the interplay between culture and language is important, when carrying out context-related research. Wong and Poon (2010: 152) point out that

> The understanding of culture – as a system of dynamic, ambiguous, and conflicting meanings, intertwined with language and discourse, mediated by power, to create and recreate the sociocultural world – is critical to the discussion and debates about translation in cross-cultural research.

The rest of this chapter will examine the different issues we encounter at various stages of the research with regard to culture, language and translation through a consideration of examples.

9.2 INTERVIEW LANGUAGE

Language issues should be taken into consideration as early as the research design stage. The official language in mainland China is Mandarin （普通话）. Yet, the family of Chinese languages includes a diverse range of languages (such as Mongolic, Turkic and Tibetan) and dialects (such as Cantonese, Sichuanese and Fukienese), to name but a few. Although over 90% of Chinese people can speak Mandarin, many people (especially those from Southern China) also speak a dialect. Since the economic reform, the number of people who can speak English has also increased. Elsewhere in other Chinese societies, many people are bilingual or even trilingual speakers. For example, most Singaporeans can switch between speaking fluent Mandarin, Cantonese and English, while in Macau, local residents can switch between Cantonese, English and Portuguese. Recently, a number of international scholars have noticed that the choice of interview language may affect the quality of the data (Welch and Piekkari, 2006; Xian, 2008). Given the prevalence of English as the language in which research is reported (such as a postgraduate dissertation), there are concerns regarding the validity of interviews using non-English. Some propose that international researchers should use English in interviews, wherever possible, to avoid the 'problematic of translation', reduce 'noise' and provide greater 'convenience in the analysis' (Chapman et al., 2004). Language, in this view, is seen merely as a tool for communication which works 'mechanically' and 'instrumentally' to transfer 'accurate' information between interviewer and interviewee (Holstein and Gubrium, 1995).

This position is, however, problematic, at least in the Chinese context, for at least three reasons. First, as argued in Xian (2008), language has significant implications for the data obtained (see also Silverman (2006) for a similar position). Welch and Piekkari (2006) maintain that the role of language in interviews should be considered in the process of knowledge production. They quote one researcher who interviewed Chinese middle managers and found that, when interviewed in English, some managers would use 'corporate English' – the English they used in the workplace to perform their professional roles. This often means repeating company policy and falling back on jargon, rather than being confident enough to formulate an extended and individualised response.

Second, language and culture are highly related. As will be demonstrated in the next sub-section, the translation of concepts between Chinese and English is highly complex and challenging. There are words and expressions in Chinese languages that are difficult to say in English. Becker (1991) argues that in every culture there is something unique and its uniqueness makes certain things unsayable in another language. Thus, when being interviewed in a foreign language, interviewees might avoid, what Becker called, 'silences', things in one language which have no counterpart in another. Two other researchers in Welch and Piekkari's study also argue that some topics in China can only be investigated in Chinese. In another Chinese-related research study, Tsang (1998) claims that 'communicating in the respondent's language is of paramount importance' for three reasons: it allows respondents to 'fully express themselves'; it establishes 'good rapport'; and it enables the interviewer to interpret the interviewee's statement with 'cultural understanding' (p. 511). This is particularly important for an interpretivist approach as it allows the researcher to primarily focus on the world as it is experienced.

Moreover, language is also employed to 're-present' or 're-frame' aspects of the identities of both the interviewer and the interviewee (Holstein and Gubrium, 1995). Welch and Piekkari (2006) report that the association between nationality and language is regarded as particularly strong, and language or dialect (we may add) is often seen as an 'illustrator' of nationality or ethnic identity. In our own experience, it would sometimes be perceived to be 'arrogant' or may make others lose 'face' when a bilingual researcher tries to communicate with a Chinese interviewee located in mainland China, in a foreign language such as English. The reason might be that overseas Chinese usually speak better English, and therefore could put the indigene into a disadvantaged position. Another reason is that if someone speaks a foreign language, the person is often seen as a foreigner or an outsider. We argue that this could extend to the choice between Mandarin and a local dialect (such as Cantonese or Shanghainese). Speaking a dialect could help the researcher gain 'insider' access to some crucial people who may not speak perfect Mandarin and make it easier to establish connections at the initial stage of data collection. Tsang (1998) suggests that when researching in China, re-enforcing the researcher's identity could win 'trust' from the interviewees who might unconsciously distinguish 'us' (an in-group) and 'them' (an out-group). Very often, there is a presumption that individuals who share the same ethnic and language background have a greater understanding of each other's experience or views. Thus, bilingual researchers should try to emphasise their social identity to avoid data quality being reduced when using a non-native language or dialect. However, Gawlewicz (2016) warns that this assumption could sometimes be dangerous as it prevents the research from capturing intersections – the complexity and diversity of experience and views – within and between various groups.

Nonetheless, we recommend that interviews should be conducted in a language or dialect that the participants are comfortable with in order to retain the rich insight of the participants' experience. Previous research suggests that it is possible to conduct interviews in a dialect that has no written form. Researchers in Hong Kong have long been using Cantonese, a dialect which only has oral form, to interview local participants, albeit residents there have a high level of English proficiency. Moreover, given the diverse range of languages and dialects spoken in China, some projects employ more than one language or dialect when interviewing respondents in different geographical locations. An example is a study conducted by Woodhams et al. (2015), in which all interviews were undertaken in the participants' native language and dialect, i.e. some in Mandarin and some in Cantonese. Another example is Tsang (2001) who investigated foreign-invested enterprises in China and conducted interviews in English, Mandarin or Cantonese.

9.3 DIFFICULTIES OF TRANSLATING BETWEEN CHINESE AND ENGLISH

Conducting research in Chinese languages and writing up results in English means that translation becomes an integral component of a study. However, translating between Chinese and English is by no means a straightforward process. Peña (2007) posits that researchers have to deal with four dimensions of equivalence while researching across languages. Linguistic equivalence is necessary to ensure that the words and linguistic meaning used in research instruments and instructions are the same for both languages. This is particularly important for comparative studies. Functional equivalence addresses the incongruity in meanings and aims to make certain research instruments, questions and elicitation methods allow for examination of the same construct or concept. Cultural equivalence focuses on the way members of different cultural and linguistic groups interpret the underlying meaning of an item or interview question, as culture may affect how people respond to research instruments. Metric equivalence refers to the level of difficulty in items of a questionnaire or interview questions.

Specifically in the Chinese context, Xian (2008) reflects on a qualitative study and outlines three difficulties. The first concerns the linguistic differences between languages, because there is little similarity in terms of grammatical structure between the two languages. Tenses are not used in Chinese. Moreover, personal pronouns are not distinguished in the verbal form. For example, the pronunciation *ta* could mean him (他) or her (她). Thus, a translator must adjust between languages by adding tense and gender pronouns from the context of the conversation.

The second problem relates to the socio-cultural differences between Chinese and Western societies. There are Chinese concepts （如，户口）, idioms （如，八仙过海）and proverbs （如，草莽出英雄）, which have come from historical events, stories or ancient mythologies. In many cases, these concepts and expressions have no true equivalence in English. If translated literally based on the typical meaning of the charters, they would become meaningless and incomprehensible. This has been reported as the most common challenge faced by bilingual researchers. The problem may be more acute in qualitative interviews conducted in a dialect (such as Cantonese), in which there is no written form for some colloquial expressions, even in Chinese languages (Twinn, 1998). Often, the translator or the bilingual researcher has to insert explanations in the form of a footnote or endnote into the translated texts. However, this addition makes the translation clumsy and less concise.

The third issue is associated with the way Chinese and English speakers interpret certain concepts, even when there is linguistic and functional equivalence between the languages. Take the word 'saint' as an example. It could be translated as 圣人 in Chinese according to the dictionary. However, saint and 圣人 are different concepts based on different cultural and religious heritages. 'Saint' refers to a holy person, an archangel (such as St Paul) or someone chosen by God, whereas 圣人 means 孔圣人 or Confucius! In Chinese society, Confucius is considered a very wise man or 'master of all knowledge'. Thus, in a cross-cultural study, there might be occasions where Chinese and Western respondents or scholars have completely different interpretations of the same research instruments or texts.

9.4 TRANSLATION STRATEGIES AND APPROACHES

There have been various translation strategies, approaches or techniques proposed in the literature to handle these linguistic, cultural and methodological challenges. Overall, the strategies and approaches suggested are linked to the philosophy and methods used by the researchers. At the risk of over-simplification, we divide them into the equivalence approach and the contextualised approach.

9.4.1 Equivalence approach

The equivalence approach has been dominating international business research (Chidlow et al., 2014). Translation has been traditionally perceived to be a technical and objective process, in which a message in a source language can be processed and transferred to the target language fluently without any change. Within this thinking, the aim of translation is to 'convey the same meaning' or produce something of 'equal value' in another language. This can be traced back to the 'science of translation' proposed by Nida (1964) who based this on two key assumptions. First, he had a 'universalist' view, typified by statements like 'anything which can be said in one language can be said in another, unless the form is an essential element of the message' (Nida and Taber, 1969: 4). Second, he promoted a 'communicative' view of the translation process, in which the emphasis is on enhancing the understanding of the receptor. He argued that the audience of the target culture should react to a translated text in the same way as the audience of the source culture would. For Nida, words and symbols are labels representing the meaning of a text and the form of the message is less important than the 'true' meaning embedded in the text. Thus, good and scientific translation would be aimed at, to achieve objectivity, comprehensiveness, explicitness and precision. This approach reflects a positivist framework which assumes an obtainable 'reality' between languages through translation (Xian, 2008).

In order to establish equivalence, many international studies have adopted various techniques in order to improve accuracy. The most common method is the use of the translation and back-translation technique, whereby 'a translator first translates the research instrument or instructions from the source language to the target language and a second translator then independently translates the target version back to the source language' (Peña, 2007: 1256). Then, the two versions (the original and the back-translated) are compared to identify variance, and any difference is to be resolved later. The second technique is to have a native speaker of the target language review the translated version to ensure it is comprehensible by the target audience. A third technique is to use multiple translators (sometimes called team translation) (Douglas and Craig, 2007). In this case, a team of translators first agrees on certain rules of functional and conceptual equivalences. Then, two or more translators make independent, parallel translations of the same text. A review meeting is held later to discuss the various versions and decide on a final and best version. Some scholars call this 'the most favoured approach' in survey methodology (Brislin, 1970; Douglas and Craig, 2007) as it allows alternatives and different perspectives to be discussed.

However, the equivalence approach is based on the assumption that a concept is understood in the same way across cultures. In practice, many researchers are confronted with the asymmetrical features of languages, as discussed in the last section. Sechrest et al. (1972) summarise the 'paradox' of equivalence: the more equivalent the translation, the less likely it is that the research will find cultural differences. Another criticism of the equivalence approach is that what is 'equivalent' is often a subjective matter. Take back translation as an example. Whether the original and back-translated versions are the 'same' relies on the subjective judgement of researchers.

9.4.2 Contextualised approach

The equivalence approach has been challenged recently by many qualitative researchers who reject the positivist conception of language as a neutral medium which transmits information between languages. It is argued that language is ambiguous, unstable and context-dependent. Many articles have been written to offer alternative thinking, which amounts to a 'cultural turn' of paradigmatic shift in translation. Proponents of the contextualised approach argue that it is impossible to produce a text in the target language, which mirrors all the features of the source language. Instead, translation is a form of communicative interaction, where human subjectivity is at the heart of it. The task of translating starts with the translator's understanding of the source text, and this understanding is influenced by a translator's knowledge, social background and personal experience. In this case, translation is first a sense-making exercise (Xian, 2008). The translator must understand and make sense of the material put in front of them, before converting it to a second language. The act of translation is shaped by the translator's interpretation of the commission and their expert judgement of what works best in the target culture. Thus, House (2006: 356) postulates that translation should be viewed as 'a process of recontextualisation, which takes a text out of its original frame and context' and places it 'within a new set of relations and culturally conditioned expectations'. Epistemologically, many scholars see meanings as socially and culturally constructed and translation as a process of reproduction or recreation of meanings between languages and between cultures.

Venuti (2008) further exposes the 'cultural politics' in translation. Venuti (1998) coins the terms of 'domestication' and 'foreignisation' to distinguish two most important translation strategies in bridging cultural differences. According to Venuti, 'domestication' is an approach to translation which, in order to combat some of the alienating effects of the foreign text, tends to promote a transparent, fluent style in the target language. On the contrary, 'foreignisation' is a strategy that deliberately breaks target linguistic and cultural conventions by retaining some of the 'foreignness' of the source text. Venuti argues that, in the Anglo-American translation tradition, translators are encouraged to 'domesticate' foreign text as well as culture so that the translated text is 'fluent' and easily 'readable' for the target audience. This, he argues, is a form of erasing foreign elements and denying differences. For Venuti, a mere pursuit of objective and seamless translation would only iron out any cultural difference that interests the researcher in the first place. Instead, he promotes the foreignising approach, whereby the translator deliberately introduces words from the source language and retains the syntax and style of the original text, so as to preserve the culturally specific features even though this might bring some discomfort to the target audience. On this perspective, a good translation is one which gives voice to the 'Others' and enriches the experience of the target audience. The influence of the contextualised approach on China-related research is evident. The last two decades have seen many Chinese concepts appearing in the form of *pinyin* in English-speaking journals. For example, in management research, the word *guanxi* （关系）is frequently used as researchers increasingly realise that its similar words – 'relationship' or 'relation' – are unable to capture its full meaning in the Chinese languages and culture. Other indigenous cultural concepts that are widely recognised in the Western world include *hukou* （户口）, *danwei* （单位）, *mianzi* （面子）and *yin-yang* （阴阳）.

9.5 TRANSLATING QUESTIONNAIRES

Consistent with a positivist philosophical stance, most quantitative research projects that use questionnaires have adopted the equivalence approach, which is associated with terms such as 'accuracy, validity, reliability and quality' (Chidlow et al., 2014). Most studies tend to implement and translate well-developed sets of items from Western literature with minimum modifications in the research undertaken in the Chinese context. This might be due to the difficulties in examining what amounts to 'equivalence', as discussed in the last section. As such, little information is revealed about who conducted the translation and how it was done. The process is most frequently written in the passive voice to avoid the problems associated with human agency, which inevitably involves subjectivity and preferences (Chidlow et al., 2014).

Example 9.1

BACK-TRANSLATION PROCESS

Many studies rely on back translation as a way to guarantee equivalence. Some examples include:

'A survey questionnaire was developed in English, translated into Chinese, and subjected to a back translation procedure.' (Luo, 2002: 173)

'As the questionnaire was originally designed in English, we undertook the translation and back-translation procedure as suggested by Brislin (1986).' (Tsai and Wang, 2013: 2205)

'The back translation process as recommended by Brislin (1993) was utilized to translate the survey instruments before distribution. The surveys were then piloted on a small number of supervisor/subordinate dyads from the firm to test their face validity and clarity. A number of small changes were made to the wording and order of the survey based on their comments.' (Miao et al., 2014: 2800)

Although many authors claim to follow Brislin's suggestions, in practice they often deviate from the procedures recommended by him. Indeed, Brislin, who has been heavily cited in international business and management research, is sceptical about using back-translation as the only technique to establish equivalence. He suggests a strategy called 'decentering', which involves adapting the questions or items so that they are culturally familiar to the populations under study. He outlines seven steps which, he believes, form the ideal procedure to follow:

1. Use simple words and sentences to re-write the original English text, so as to make it easily translatable.
2. Employ competent translators who are familiar with the content involved in the source language.
3. Have one bilingual translate from the source to the target language, then have another back-translate it from the target to the source language.
4. Have the research instrument independently reviewed by other bilinguals to identify meaning errors.
5. Pilot-test the translated materials with a small number of the target population.
6. Pilot-test the research instrument with bilinguals, whereby one group uses the original version and another group uses the translated version.
7. Compare the experiences of the groups to make sure the responses are similar across the groups. (Brislin, 1970)

Example 9.2

INDIVIDUALIST/COLLECTIVIST TENDENCY

Below is a set of 16 items and their Chinese versions to measure the individualist/collectivist tendency, adopted from Triandis and Gelfand (1998):

1. I'd rather depend on myself than others.
2. I rely on myself most of the time; I rarely rely on others.
3. I often do 'my own thing'.
4. My personal identity, independent of others, is very important to me.
5. It is important that I do my job better than others.
6. Winning is everything.
7. Competition is the law of nature.
8. When another person does better than I do, I get tense and aroused.
9. If a coworker gets a prize, I would feel proud.
10. The well-being of my coworkers is important to me.
11. To me, pleasure is spending time with others.
12. I feel good when I cooperate with others.
13. Parents and children must be together as much as possible.
14. It is my duty to take care of my family, even when I have to sacrifice what I want.
15. Family members should stick together, no matter what sacrifices are required.
16. It is important to me that I respect the decisions made by my groups.

(Continued)

The Chinese version/translation:

1 我宁愿依靠自己而不是其他人
2 大部分时间我都靠我自己，我很少指望其他人相助
3 我经常自我行事
4 我要有自己的，与别不同的个性，这对我来说很重要
5 我的工作要做得比被人好，这对我来说很重要
6 胜利就是一切
7 竞争是自然规律
8 当其他人的工作做得比我好时，我会很紧张，不高兴
9 如果同事获奖了，我也感到自豪
10 同事生活幸福对我也很重要
11 对我来说，快乐的是能和其他人在一起
12 在工作中能和他人合作是很愉快的事
13 父母和孩子应尽量住在一起
14 照顾家庭是我的责任，即便有时我要牺牲我想要的东西
15 不管付出什么样的牺牲，家庭成员应尽量在一起
16 尊重集体的决定对我来说是重要的

9.6 TRANSLATING INTERVIEW QUESTIONS AND DATA

Qualitative researchers do not always mention translation issues in their cross-cultural studies. Chidlow et al. (2014) speculate that this might be because the dominating equivalence approach is associated with positivist assumptions, which qualitative researchers find it hard to subscribe to. Some qualitative researchers do follow the equivalence approach, especially when translating interview questions. For example, Buckley et al. (2006) examine the role of cultural awareness in knowledge transfer by using a case study method. These authors first developed their interview questions in English and then translated the questions into Chinese. They further use back translation 'as suggested by (Brislin, 1970)' to 'verify the content consistency between the two versions' (Buckley et al., 2006: 279). Data translation was not mentioned in their journal article. Indeed, questions such as how interview data are translated and by whom, often remain in a 'black box' in most academic publications. However, most qualitative researchers do not make claims of equivalence in the translated data. A possible explanation is that back translation is time-consuming and often seen as impractical for handling a large amount of interview data (Twinn, 1998).

An emerging trend, though, is to see translation as a decision-making process involving researchers and maybe translators. These decisions include whether or not to translate, who will translate, how much needs to be translated, what the purpose is, the approach to be taken, and so on. Chidlow et al. (2014) argue that the contextualised approach, which recognises this negotiation, adjustment and discussion during the course of research, is more appropriate. In terms of translating interview data, this approach has two advantages. First, as equivalence is no longer the main purpose, it allows the translator to explore the cultural meaning deeply embedded in the interviewees' stories or accounts. Second, the approach promotes the preservation of native expressions in the text to avoid losing culturally specific meaning. This is particularly important for qualitative research following an interpretivist framework, which aims to produce contextualised knowledge.

Example 9.3

AN INTERVIEW SCRIPT AND ITS ENGLISH TRANSLATION

问: 那你觉得你一直以来的发展还顺利吗?

答: 我觉得我是比较顺利的。我自己感觉是这样。就是在我这个年纪做到公司总经理或CEO的应该不是特别多。而且我属于完全没有背景的，完全是毕业后分配来的，不象有些人的父母在这个单位有什么关系。我们那时候分到北京也是比较幸运的。后来在这几次工作中把握机会还是比较好。进入的行业比较好吧，一个进入的是IT行业，另一个是进入互联网和无线互联网行业。反正这两个行业在我在的时候都在上升的阶段，应该来说对我自己也是得到提升。所以总体来说我还是比较幸运的。

问: 哪份工作对你的影响最大呢答: 应该是两份吧，一个是[公司A]，是这样的：因为我在[公司B]呆得比较短。但是在短短的时间内我去要了解一个大公司的运作和企业文化是有帮助的，包括也结交了一群人。[公司A]我觉得是一个很伟大的公司。在这个公司对我个人来讲实现了从单兵作战到团队管理的一个转变。另外，实际上在[公司A]我也实现了从技术人员转变到市场管理人员，从事商务了。第二个对我帮助最大的应该是上一家公司[C]。他们一开始也没有收入，也没有机制，也没有什么。等于我是从零做起来的。其实刚开始我也不懂，不是这个位置，工资也不高。但是后来做起来以后呢，就慢慢地工资涨得比较高了。然后走的时候他们也特别不舍得我走。但后来我还是不想一辈子光做打工，所以就想做别的。[公司C]是对我经历了从管理一个部门到管理一个公司这样的转变。就是包括人事，财务，公司的策略，方向。你出去也代表你公司的形象来开会。我觉得也是实现了第二次的转变。所以这两个公司从我职业来讲，我觉得还是对我印象比较深的。

Q: Do you think your career development has gone well?

A: I think it has gone quite smoothly. I feel this is the case. There are not many people who have become a general manager or CEO at my age. And I did not have any particular background. My development depends entirely on my hard work after graduation and job allocation. I am not like some people whose parents have some special *guanxi* in some SOEs. I was lucky to be allocated to Beijing [in the job allocation]. Later, I was lucky to have a few good opportunities. I entered two good industries, both in their expanding stages. First, I entered the IT industry, and then I entered the internet and mobile internet industry. I feel I have really benefited from these opportunities. So, generally, I am a lucky person.

(Continued)

Q: Which job has had the greatest influence on you then?

A: There should be two: one is in [company A], since I only stayed at [company B] for a short period of time. However, this was very helpful, as I managed to get to know the operations and corporate culture of a big company in a short time. I also got to know a group of excellent people. Then I moved to [company A], which is a great company. At the company, for me personally, I had experience of a change: I changed from working individually to working as a team leader. In addition, at [company A] I realised another change: from working as technical staff to working in the marketing and business operation. The second company that benefited me greatly is [company C] – my last company. It did not have positive revenue at the beginning. Neither did it have any kind of management mechanism. That means I had to start from ground zero. To be honest, I did not know what to do at the beginning. I had not been in this position before. My wage was not particularly high. But, after a while, I helped them to establish a structure and all the management mechanisms. Gradually, my salary increased. When I told them I wished to leave, they were reluctant to let me go. But then I did not want to work for someone all my life. I wanted to try something new. At [company C], I experienced a change from managing a department to managing a whole organisation, including personnel, financial, corporate strategy and overall business direction. When I went out for a meeting, I represented the company. I think it was a second significant change. So, from a career point of view, these two companies had the biggest impact on me.

FURTHER READING

Chidlow, A., Plakoyiannaki, E. and Welch, C. (2014) Translation in cross-language international business research: Beyond equivalence. *Journal of International Business Studies* 45(5): 562–82.

Xian, H. (2008) Lost in translation? Language, culture and the roles of translator in cross-cultural management research. *Qualitative Research in Organizations and Management: An International Journal* 3: 231–45. This article discusses language and translation issues, particularly in the Chinese–English context.

REFERENCES

Becker, A. (1991) A short essay on language. In F. Steier (ed.) *Research and Reflexivity*. London: Sage.

Brislin, R.W. (1970) Back-translation for cross-cultural research. *Journal of Cross-Cultural Psychology* 1: 185–216.

Buckley, P.J., Clegg, J. and Tan, H. (2006) Cultural awareness in knowledge transfer to China: The role of guanxi and mianzi. *Journal of World Business* 41: 275–88.

Chapman, M., Gajewska-De Mattos, H. and Antonious, C. (2004) The ethnographic international business researcher: Misfit or trailblazer? In R. Piekkari and C. Welch (eds) *Handbook of Qualitative Research Methods for International Business*. Cheltenham: Edward Elgar, 287–305.

Chidlow, A., Plakoyiannaki, E. and Welch, C. (2014) Translation in cross-language international business research: Beyond equivalence. *Journal of International Business Studies* 45(5): 562–82.

Douglas, S.P. and Craig, C.S. (2007) Collaborative and iterative translation: An alternative approach to back translation. *Journal of International Marketing* 15: 30–43.

Gawlewicz, A. (2016) Language and translation strategies in researching migrant experience of difference from the position of migrant researcher. *Qualitative Research* 16(1): 27–42.

Hofstede, G. and Bond, M.H. (1988) The Confucius connection: From cultural roots to economic growth. *Organizational Dynamics* 16: 5–21.

Holstein, J.A. and Gubrium, J.F. (1995) *Active Interview*. Los Angeles, CA: Sage.

House, J. (2006) Text and context in translation. *Journal of Pragmatics: An Interdisciplinary Journal of Language Studies* 38: 338–58.

Luo, Y. (2002) Stimulating exchange in international joint ventures: An attachment-based view. *Journal of International Business Studies* 33(1): 169–82.

Marschan-Piekkari, R. and Welch, C. (2004) *Handbook of Qualitative Research Methods for International Business*. Cheltenham: Edward Elgar.

Miao, Q., Newman, A. and Huang, X. (2014) The impact of participative leadership on job performance and organizational citizenship behavior: Distinguishing between the mediating effects of affective and cognitive trust. *The International Journal of Human Resource Management* 25: 2796–810.

Nida, E.A. (1964) *Towards a Science of Translating*. Leiden: Brill.

Nida, E.A. and Taber, C.R. (1969) *The Theory and Practice of Translation*. Leiden: Brill.

Peña, E.D. (2007) Lost in translation: Methodological considerations in cross-cultural research. *Child Development* 78: 1255–64.

Sapir, E. (1921) *Language: An Introduction to the Study of Speech*. New York: Harcourt Brace.

Sechrest, L., Fay, T.L. and Zaidi, S.M.H. (1972) Problems of translation in cross-cultural research. *Journal of Cross-Cultural Psychology* 3: 41–56.

Silverman, D. (2006) *Interpreting Qualitative Data: Methods for Analysing Talk, Text and Interaction*. London: Sage.

Triandis, H.C. and Gelfand, M.J. (1998) Converging measurement of horizontal and vertical individualism and collectivism. *Journal of Personality and Social Psychology* 74: 118–28.

Tsai, C.-J. and Wang, W.-L. (2013) Exploring the factors associated with employees' perceived appraisal accuracy: A study of Chinese state-owned enterprises. *The International Journal of Human Resource Management* 24: 2197–220.

Tsang, E.W.K. (1998) Inside story: Mind your identity when conducting cross-national research. *Organization Studies* 19: 511–15.

Tsang, E.W.K. (2001) Managerial learning in foreign-invested enterprises of China. *Management International Review* 41: 29–51.

Twinn, S. (1998) An analysis of the effectiveness of focus groups as a method of qualitative data collection with Chinese populations in nursing research. *Journal of Advanced Nursing* 28: 654–61.

Venuti, L. (1998) *The Scandals of Translation: Towards an Ethics of Difference*. London: Taylor & Francis.

Venuti, L. (2008) *The Translator's Invisibility: A History of Translation*. London: Routledge.

Warner, M. (2010) In search of Confucian HRM: Theory and practice in Greater China and beyond. *The International Journal of Human Resource Management* 21: 2053–78.

Welch, C. and Piekkari, R. (2006) Crossing language boundaries: Qualitative interviewing in international business. *Management International Review* 46: 417–37.

Wong, J.P.-H. and Poon, M.K.-L. (2010) Bringing translation out of the shadows: Translation as an issue of methodological significance in cross-cultural qualitative research. *Journal of Transcultural Nursing* 21: 151–8.

Woodhams, C., Xian, H. and Lupton, B. (2015) Women managers' careers in China: Theorizing the influence of gender and collectivism. *Human Resource Management* 54: 913–31.

Xian, H. (2008) Lost in translation? Language, culture and the roles of translator in cross-cultural management research. *Qualitative Research in Organizations and Management: An International Journal* 3: 231–45.

Zhu, Y. (2009) Confucian ethics exhibited in the discourse of Chinese business and marketing communication. *Journal of Business Ethics* 88: 517–28.

10
WRITING UP

10.1 KEY COMPONENTS OF A DISSERTATION

In the UK HE environment, an undergraduate dissertation normally requires 8,000 to 10,000 words and it is very common for the postgraduate dissertation to be slightly longer, ranging from 10,000 to 12,000 words. In general, a dissertation comprises of five main parts. We are now going to discuss what should be included in each part.

10.1.1 Introduction 引言

In this section, you should define the wider context of your research topic and/or background of the study. Ask yourself a few questions: What is your interest in this topic? Is it original? Why is this topic important to study? In other words, what are the main contributions of your study to the existing knowledge or practice?

At the end of the introduction, you should provide an outline of the structure of the dissertation, so that the reader knows what to expect and to help prepare them for what follows.

Depending on the individual supervisor's suggestion, you may include your research aims and objectives either in the introduction or at the beginning of the methodology chapter. You should ask your supervisor for advice.

TOP TIPS 小建议

引言部分是整个论文的亮点，我们要想拿高分，一定要在这个部分下功夫。我们的建议是，引言部分留在论文其他部分完成以后写。要能一下子吸引读者的阅读兴趣。直接点题，迅速的引出论文的研究背景和主要论点。注意这个部分同样要运用 'references'，非学术的文献资料也可，注意不要说空话。

10.1.2 Literature review 文献综述

In this section, you will need to demonstrate your understanding of relevant academic theories and the extent to which these inform the study. A literature review demonstrates your awareness and knowledge of what exists in the subject area you are researching. It helps you to build on the work that has already been done in that field (Reardon, 2006). It is important to ensure that you have searched the literature thoroughly and have identified the key findings which are relevant to your project. The literature review should also provide a critical examination of these previous studies (Fisher, 2007). A well-written literature review is critically engaged with debates, readings and theory.

Searching for literature

Students often ask: 'How many references should I cite in my dissertation?' The answer that you will get from your supervisor is likely to be: 'It depends' or 'Quality is more important than quantity'. Yes, the number of references all depends on what material is available and how you use the literature to form your own ideas. You need a mixture of sources for your literature review, often comprised of a combination of books (textbooks and academic monographs), journal articles (peer-reviewed academic journal articles and non-peer-reviewed journals including professional or trade journals), web pages and unpublished dissertations or PhD theses.

TOP TIPS 小建议: WHERE DO I FIND ELECTRONIC SOURCES FOR MY LITERATURE REVIEW?

- Electronic journals, e.g. *Journal of Management, British Journal of Management, Journal of Business Ethics, Journal of International Business Studies, Journal of Marketing, Journal of Consumer Research, Human Relations, Asia Pacific Journal of Management.*
- Full-text databases, e.g. Academic Search Complete, Business Source Complete, Emerald Management, Asian & European Business Collection.
- Electronic newspapers and magazines, e.g. *Financial Times, The Guardian, The Independent, The Times, Marketing Week, HR Review.*
- Industry databases, e.g. FAME (main financial database) and Mintel (main marketing database).

Your subject librarians or bibliographic specialists will be able to help in providing guidance on the choice and use of the sources available.

Conceptual framework

You may be asked to include a 'conceptual framework' and to use it as the basis of your research.

KEY CONCEPTS IN CHINESE: CONCEPTUAL FRAMEWORK

概念框架是一种有多变形式的分析工具。它对于组织你对论文选题的具体想法、描绘各个关键概念之间的联系、和构建需要验证的假设至关重要。也和你的研究目的、研究设计和分析都息息相关。

—————— **Example 10.1** ——————

A TYPICAL CONCEPTUAL FRAMEWORK (MENG-LEWIS ET AL., 2013)

The conceptual framework shows the key areas of importance to the research and how they are linked. For example, in Figure 10.1, the main area under investigation is how consumers respond to sponsorship initiatives by sponsors from different countries of origin. The conceptual framework shows how the key areas are linked in a diagrammatic form. As illustrated in the figure, the proposed conceptual framework shows the key *constructs* （抽象概念，比如以上例子中的 attitudes toward the sponsor，对赞助商的态度）and the connections or relationships amongst the constructs.

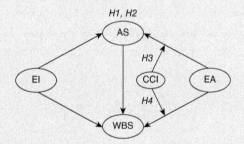

Figure 10.1　A typical conceptual framework

Source: Meng-Lewis et al. (2013)

Notes: EI = Event Involvement; EA = Economic Animosity; AS = Attitudes toward the Sponsor; WBS = Willingness to Buy from the Sponsor; CCI = Current Competitiveness Index

TOP TIPS 小建议：LITERATURE REVIEW DOS AND DON'TS

优秀的文献综述要概括与你选题相关的知识认知，并且做到应该 (dos)：

- 找出最新、最关键、最有标志性的文献，并对其论点结果进行讨论分析；
- 将分散的知识点总结成不同的主题，或者小论点；

(Continued)

- 比较不同文献的研究结果；
- 讨论这些以往研究的不足之处或者矛盾的地方；
- 根据你对已知文献的了解，确认现今研究的空缺点。

此外，你还要不断深入的对你的这个特定选题进行研究意义的论证，从而凸显此选题的重要性（比如:对于其他研究人员，业界人士，或者政策制定者们的意义和贡献）。

此外，尽量避免以下的错误 (don'ts):

- 忽略经典的文献和研究结果；
- 引用过时老旧的观点和研究；
- 简单直白的罗列不同文献的研究结果，而缺乏对于以往研究的归纳和系统的分析总结；
- 缺乏对于引用出处的深一步考察，轻易相信或者直接挪用间接引用的结果；
- 不规范的引用文献资料或者遗漏文献出处；

未经改写直接'使用'他人文章中的文献，这有抄袭嫌疑。

It is very common to propose your research aim(s) and 3–5 research objectives at the end of the introductory chapter. For more details, see Chapter 2 of this book. These research objectives are going to link directly to the next chapter in your dissertation – Methodology.

--- FURTHER READING ---

Hart, C. (1998) *Doing a Literature Review: Releasing the Social Science Research Imagination.* London: Sage. The book provides advice on how to search out existing literature, analyse and map arguments and ideas, and construct a literature review.

Fisher, C. (2007) *Researching and Writing a Dissertation: A Guidebook for Business Students*, 2nd edition. Harlow: Pearson Education. Chapters 2 and 3 provide step-by-step guidance on writing a critical literature review and developing conceptual frameworks.

10.1.3 Methodology 研究方法

In this chapter, you explain how you conducted your research, with the chapter closely connected to your research question. On the basis of the defined scope of your research, you need, first, to formulate a research design, in terms of research strategy, methods including primary and/or secondary data collection methods, sampling and time frame. You need to demonstrate how the research approach builds on ideas drawn from your literature review. It is always helpful to provide details about how you designed and piloted your data collection instruments, and any improvement in your research design before and after your pilot study.

Second, you need to consider the limitations of the approach selected and the implications for generalising from your findings. Third, it is necessary to discuss the intended data analysis approach. Finally, you need to include any ethical issues or potential problems (reliability and validity) with your research and how you have overcome them. (See Chapter 4 in this book for further information on this latter point.)

TOP TIPS 小建议

The methodology chapter should contain:

- An evaluation of the data collected and not collected (type, scope, alternatives, relevance, problems and issues).
- The adopted data collection methods (tools, levels of measurement, sampling procedures).
- An evaluation of the methods used (reliability type, construct and internal validity).
- The techniques used for data analysis (content, semiology, thematic and/or statistical analysis).
- The quality of the data collected (reliability, external validity and generalisation).
- The limitations of the data and methods (scope, quantity, depth).

Source: adapted and modified from Hart (2005)

TOP TIPS 小建议：同学们在写这一章的时候，请注意以下几点

- 用过去时态叙述，告诉读者你做过了什么而不是你将要做什么。
- 要解释清楚你关于研究方法的选择，比如，为什么你选择了质性研究而不是量化研究？为什么你选择用问卷调查而不是深访？
- 认识到不同种研究方法的优缺点、不足之处以及解决之道。

10.1.4 Research findings 研究结果

In this chapter, you need to provide your data analysis, and present and critically evaluate the results and findings from your data. Your discussion and analysis should be insightful, showing readers what your data really says in a clear, meaningful and engaging way.

To present your qualitative findings, you will need to categorise them into a number of themes. Within each theme, you should use your own words and quotes to illustrate the theme, explaining to the reader why each finding happened and referring them back to your literature review. Try to explain how your research findings relate to existing knowledge in the field. How do your findings support or contradict the previous literature? And why is this interesting and/or valuable?

To present your quantitative findings well, it is important to use a combination of text and visuals. Nevertheless, note that the reader should be able to understand both your text and tables (graphs/charts) independently. Always provide a description in the main text of the important information that is in a table or in your SPSS output. Finally, don't forget to tell the readers whether your proposed hypotheses are accepted or rejected.

TOP TIPS 小建议：本章的三个关键词

- Analysis （数据分析）- *what* you found out from your data.
- Interpretation （解释）- *why* it is the case, and the contribution to existing knowledge.
- Presentation （展示）- communication and explanation of the *what* and the *why*.

10.1.5 Conclusion 结论

In this chapter, you are expected to achieve three goals. First, summarise and evaluate your research findings and discuss how they are aligned to the research objectives. Meanwhile, explore the connections between your findings and previous studies. Second, review the implications (both theoretical and practical) and state the theoretical, empirical or methodological contributions of your research. Discuss the implications of your research for any *research stakeholders* (e.g. organisations, managers, workers, consumers, policy-makers). Finally, acknowledge any research limitations and make recommendations for further research. Some programmes require you to write a section of personal reflection where you reflect on the research process, discuss the skills and knowledge you have developed over this period of time and how these skills and knowledge may relate to your future career development.

KEY CONCEPTS IN CHINESE: RESEARCH STAKEHOLDERS

研究干系人 是指对你的研究结果感兴趣的机构或群体，或者对你的研究结果有影响的机构或群体。

> ## TOP TIPS 小建议
>
> 在写你的研究贡献时，不要过分自信，夸大其词。Don't oversell your work! 要知道你的论文会存在很多研究方法或理论上的不足之处，而这些你的导师和读者也都是明白的。

Example 10.2

KEY ELEMENTS OF THE BASICS OF A UNIVERSITY DISSERTATION

Prelims Title page (title, author, degree, date); acknowledgements; abstract; contents; list of tables and figures

Chapter 1 Introduction

Chapter 2 Literature Review

Chapter 3 Methodology

Chapter 4 Research Findings; this may need to be divided into two chapters: Data Analysis and Discussion of Findings

Chapter 5 Conclusions

Bibliography

Appendices

10.2 WRITING STYLE

Your dissertation mark is also determined by your ability to communicate the extent of your knowledge and understanding according to the marking criteria (Cameron, 2005). Expressing yourself in an appropriate academic writing style is therefore a critical skill for your dissertation success. As a Chinese student studying in the UK, you first need to push through any fear around whether you will be able to write as well as a native speaker. You wouldn't have been accepted on the course if your language skills were not good enough. In addition, academic writing is very different to other forms of English writing. You will be able to produce a well-written piece of work once you have mastered the essentials of academic writing. Below, we list a number of points on dissertation writing style.

10.2.1 Simplicity and clarity

Avoid using any long and complicated sentences as it is much easier to make grammatical errors once the sentences get longer – this is particularly true for students using English as their second language. For your markers and readers, complex long sentences are always more difficult to read and require more time to make sense of. Cameron (2005) suggests that 25 words or 2.5 lines should be plenty for a sentence.

Meanwhile, over-lengthy paragraphs should be avoided as well. Each paragraph should only contain one idea/theme of yours. However, paragraphs that are too short can seem disjointed or superficial. The ideal length of a paragraph is 75–100 words (Cameron, 2005).

At times, you may wish to link several paragraphs when building an argument or expressing a viewpoint. Transitions between these paragraphs should be smooth. It is important that you link the paragraphs so that your arguments/ideas flow from one to the other.

Example 10.3

A LIST OF FREQUENTLY USED TRANSITION WORDS AND PHRASES

- Agreement/Addition/Similarity 附加信息，强化观点，表示同意 ：

Also, in addition, additionally, likewise, not only ... but also, moreover, as well as, together with, comparatively, correspondingly, similarly, furthermore.

- Opposition/Limitation/Contradiction 提出不同点，对比 ：

Although, in contrast, different from, on the other hand, on the contrary, at the same time, in spite of, even so/though, after all, unlike, while, even though, although, instead, whereas, despite, otherwise, however, nevertheless, nonetheless, regardless, notwithstanding.

- Cause/Condition/Purpose 提出条件、意图 ：

As/so long as, for the purpose of, with this intention, in the hope that, in order to, in view of, if, unless, when, whenever, while, because of, since, as, in case, provided that, given that, only/even if, so that, so as to, owing to, due to.

- Examples/Support/Emphasis 举例、强调、支持 ：

In other words, to put it differently, as an illustration, in this case, for this reason, to put it another way, to point out, including, namely, indeed, certainly, such as, especially, explicitly, specifically, surprisingly, significantly, particularly, in fact, in general, for instance, to emphasise, to clarify, to explain.

- Effect/Consequence/Result 提出结果、结论 ：

As a result, under those circumstances, in that case, for this reason, in effect, thus, then, hence, consequently, therefore, accordingly.

- Conclusion/Summary/Restatement 总结、综述 ：

Generally speaking, as shown above, given these points, as has been noted, in a word, in fact, in summary, in conclusion, in short, in essence, to summarise, altogether, overall, to sum up, on the whole, all in all, ultimately.

- Time/Sequence 表时间先后、序列 ：

At the present time, from time to time, at the same time, to begin with, as soon as, as long as, in the meantime, in the first place, finally, after, later, last, until, till, since, then, before, once, next, formerly, suddenly, whenever, eventually, meanwhile, further, during, prior to, straightaway, until now, presently, occasionally.

10.2.2 First person or third person

It is a common requirement for university dissertations to use the third person as this is more formal in tone and is considered to reflect the desire for objectivity in academic research. However, some supervisors may allow you to use the first person, especially if you are doing a piece of qualitative research. Using the first person is a more personal way of expressing yourself and is accepted in research which has reflective aspects. Always check this with your supervisor before you start writing. (See Table 10.1.)

Table 10.1 Examples of first, second and third person

First person	Third person
I argue that ...	This essay argues that ...
We researched the issue of ...	The researchers/group researched the issue of ...
I used semi-structured interviews as my methodology	The chosen methodology was semi-structured interviews
After this I will analyse topic x	Subsequently, topic x will be analysed
I found that ...	It was found that ...
We thought the results were ...	The results appeared to be ...

(Continued)

Table 10.1 (Continued)

Second person	Third person
You can read further about this in the work of x	Further discussion of this topic is found in the work of x
You may find it difficult to replicate this experiment	Replication of this experiment may be difficult
Your reading will be more effective if you have a study plan	Use of a study plan will improve the effectiveness of one's reading

Source: adapted from Griffith University (2011)

10.2.3 Using quotations and paraphrasing

You may quote an author's words directly if the point made has been summed up in a particularly precise and logical way. For example, Booth et al. (2008) suggest that writing a piece of research is to think with and for your readers. Nevertheless, you should seek to strike a balance between using quotations and your own words. Quotations should be brief and used to back up your arguments. In your dissertation, you should be able to demonstrate your ability to explain an idea in your own words. Interpreting and paraphrasing another author's writing show that you have understood what you have read in the literature, and are therefore key skills in academic writing.

TOP TIPS 小建议

当你阅读每篇文献资料时，不要直接摘抄作者的原话，而要尽量用自己的话做笔记。不要忘记记录下你笔记的出处。然后当你在写论文时，只需要浏览你的这些笔记，从中总结组织你的论点就可以了，并不需要再次阅读你的原始资料。那么，如何意译别的作者的原话呢？

- 运用同义词替代原句中的关键词
- 重新组织原作者主要论点的结构

请看以下例子。

McCutcheon et al. (2002) suggest that celebrity worship and modelling is a process that typically begins in adolescence and continues over the following years.

Or

Young people are likely to be susceptible to celebrity influence and the influence of celebrities on their personal development can last many years (McCutcheon et al., 2002).

10.2.4 Construction of arguments

Good dissertations always offer well-reasoned arguments that are backed up with evidence. The supporting evidence should be sufficient, reliable and clearly connected to your claims (Booth et al., 2008). Many things can count as evidence – for example, summaries, paraphrases, quotations, facts, figures, graphs, tables, and so on; that is, anything you refer to from either a primary or secondary source. Try to avoid making any strong statements using words like *absolutely*, *definitely*, *certainly*, *prove*, *confirm*. Meanwhile, linking words or phrases is helpful in assembling a logical argument.

Example 10.4

LINKING WORDS AND PHRASES

Addition

Also, in addition/additionally, similarly, not only did …, but … also, moreover, furthermore, as well as, …

Contrast

However, although, on the other hand, on the contrary, yet, nevertheless, in contrast (to)/ in comparison, despite/ in spite of, …

Illustration

For example, for instance, such as, that is, namely, including, …

Sequence

Next, then, thereafter, after this/that, as soon as, following, subsequently, …

Result

So, therefore, as a result, consequently, as a consequence (of), hence, thus, due to, …

Conclusion

Finally, in all, in conclusion, to conclude, to summarise, in summation, …

Here we recommend that students read part III, 'Making a claim and supporting it', in Booth et al.'s book *The Craft of Research* (2008), which provides detailed guidance on and rich examples of how to assemble a research argument. This reading is helpful for those Chinese students who have not had any systematic academic writing training.

If you believe you need to improve your academic writing skills, you can seek help from the academic skill group within your school or university.

FURTHER READING

We also recommend the following book for your self-learning and practice:

Bailey, S. (2011) *Academic Writing: A Handbook for International Students*, 2nd edition. Oxon: Routledge.

10.2.5 Revisions

A well-written piece of work needs numerous revisions and editing. When writing a university dissertation, you will usually be expected to follow some conventions.

TOP TIPS 小建议： 如何修改论文

- 删掉那些显而易见的论点。用长篇大论去反复论证一个浅显易懂的问题是不可取的。
- 不要用英语口语, 俚语，或者惯用语。比如，buddy, you know; buzz (feeling of pleasure or excitement), chicken (coward), homeboy (very close male friend); up a gum tree (in a difficult situation), let the cat out of the bag (reveal a secret), to be in someone's good/bad books (to be in favour/disfavour with someone)
- 去掉不必要的词语，例如， absolutely essential (只用 essential); combined together (只用 combined); the great majority of (只用 the majority of)
- Always re-read long sentences a few times to extract their meaning and to check if there are any grammatical errors. 不用长句或者复杂的句式，每句话只包含一个观点。
- Apart from the introductory chapter, it is a good idea to include a brief introduction at the beginning of each chapter. 这一两句引言会起到很好的承上启下的作用，便于读者阅读。
- 注意上下文的逻辑性，不要只罗列句子。如一段话里有5个句子，你要确保这些句子的意思是关联的。
- Ensure that any figures, tables, graphs and appendices are referenced correctly in the text and are clearly presented.
- Get someone to proofread your work throughout to minimise the grammatical and spelling errors. 这一点对于我们中国学生非常重要，导师不会去读你没经过 proof read 的草稿，它们会直接被发还给你，直到语言过关。

10.3 REFERENCING

When you are writing your dissertation, inevitably your work should build on existing knowledge, i.e. other people's thoughts, ideas or findings. When you are borrowing an idea from someone, you must give them credit. You should use references whenever you make a statement, use the data or other information – that is, from another author and not your own. Failure to do this is considered plagiarism, which may have significant consequences.

There are many different referencing styles in common use. Each department within a university may also have its own preferred format. For example, a business law department may have different referencing requirements to a marketing department. Most universities have made referencing guidance available online or through their library. We provide here some general principles of the most commonly used format – the Harvard style (also called the 'author–date method'). This system is most used in the social sciences, where the date follows the author. Referencing in the Harvard Style has two parts: citing your source in the text and listing the reference details in the bibliography or reference section at the back.

10.3.1 Citing your source in the text

The citation in the text should include the author's surname and the year of publication, and also the page number when using a quote. Where there are more than two authors, put 'et al.' after the first surname. This information should be included in brackets at the most appropriate point in the text. Here are a few examples to show the variations when citing within the text:

> In 2011, sports sponsorship spending increased by 6.2%, making it the fastest-growing sector (IEG, 2012). (注意这里 IEG 是个组织机构，不是个人)

> As China gains increasing dominance in the world economy, it has captured worldwide attention (Melewar et al., 2004). (注意当有3个或者以上作者时，只引用第一个作者，然后加上 *et al.*)

> *Event involvement* represents 'the extent to which consumers identify with and are motivated by their engagement and affiliation with particular leisure activities' (Meenaghan, 2001: 106). (注意这里因为直接引用了作者的原话，要加上引号还有出处页码)

10.3.2 Reference list/bibliography at the end of the work

Every source that you have cited in the text must have a corresponding full reference at the end of your work, under the heading *References* or *Bibliography*. The reference list should appear alphabetically by author surname.

- Book:

Hair, J.F., Anderson, R.E., Tatham, R.L. and Black, W.C. (1998) *Multivariate Data Analysis*, 5th edition. New York: Macmillan. (注意引用书的顺序是：作者，年，书名（斜体），地点：出版社)

- Journal article:

Cheng, H. and Schweitzer, J.C. (1996) Cultural values reflected in Chinese and US television commercials. *Journal of Advertising Research*, May/June: 27–45. (注意引用期刊论文的顺序是：作者，年，文章名，期刊名（斜体），期刊号，页码)

- Chapter in an edited book:

Fredrickson, B.L. and Cohn, M.A. (2008) Positive emotions. In M. Lewis, J.M. Haviland-Jones and L.F. Barrett (eds) *Handbook of Emotions*, 3rd edition. New York/London: The Guilford Press. (注意引用被编辑的书中特定张记的顺序是：作者，年，章节名，in 编辑的名字 ed/eds, 书名（斜体），地点：出版社，章节页码)

- Electronic journal article:

Dehghan, M., Akhtar-Danesh, N. and Merchant, A.T. (2005) Childhood obesity, prevalence and prevention. *Nutrition Journal* 4. [Online] Available at: www.nutritionj.com/content/pdf/1475-2891-4-24.pdf (accessed: 15 September 2015). (注意如果一篇论文同时有电子版和印刷版，而且两者的排版，页码，文字和图片都一样，你也可以按照印刷版论文的方法引用。如果这篇论文只有电子版，或者电子版和印刷版不同，你需要加入你看到此文的日期和网址。

引用电子版论文的顺序是：作者，年，文章名，期刊名（斜体）[Online] 期刊号，Available at: 网址，(accessed: 日月年))

- Web document:

IOC (2008) Olympic marketing fact file [Online]. International Olympic Committee. Available at: http://multimedia.olympic.org/pdf/en_report_344.pdf (Accessed: 5 November 2009).
(引用网络文档的顺序是：作者，年，名称（斜体）[Online]，地址：出版社 （如果有） Available at: 网址，(accessed: 日月年))

- Chinese-language sources:

For sources in Chinese, you must transliterate the reference into the English alphabet. The most common way is to use *pinyin*, but you don't need to include any tone marks. For example, if the Chinese source information is as below:

Authors: 张华鑫，田坤

Title: 论我国企业品牌国际化体育营销战略

Journal title: 体育科学

Using Harvard style to cite this article would be as follows:

Zhang, H.X. and Tian, K. (2005) Lun woguo qiye pinpai guoji hua tiyu xingxiao zhanlue. [The sports marketing strategies of Chinese brands as a result of internationalization.] *Tiyu Kexue*, 25(4): 13–16. (注意这里和引用英文期刊论文的顺序是一样的：作者，年，文章名（汉语拼音）［括号里加入英文翻译］，*期刊名（斜体，汉语拼音）*，期刊号，页码)

FURTHER READING

Cardiff University provides a very detailed tutorial for Harvard referencing. You can find this at the following web page: https://ilrb.cf.ac.uk/citingreferences/tutorial/index.html

---

10.4 PLAGIARISM

Plagiarism is a serious academic offence and is defined as 'The practice of taking someone else's work or ideas and passing them off as one's own' (Oxford Dictionaries, 2017). Within the UK higher education system, plagiarism can lead to failing a paper or even a degree. Universities use plagiarism-prevention software (such as 'Turnitin') to check students' documents for unoriginal content. Some students may not have intended to plagiarise, or perhaps may not have understood the consequences of plagiarism. This can result from simply being careless or by being misled by others. Try to ask yourself the following questions to help identify plagiarism:

1. Have I quoted, paraphrased or summarised a source but failed to cite it?
2. Have I used ideas or methods from a source but failed to cite it?
3. Have I used the exact words of a source and cited it, but failed to put those words in quotation marks or in a block quotation?

(Booth et al., 2008)

The above questions identify clear examples of plagiarism. However, there are other plagiarism cases that may not be that obvious to Chinese students.

10.4.1 Paraphrasing

You can be charged with plagiarism if you paraphrase too closely the source, even if you have acknowledged the source. What is too closely paraphrasing? This happens when you largely maintain the author's method of expression and sentence structure; or your paraphrases still contain words/phrases in the original author's language, although you have rearranged them into a new structure. In order to avoid this kind of plagiarism, you should always use quotation marks which indicate the words that are taken directly from the original source.

10.4.2 Self-plagiarism

Self-plagiarism is a situation where you submit the same piece of work twice, or include any material that is substantially similar to your previous work, as determined by examiners. In essence, a piece of coursework, or a dissertation, or a project can only be submitted for assessment once.

TOP TIPS 小建议：以下情况不算自我抄袭

- 按规范引用了你在以前作业中用过的文献或者摘录；
- 当你写毕业论文的时候，你的选题可以是以写过的作业选题为基础，进一步发展起来的。当然，整句整段抄袭以前的作业是不允许的。

10.4.3 Translated plagiarism

Many Chinese students may ask: is it acceptable to find a source online in Chinese, translate it into English and put it in my dissertation? The answer is 'No' and it is a type of plagiarism if you don't cite it properly. You will probably get caught! Turnitin, for example, is able to detect any matches within documents written in English, compared to the sources written in Chinese.

If you have any questions about plagiarism and/or require assistance with academic referencing conventions, please seek guidance from your supervisor or the library.

10.5 MANAGING YOUR RELATIONSHIP WITH YOUR SUPERVISOR

Spending a few months on your dissertation is a very challenging task (probably for most students, it is the most important academic project undertaken in their life so far!). A lot of Chinese students studying in the UK suffer from various issues during this process – for example, isolation, time management, language and cultural difficulties. It is thus very helpful for you to maintain a good relationship with your dissertation supervisor, so that you can exchange ideas and seek guidance and feedback (Wisker, 2008). How do Chinese students manage this vital relationship, which is critical to the success of their project?

10.5.1 Be proactive: ask, ask and ask

Chinese culture has traditionally emphasised humility and modesty and this has had a great impact on the Chinese education system. Lecturers within UK higher education tend to hold a stereotype of Chinese students as being hard working and polite, but rarely asking any questions. In our experience as dissertation supervisors, it is true that most Chinese students are reluctant to ask for help from their supervisors.

However, are you absolutely clear about all the requirements of your dissertation and do you totally understand every point of your supervisor's feedback? If you have doubts here or there, you should ask your supervisor directly through emails, phone calls or face-to-face meetings. You may be surprised, but supervisors like students asking questions. Through these questions, supervisors will identify the potential issues and your weaknesses, and help to find a solution. After all, all supervisors would like to see good results from their students' dissertations. So, don't be afraid or too shy to ask.

Although different universities have different time allocations for dissertation supervision (for example, some universities give a specified time for the whole project, and some don't), don't wait to be contacted, and do knock on your supervisor's door or drop him or her an email to arrange your meeting time. Of course, don't send them a mountain of enquiries day by day. Try to see, first of all, if you can find the answer through other means. For example, you can certainly find the information on how to reference a web document yourself.

10.5.2 Be flexible but have your own stance

Traditional Chinese education tends to suppress creative and innovative thinking, whilst promoting obedience to teachers. This may lead students to seek very detailed instructions from their supervisors. Nevertheless, the majority of supervisors here in the UK only provide students with general advice – for example, helping you to clarify and define a research topic, directing you to appropriate sources, and advising you on methodology, data analysis and draft chapters. It is still up to you to identify your specific research topic and questions, to find the academic and non-academic sources in your area, to identify your respondents for the study and to learn a specific analytical tool, such as SPSS or NVivo. It is YOUR project and YOU are responsible for it.

When meeting with your supervisor, you may be questioned on many areas, so do some preparation before your meetings. Provide evidence to defend yourself and your ideas. Some of your supervisor's suggestions may be good for other students, but may not be the most appropriate for you. In this case, do not be afraid to raise your concerns and suggest alternatives. Remember, you are the person who knows more about the project than anyone else.

10.5.3 Peers versus supervisor

Coming from a collective culture, Chinese students often quickly form their own groups from the start of their study overseas. It is understandable: it is perhaps easier to stick to your own cultural and ethnic group, and to share your knowledge and study tips between yourselves. However, this can be dangerous. Often, students prefer to ask their classmates questions relating to their dissertation rather than going to their supervisor. However, these other students may have a different supervisor, and there is always a great deal of difference across various supervisors' personalities, specialties, supervision styles and specific requirements. You should hold questioning attitudes towards indirect knowledge or information from your peers and be aware of the spread of possible rumour when well-meaning but possibly misinformed advice is spread amongst students.

REFERENCES

Booth, W.C., Colomb, G.G. and Williams, J.M. (2008) *The Craft of Research*, 3rd edition. London: University of Chicago Press. Available at: https://scholar.google.co.uk/scholar?q=Booth+colomb+williams+2008&btnG=&hl=en&as_sdt=0%2C5#0 (accessed 22 November 2015).

Cameron, S. (2005) *The Business Student's Handbook: Learning Skills for Study and Employment*, 3rd edition. Upper Saddle River, NJ: Prentice Hall.

Fisher, C. (2007) *Researching and Writing a Dissertation: A Guidebook for Business Students*, 2nd edition. Harlow: Pearson Education.

Griffith University (2011) Writing in the Third Person. Available at: www.griffith.edu.au/__data/assets/pdf_file/0004/320179/writing-in-the-third-person.pdf (accessed 14 September 2015).

Hart, C. (2005) *Doing Your Masters Dissertation*. London: Sage.

McCutcheon, L.E., Lange, R. and Houran, J. (2002) Conceptualization and measurement of celebrity worship. *British Journal of Psychology* 93(1): 67–87.

Meng-Lewis, Y., Thwaites, D. and Pillai, K.G. (2013) Consumers' responses to sponsorship by foreign companies. *European Journal of Marketing* 47(11/12): 1910–30.

Oxford Dictionaires (2017) Available at: https://en.oxforddictionaries.com/definition/plagiarism (accessed 19 October 2017).

Reardon, D. (2006) *SAGE Essential Study Skills Series: Doing Your Undergraduate Project*. London: Sage.

Wisker, G. (2008) *The Postgraduate Research Handbook: Succeed with Your MA, MPhil, EdD and PhD*, 2nd edition. London: Palgrave Macmillan.

APPENDIX 1
LIST OF USEFUL RESOURCES

ACADEMIC JOURNALS

Asia Pacific Business Review

Asia Pacific Journal of Human Resources

Asia Pacific Journal of Management

Australasian Marketing Journal

China Economic Journal

China Economic Review

China Journal of Accounting Research

China Journal of Economic Research

Europe–Asia Studies

International Journal of Chinese Culture and Management

International Journal of Human Resource Management

Journal of China Marketing

Journal of Chinese Economic and Business Studies

Journal of Chinese Human Resource Management

The China Business Review

The China Quarterly

CODES OF ETHICS FOR BUSINESS AND MANAGEMENT RESEARCHERS

Academy of Management (AoM), Code of Ethics (2006):

http://aom.org/uploadedFiles/About_AOM/Governance/AOM_Code_of_Ethics.pdf

Association of Business Schools (ABS), Ethics Guide (2015):

http://charteredabs.org/publications/ethics-guide-2015-advice-guidance

British Academy of Management (BAM), Code of Ethics and Best Practice (2013):

https://www.bam.ac.uk/sites/bam.ac.uk/files/The%20British%20Academy%20of%20Management%27s%20Code%20of%20Ethics%20and%20Best%20Practice%20for%20Members.pdf

FINANCIAL NEWS

http://business.sohu.com 搜狐财经

http://finance.people.com.cn 人民网的财经专栏，是由《人民日报》主办，涵盖丰富的中央政府的财经政策、事实要闻及专业解读

http://finance.sina.com.cn 新浪财经

http://finance.yahoo.com 雅虎财经，以上三个财经网站提供中国及时财经新闻，股票信息和数据。

GOVERNMENTAL AND NON-GOVERNMENTAL AGENCIES

www.un.org 联合国官方网站，公布各种国际公约，人道主义和非政府组织目录。也可在网站中找到每次会议的相关记录和录像。

http://data.worldbank.org 世界银行每年会收集并发表各个国家的各种数据，最著名的包括 World Development Indicators, GDP Ranking, Country Profiles, Global Economic Monitor 等。

www.imf.org 国际货币基金组织网站，包括各国的金融和经济发展数据和研究报告。

www.ilo.org 国际劳动组织网站，包括各国劳动就业统计信息，也发表国际公认的劳动规范和公约。

www.cia.gov/library/publications/the-world-factbook 美国中央情报局也有很多各国的基本信息。

www.stats.gov.cn《中国统计年鉴》。近些年的可以在中华人民共和国国家统计局网站免费下载。

还有一些收费网站提供更详实的中国宏观经济数据，如中国资讯行数据库 www.infobank.cn 中国经济信息网 www.cei.gov.cn 等。

INDUSTRIAL INFORMATION

www.ctei.cn 中国纺织经济信息网， 提供国内外纺织行业信息资源，相关政策和数据。

www.chinafoods.com.cn 食品信息网，包含各类国内外食品咨询、市场行情以及进出口数据统计。

www.realestate.cei.gov.cn 中国房地产信息网，是由国家信息中心主办，涉及市场咨询、法律政策，并提供庞大的统计数据库，可以查询到分城市、地区、年、月的详尽资料。

www.autoinfo.org.cn 中国汽车工业信息网，提供关于行业咨询，政策法规，各类型汽车的市场统计，专题分析和研究报告。

LIBRARY SEARCH ENGINES

中国知网（CNKI），现在很多国外的大学都会订阅中文的学术期刊，但必须从大学图书馆的网站进入。

很多省市的图书馆也对其会员提供各种信息和数据资源。例如，广东省立中山图书馆 www.zslib.com.cn 的会员可以访问CNKI知识资源总库，维普期刊资源整合服务平台， 国务院发展研究中心， 超星数字图书馆等。

www.library.sh.cn 上海图书馆，是与上海科学技术情报研究所联合创办，提供综合情报研究和文献服务。

中文文献期刊和学术论文的查询可以参阅万方数据库 www.wanfangdata.com.cn 这个数据库对于全国大多数高校的师生以及图书馆会员开放。

APPENDIX 2
RESEARCH ETHICS APPLICATION FORM

1. Project details

   Date of submission: Student no.

   Title of proposed project:

2. Responsible persons

   Name and email address of principal researcher/student/programme member *(delete as appropriate)*

   Name and email address of supervisor *(if applicable)*:

   Nature of project (mark with an 'x' as appropriate)

Staff research	☐	Masters	☐
Undergraduate	☐	Doctoral	☐
MBA	☐	Other	☐

BRIEF SUMMARY OF PROPOSED PROJECT AND RESEARCH METHODS

☐ I confirm that, where appropriate, a consent form has been prepared and will be made available to all participants. This contains details of the project, contact details for the principal researcher, and advises subjects that their privacy will be protected, that their participation is voluntary and that they may withdraw at any time without reason.

☐ I confirm that research instruments (questionnaires, interview guides, etc.) have been reviewed against the policies and criteria noted in The University Research Ethics Committee Notes for Guidance. Information obtained will be safeguarded and personal privacy and commercial confidentiality will be strictly observed.

☐ I confirm that, where appropriate, a copy of the *Consent Form* and details of the *Research Instruments/Protocols* are attached and submitted with this application.

3. Please reply to **all** of the following questions regarding your proposed research project:

		Yes	No
1.	Are the participants and subjects of the study patients and clients of the NHS or social services to the best of your knowledge?	☐	☐
2.	Are the participants and subjects of the study subject to the Mental Capacity Act 2005, to the best of your knowledge (and therefore unable to give free and informed consent)?	☐	☐
3.	Are you asking questions that are likely to be considered impertinent or to cause distress to any of the participants?	☐	☐
4.	Are any of the subjects in a special relationship with the researcher?	☐	☐
5.	Is your project funded by a research council or other external source (excluding research conducted by postgraduate students)?	☐	☐

4. Please reply to **all** of the following questions regarding your proposed research project:

		Yes	No
1.	The research involves archival research, access of company documents/records, access of publicly available data, questionnaires, surveys, focus groups and/or other interview techniques.	☐	☐
2.	Arrangements for expenses and other payments to participants, if any, have been considered.	☐	☐
3.	Participants will be/have been advised that they may withdraw at any stage if they so wish.	☐	☐
4.	Issues of confidentiality and arrangements for the storage and security of material during and after the project and for the disposal of material have been considered.	☐	☐
5.	Arrangements for providing subjects with research results if they wish to have them have been considered.	☐	☐
6.	Arrangements for publishing the research results and, if confidentiality might be affected, for obtaining written consent of this have been considered.	☐	☐

7.	Information sheets and consent forms have been prepared in line with university guidelines for distribution to participants.	☐	☐
8.	Arrangements for the completed consent forms to be retained upon completion of the project have been made.	☐	☐

If the research is to be conducted outside of an office environment or normal place of work and/or outside normal working hours, please note the details below and comment on how the personal safety and security of the researcher(s) has been safeguarded.

Please confirm that at the conclusion of the project primary data will be:

Destroyed ☐   Submitted to the Research Ethics Committee ☐

APPENDIX 3
PARTICIPANT CONSENT FORM

Title of research project:

Name of researcher:

Participant identification number for this project: **Please initial boxes**

1. I confirm that I have read and understand the information sheet explaining the above research project and I have had the opportunity to ask questions about the project.

2. I understand that my participation is voluntary and that I am free to withdraw at any time without giving any reason and without there being any negative consequences. In addition, should I not wish to answer any particular question or questions, I am free to decline.

3. I understand that my responses will be kept strictly confidential.

   I give permission for members of the research team to have access to my anonymised responses. I understand that my name will not be linked with the research materials, and I will not be identified or identifiable in the report or reports that result from the research.

4. I agree for the data collected from me to be used in future research.

5. I agree to take part in the above research project.

6. I agree to have the interview audio recorded.

_____   _____   _____

Name of participant   Date   Signature
(*or legal representative*)

_____   _____   _____

Name of person taking consent   Date   Signature
(*if different from lead researcher*)

To be signed and dated in presence of the participant

_____   _____   _____

Lead researcher   Date   Signature

To be signed and dated in presence of the participant

INDEX

Page numbers in *italics* indicate figures; page numbers in **bold** indicate tables.